The
Priesthood
Manual

Reorganized

CHURCH OF JESUS CHRIST

of Latter Day Saints

The Priesthood Manual

HERALD PUBLISHING HOUSE

REVISED AND ENLARGED EDITION

COPYRIGHT © 1985
HERALD PUBLISHING HOUSE
Independence, Missouri

Library of Congress Cataloging in Publication Data

The Priesthood Manual for the Reorganized Church of Jesus Christ of Latter Day Saints.
    Compiled by Clifford A. Cole.
    Includes index.
    1. Pastoral theology—Restoration Movement I. Cole, Clifford Adair, 1915-   . II. Reorganized Church of Jesus Christ of Latter Day Saints.
BX8675.P74   1985   262'.149333   85-14044
ISBN 0-8309-0420-4   AACR2

Printed in the United States of America

FOREWORD

For many years the First Presidency has endeavored to keep in the hands of the priesthood members in the church a basic library of literature that will allow them to pursue their ministry from an informed point of view. One volume of that library is *The Priesthood Manual.*

Because of changes which occur in the world to which the gospel is addressed, and because new structures are sometimes indicated, there is need for an updating of these resources from time to time. The last such reediting was in 1982.

The reason for such a volume is contained in Doctrine and Covenants 104:44

Wherefore, now let every man learn his duty, and to act in the office in which he is appointed, in all diligence. He that is slothful shall not be counted worthy to stand, and he that learns not his duty and shows himself not approved, shall not be counted worthy to stand.

There is no responsibility in life which justifies greater effort in the development of insight and skill than those functions which relate to the ministry of the several offices of the Melchisedec and Aaronic orders.

The Priesthood Manual was virtually rewritten in 1982. That edition now has been revised and enlarged. Because of the importance of this task we asked Elder Clifford A. Cole to accept the responsibility of writer, editor, and coordinator of its contents. We feel that he has achieved remarkable success in that task and we are grateful for his efforts.

Clifford A. Cole became an appointee minister in 1947. He was called and ordained to the Council of

Twelve Apostles in 1958 and became President of the Twelve in 1964 in which office he served until 1980. During the latter part of his ministry in the Twelve he was appointed as Director of Field Ministries by the First Presidency. In this role he became well acquainted with the church in many lands and was related closely to the members of the First Presidency in their task of presiding over the church in all the world.

Brother Cole brings to this task a vast experience and knowledge gleaned from many years of ministry. Known for his kindness and wisdom, and his ability to penetrate deeply to the core of an idea, Brother Cole reflects these gifts and developed skills in his work on the current *Priesthood Manual.*

We commend this volume to the ministers of the church in grateful appreciation for all who have contributed to it.

THE FIRST PRESIDENCY
Wallace B. Smith
Howard S. Sheehy, Jr.
Alan D. Tyree

PREFACE

The Pastors' Reference Library has been of great value to the priesthood and leadership of the church. It has formed the central corps of books considered by priesthood as essential to their ministry. It has set standards for our work and helped to unify the church. *The Priesthood Manual* is one of this group of publications.

From time to time it has been necessary to revise and update *The Priesthood Manual* to keep it current with the growth of the church. This edition is our latest attempt to bring the *Manual* up-to-date. It is a revision of the former edition of *The Priesthood Manual*. It is expanded and enriched by the "Guidelines for Priesthood: Ordination, Preparation, Continuing Commitment" which is included as an appendix. In our work of updating the *Manual*, many contributions have been made and some chapters rewritten by various church leaders. Many have given valuable counsel and advice in the revision of the text.

I shall not name the persons who have contributed to this edition. First, because they are so numerous I am sure I would overlook some, and second, because this, like other standard publications of the church, should be regarded as expressing the composite understanding of the church at this time in its history. No part of the book should be regarded as one writer's opinion or identified as the notion of some private individual. Through committees, group and individual advisors, and a wide range of writers we have hoped to prepare this book to speak for the church.

I take no personal credit for the work done in preparing this publication, but since I have been responsible for coordinating the contributions to the manuscript and selecting its content I must accept responsibility for its limitations. It is my hope that in spite of those limitations, members of the priesthood will find this *Priesthood Manual* a valuable resource for their ministry.

Clifford A. Cole

CONTENTS

FOREWORD 5
PREFACE 7

PART ONE—PRIESTHOOD AND PRIESTHOOD
   FUNCTION 11

   Chapter 1 The Nature of Priesthood 12
   Chapter 2 The Authority of Priesthood 22
   Chapter 3 God's Continuing Concern
                   in Priesthood 32
   Chapter 4 Priesthood Offices 41
   Chapter 5 Ministerial Ethics 62
   Chapter 6 Administrative Functions and
                   Procedures 74
   Chapter 7 Priesthood Calls 124
   Chapter 8 Priesthood Status and
                   Accountability 132

PART TWO—WORSHIP 138

   Chapter 1 Worship in the Life of the Church . . 139
   Chapter 2 The Ministry of Preaching 154
   Chapter 3 Conducting the Prayer Service 165
   Chapter 4 Home Ministry 172
   Chapter 5 Visiting the Ill 184
   Chapter 6 The Funeral Service 191
   Chapter 7 Ministry and the Armed Forces 204

PART THREE—ORDINANCES
AND SACRAMENTS 213

Chapter   1   Ordinances and Sacraments 214
Chapter   2   The Baptismal Service 220
Chapter   3   The Confirmation Service 228
Chapter   4   The Sacrament of the
                  Lord's Supper 232
Chapter   5   Administration to the Sick 237
Chapter   6   The Blessing of Children 243
Chapter   7   Ordination 246
Chapter   8   Sacrament of Marriage 249
Chapter   9   Marriage Counseling 273
Chapter 10   Patriarchal Blessing 281

PART FOUR—STEWARDSHIP OF
TEMPORALITIES 283

PART FIVE—HEADQUARTERS
ORGANIZATIONAL STRUCTURE,
INSTITUTIONS, AND
SPECIAL SERVICES 302

Chapter   1   Headquarter's Organizational
                  Structure 303
Chapter   2   Institutions and Special Services of
                  the Church 315

INDEX 325

Appendix A Guidelines for Priesthood 329

PART ONE

PRIESTHOOD AND
PRIESTHOOD
FUNCTION

Chapter 1

THE NATURE OF PRIESTHOOD

Priesthood Enables the Church

Every human organization must have people who perform certain special functions. These functions are necessary to help the group be united in its purposes, mobilize and use its resources effectively, carry out its decisions, and meet the needs of its members. In order for the group to function smoothly without internal conflict, it is important for the people who perform these functions to understand their roles and be accepted by the group. When the members of a group have well-defined roles and accept their roles affirmatively, it is easier for each one to find fulfillment and happiness in life.

Many of the specialized functions in the church are carried out by priesthood members; however, every member is called into service by God. We are informed by the scripture that "All are called according to the gifts of God unto them."[1] Divine calling into special functions emphasizes the involvement of God in those aspects of life. God is concerned about all of life and is involved with us in every part of our experience. When one considers the range of life's activities in which we are called to be involved with God, one is aware that all of life is sacred. There are no areas in which God is not present. God joins with us in our organizations and activities as the Supreme Being who created and loves us. God calls us to share in the divine purpose. This, to some extent, accounts for the wide range of ministries inherent in the several orders and offices of the priesthood. The church recognizes in its priesthood structure that activities considered by many to be secular have a ministerial dimension.

At this time people are reviewing the roles and work of the various persons who compose society. Roles which once were well accepted by most people are now being challenged. In the church this is especially true of priesthood. The idea that many functions, once thought to be the province of priesthood only, should still be reserved for priesthood is being questioned because persons today recognize that many of the unordained have skills and insights needed by the church. These unordained people want to contribute to the church in ways that are not possible when these ministries are reserved to priesthood. Questions about the roles of ordained and unordained members of the church have come increasingly into focus. Unordained persons are more concerned now than in former years about ways in which they may function appropriately in the church and how they should relate to priesthood.

While this manual will deal with the ministry of priesthood, it is nevertheless true that all, both priesthood and unordained, are called according to the gifts God has given them. Therefore, unordained persons share in the work of God and may perform ministries of great value to the church and its members. It is primarily in administering the ordinances and sacraments of the church and in some presiding functions that those in the priesthood have exclusive roles which cannot be performed in the church by anyone else.

The Source of Priesthood

Priesthood has its origin in Jesus Christ. In Christ we see God ministering to the human race and humans responding to God's ministry. According to scripture "For in him [Jesus] dwelleth all the fullness of the Godhead bodily."[2] Jesus has revealed the full response of our humanness to the divine will. He lived out in practice the meaning of his prayer in Gethsemane, "Not as I will, but as thou wilt."[3]

A divine call to minister is a call to join the Lord Jesus in the continuing interpretation of the purposes of God in terms of earthly human life. In a sense, this is what it means to be prophetic. Priesthood is to give form and substance to the Word of God. It is to make the Word flesh in each generation so that God's truth and will may be understood among the people. This requires our personal response to the spirit of revelation and the discipline appropriate to those who are "laborers together with God." The church is the divinely established structure which permits human beings to relate to God and each other in effective group life.

Priesthood Is Granted for Ministry, Not Glory

Priesthood is a call to serve. According to a well-known scriptural passage persons do not take priesthood honor unto themselves, but are "called of God as was Aaron."[4] If one's ministry is to be effective he or she must respond to such a call humbly and with a desire to serve. In the scriptures we are informed that even Jesus "glorified not himself to be made a high priest."[5]

Those ordained must be willing to yield their lives to

the leadings of the Holy Spirit. Through study, experience, and the ministry of the Holy Spirit they grow in their capability to express and share this ministry with other persons. They must concern themselves continually with the welfare of all people everywhere and in every condition. Priesthood members are responsible for creating conditions which contribute to the full growth and development of all people. They should be patient and long-suffering, willing to sacrifice and be sacrificed for others. They must be able to lead people to dedicate themselves to discipleship as followers of Christ.

Both personal ministry and sacramental functions performed by priesthood members are channels of ministry. When properly administered by authorized officials they bind the church to the legal provisions such as church membership, child blessing, ordination, marriage, etc. The spiritual content of these relationships is not guaranteed by the official action. The spiritual dimension of ministry is a gift from God but is usually made possible by discipline, study, moral righteousness, and compassion for people. These are personal elements. Official functions should contribute to them, but cannot replace them.

Priesthood Is a Covenant

Latter Day Saints have long believed that life should be lived as a stewardship. The commitment made at the time of baptism is a covenant. On our part we promise in that covenant to accept Christ as our savior and to serve him. He is our Lord. In latter-day scriptures we are told that "Stewardship is the response of my people to the ministry of my Son and is required alike of all those who seek to build the kingdom."[6]

Each one of us is accountable for the investment God has made in us for divinely wise purposes. What we do with our lives is therefore of profound importance. When we are called to the priesthood our response is a part of that stewardship. Ministerial responsibility should not be lightly accepted, and failure to function actively in the responsibilities of our priesthood office is a serious matter. Such failure violates the covenant we have made with God and the people who accepted us.

On the other hand the covenant we made at baptism makes it a grave matter to refuse ordination. It involves not only our unwillingness to serve but also the most serious kind of embezzlement in which we take the gifts of God to use in our self-interest while withholding them from service. This is a mismanagement of our stewardship. In choices like this we determine the character of our lives and finally our eternal destiny. Priesthood, therefore, is not accepted, rejected, or laid aside casually, but requires an earnest search to know and respond to God's will.

Priesthood Is a Witness of Truth

Jesus said "I am the way, the truth and the life."[7] He is the revelation of God's intent for us. Again he said, "I will pray the Father, and he shall give you another Comforter, that he may abide with you forever; even the spirit of truth."[8] It is important that we grow in knowledge and understanding. We are told "The glory of God is intelligence, or, in other words, light and truth."[9] It is that truth found in Jesus Christ that makes us free and whole. Jesus therefore is both our guide and the source of power which enable us to become sons and daughters of God.

Thoughtful consideration of the gospel shows, however, that our ministry is not only a call to communicate knowledge but also to be witnesses of divine grace. It is possible to dispense ideas without bringing people to God. In a real sense the priesthood member must become the embodiment of divine grace. Ministry is of the spirit as well as of knowledge. In the great crises of life persons need to know that God has really come into their lives through the ministry of those God has called.

The proof of ministry is not so much in argument as in its function. When John the Baptist sent from prison to ask of Jesus whether or not he was the one "of whom it is written in the prophets that he should come," Jesus answered, "Go and tell John again of those things which ye do hear and see; how the blind receive their sight, and the lame walk, and the lepers are cleansed, and the deaf hear, and the dead are raised up, and the poor have the gospel preached unto them."[10] The proof of the messiahship of Jesus was in his life and work. So it is with us.

Priesthood Members Must Keep Growing

Those in the priesthood must continue to grow in understanding and ministerial effectiveness. This means that priesthood members are to serve and are to lead others into service. They are commanded to study, to read all good books and to do those things which will help them be prepared to serve effectively. Skill in ministry, however, will also require actual pastoral care of members of the church and nonmembers. As priesthood members seek to qualify for ministry their training programs will for the most part be in conjunction with actual ministry. This has sometimes been called "on the job training."

A Power of Life

Priesthood is involved with the power of life emanating from God. It is manifest in the new birth by which persons come to possess a higher life than they would otherwise achieve. Under this power there are times when there is a quickening of the mind to understand divine truth beyond that which is obtainable through the physical senses. Such spiritual insight may increase one's powers of ministry, understanding, and maturity of judgment. Through the quickening of the Holy Spirit persons perceive a higher standard of righteousness far above that which would otherwise be understood. It adds to one's powers of attainment enabling that person to become a son or daughter of God, according to the promise of the scriptures.[11] This is not a power reserved to priesthood alone, but it is certainly one which priesthood members should seek and experience.

A Sacred Trust

Priesthood is a sacred trust, and those accepting it must account for the manner in which it is used. It is not an earthly honor, for honor's sake, not a privilege for human glory.[12] It is not like an earthly bequest, controlled and administered for personal selfish interests. Priesthood is the highest conceivable kind of stewardship, involving responsibility to both God and humankind.[13] Because this is so no person should demand to be ordained as if it were a right.

A Great Commission

The purpose of priesthood is to bear witness of the love of God and of the saving grace and sacrifice of Jesus Christ. It is called to bear the message of salvation to the world and to win persons to God. The testimony it bears centers in Christ, as when the Spirit of God declared to the disciples, "This is my beloved Son, in whom I am well pleased; hear ye him."[14] The gospel it teaches is joyous, because it is the "good news" of the kingdom of God. This gospel is universal in its power to meet human need and is for all people. The gospel must be shared with others. There is a sense of great urgency in this mission because the life of every person is short. Those who are here and have the opportunity today may not be here tomorrow. Much can happen in a little while that will affect life eternally. The soul that needs salvation needs it now.

When Jesus sent the first apostles forth he said, "All power is given unto me in heaven and in earth. Go ye therefore and teach all nations, baptizing them in the name of the Father, and of the Son, and of the Holy Ghost; teaching them to observe all things whatsoever I have commanded you; and, lo, I am with you always, unto the end of the world."[15]

While this commission was first spoken to the original apostles it speaks to every one of us. It is our commission, too. The most meaningful part of the world for us may not be in distant places. It may be in our town or on our block.

A Humanitarian Ministry

Good ministers are always keenly aware of human need and human suffering. They must be willing to help bear the burdens of humanity. One of the finest things said of Jesus was that he "went about doing good." It is a simple model for all who represent him. But the attention and interest of ministers are not confined to the affairs of this earth; they must always be seeking to represent people before the throne of God, praying that the divine love and power will intercede where human power meets its limits and can go no further. They must interpret God to the minds and hearts of people.

A Pastoral Ministry

Genuine ministry, of whatever order, quorum, or office, always evidences a rich pastoral quality. The good minister is a true shepherd. The bad shepherd is one who does not feed the flock.[16] The good shepherd's life is laid down for the sheep. Jesus briefly designated the duties of the shepherd as they are recorded in John 10:1-16. The shepherd provides protection and guidance, as we find illustrated in Psalm 23. It is a saving ministry. "The Son of man is come to save that which was lost."[17]

A Teaching Ministry

Christ set a high standard for teaching. He had a clear concept of his purpose. He knew his material thoroughly. He was a master of technique and method. He was the living example of the truth he revealed. He was deeply devoted to those he taught.[18]

Teaching at its best is concerned with life. Those who teach deal with living persons more than with materials. They seek to understand the possibilities, meanings, limitations, and dangers of the life processes that affect the welfare of people, and use them for good purposes.

NOTES

1. Doctrine and Covenants 119:8b.
2. Colossians 2:9.
3. Matthew 26:36.
4. Hebrews 5:4.
5. Ibid., 5:5.
6. Doctrine and Covenants 147:5a.
7. John 14:6.
8. Ibid., 14:16-17.
9. Doctrine and Covenants 90:6a.
10. Matthew 11:3-5.
11. Docrine and Covenants 50:6; 83:8; 90:4.
12. John 7:18.
13. Doctrine and Covenants 50:6.
14. Matthew 17:4.
15. Ibid., 28:17-19.
16 Ezekiel 34:8.
17. Matthew 18:11.
18. John 10:17.

Chapter 2

THE AUTHORITY OF PRIESTHOOD

Priesthood and the Church

The Reorganized Church of Jesus Christ of Latter Day Saints believes that God acted through the prophet, Joseph Smith, Jr., to establish the church in modern times. As a part of this act God provided for a divinely authorized ministry. There is vested in the church a priesthood authority to represent God in administering the ordinances, ministering to persons, and establishing the kingdom of God. In latter-day scriptures we are informed that "the Lord confirmed a priesthood also upon Aaron and his seed throughout all their generations, which priesthood also continueth and abideth forever, with the priesthood which is after the holiest order of God. And this greater priesthood administereth the gospel and holdeth the key of the mysteries of the kingdom, even the kingdom of the knowledge of God."[1]

It is our belief that authority has been granted the church and that God works through it in ministering to people both for the present and for eternity. The authority held by the church and exercised by its priesthood has its basis in many facets of the church's life.

Legal Authority

When considering authority probably most people think of legal authority first—the legal right to act for another or to command, or to exercise dominion over others. Legal authority is bestowed through ordination after one has been called and the church has approved the ordination by vote. The authority which is exercised by the priesthood member is defined in the duties of the office to which that person is called and ordained.

Under the government of our land we are subject to authority which is imposed by the law. Absolute compliance is ofttimes required. Subjection to authority within the church is modified by the fact that membership in the church is voluntary. We can discipline or disfellowship unruly members but we cannot compel them to obey the law.

There are times when legal authority must be employed with full power. There should be no pride, selfishness, vanity, oppression, greed, or personal ambition used in this exercise of authority. However, the one who is appointed to take charge of a meeting is expected to do so, and must do so if the work of the church is to be done. Someone must make decisions, and the government of the church provides that various offices of the priesthood have the right to lead in ways which are prescribed as the legal rights of that office. The application of the law of the church must sometimes be interpreted in specific cases. This authority to interpret rests with those who are given priesthood and administrative responsibility.

The traveling and supervising ministers occasionally find situations in which they must use their legal authority to protect the church and its people. Legal authority must be exercised sometimes when it is necessary to silence a member of the priesthood who is in sin or error.

Legal authority applied for disciplinary purposes, however, should be used only as a last resort. The labor of love and kindly persuasion should be employed as far as possible. Priesthood members should apply the principles of reconciliation and repentance. If persons can be led to see the value of the law, and persuaded to take the right course of action voluntarily, we have succeeded in the exercise of our authority on a very high level. We are told that "all things shall be done by common consent in the church."[2] This is one of the wisest and finest laws of the church. The idea of common consent does not preclude the need for moral persuasion and loving-kindness which may modify people's actions.

There are situations, however, in which moral persuasion is rebuffed and the maintenance of order requires the force that is found in legal authority. The law of the land in many nations respects the legal authority of the church and its representatives in some acts such as marriage ceremonies, or the right of the church to regulate its internal affairs. In these the church is held accountable for the actions of its representatives.

We believe God has established the church and granted it legal authority to act to bring about divine purposes. We have felt God's power at work in the church and are assured that God is accepting us and participating with us in this work. We have a testimony that God has called us into service. We are assured of the authority resident within the church to do those things which bring ministry to people and build the kingdom of God. The legal authority which we have as priesthood members is limited to the right to function within the church and those ways in which the church may be recognized to function for society.

God, however, is not limited to working within the confines of the Reorganized Church of Jesus Christ of Latter Day Saints. God is at work in many places in the world and grants to those chosen the authority to accomplish the task they are called to do. It is not wise for us to become concerned about what authority others may have. It is important to know that we function with authority given by God through the church.

Moral Authority

Moral authority is an important element in the authority exercised by a priesthood member. This is the authority which comes to a person because of the goodness or moral quality of one's life. An honest, compassionate and righteous person carries a quality about his or her life which gives authority far beyond the one who is known to be deceitful, crafty, or untrustworthy.

Part of the authority exercised by Jesus was the goodness and righteousness of his own life. This moral authority was seen in such situations as that when the scribes and Pharisees brought Jesus a woman taken in adultery stating that Moses commanded such should be stoned. Jesus replied to his questioners, "He that is without sin among you, let him first cast a stone at her" and the scriptures record that "They which heard it, being convicted by their own conscience, went out one by one, beginning at the eldest, even unto the last."[3]

This moral right to act is felt by the priesthood member and by the people who receive that ministry. Seldom will a priesthood member who deliberately fails to pay

25

tithing owed, teach the financial law with authority and conviction. The priesthood member who is unwilling to forgive or be reconciled with a brother or sister will not be fully authoritative in the ministry of reconciliation.

There is a moral authority which grows out of the quality of the action or ministry of the priesthood member. People often reflect this when they say "Is this right? Is this good? Will this be fair?" The letter of the law is legal but the spirit of the law is reflected in moral rightness, and this carries an authority which is very important.

Spiritual Authority

At the time of his ascension Jesus promised, "Ye shall receive power, after that the Holy Ghost is come upon you."[4] This, of course, points particularly to Pentecost, but in the larger sense God empowers the church and those called through the gift of the Holy Spirit. An important element in priesthood authority should be the quickening influence of the Holy Spirit expanding and using those abilities, talents, and skills which may be latent within the priesthood member.

It is unfortunate that many people think of spiritual authority as being primarily exercised in such gifts as speaking in tongues, prophesying, or healing the sick. While it is true that these gifts of the Spirit sometimes occur, it is often the case that the power of the Spirit is present and quickening the priesthood member in much more subtle ways. Those ordained to the priesthood will many times be able to speak publicly, offer public prayers, and perform ministries in a way they never supposed possible. Occasionally it becomes necessary for priesthood members to perform tasks which call for gifts they feel they do not have. If they will prayerfully do their best they will sometimes find the quickening power of the Holy Spirit giving them insights and abilities to act beyond anything they had felt possible. In a very real sense while knowing one's capacities have been quickened by the Spirit, the ministry is of such new dimensions that a person may say, "it wasn't so much me as God working through me that brought the ministry."

Priesthood members need the ministry of the Holy Spirit to enlighten their minds, quicken their abilities, and increase their love and compassion for those who are in need. They should avoid any attempt to substitute a pseudospirituality for lack of preparation. The Holy Spirit is not a substitute for study, but will help those who prayerfully enter into study.

Priesthood members should expect the Holy Spirit to bless their ministry with authority as they prayerfully give their best in service to God and the people.

The Authority of Competence

Competence is an indispensable element in priesthood. Legal authority may be given through ordination, but incompetence or lack of discipline make that authority hollow. Priesthood members should study to become skilled in ministry. Each task requires preparation so that the very best service can be given.

The Apostle Paul advised Timothy to "Study to show thyself approved unto God, a workman that needeth not to be ashamed, rightly dividing the word of truth."[5] Similar advice is given us in latter-day scriptures.

Authority is dependent upon the ministers having the

skills, understanding, and insights to be competent in their ministry. Priesthood members should learn the duties of the office to which they are ordained and make as much preparation as possible to perform the ministries required.

Much of our discussion centers around the legal authority to represent God in performing those ordinances and rites which affect one's eternal life or life after death. This question is of concern to the legal right to function for God considered earlier in this chapter. However, when one considers the authority to effect those conditions here and now which bring about the kingdom of God on earth, then competency assumes a much more significant role. Ordination in and of itself does not make one an architect capable of drawing up plans for a church building, or knowledgeable regarding finances qualifying one to advise others about stewardship associations, or skilled in medicine to treat the sick. Ordination to priesthood may well bring a ministerial dimension which supplements and adds to the authority of competency, but in the total work of the priesthood member skill and competency are essential to exercising authority.

Priesthood's Relationship to the Church

Some have accepted priesthood believing that their call which came from God makes them responsible in their ministry to God only. Perhaps our consideration of this would be helped if we remember that God establishes and nurtures the church. God authorizes the church as the body of Christ to minister in Christ's stead. This does not mean that the church is free from sin or error. It does mean that by grace God accepts the immaturity, rebellion, and ignorance of the church as well as the glory. God works with the church through the power of the Holy Spirit to draw it ever nearer to the divine will and to use the church for the salvation of the human race.

Since the church is called to accomplish the ministries of salvation, it may be expected that the Holy Spirit will work in it to designate persons for special priesthood ministries. The call comes through and for the church, and ordination is authorized by the church through the common consent of the body.

Persons who are ordained, therefore, are responsible to the church and its administrative officers. They should function in their priesthood as a part of the team. Priesthood members are not free to flaunt the church or frustrate the work of the body; and when they persist in doing so, they may be silenced and their authority to represent the church taken from them. Neither are priesthood members free to engage in activities or a style of living which bring disrepute on the church.

The church has a right to expect that those it authorizes to represent it in the priesthood will affirmatively support and promote the work of the church.

Priesthood Is Conferred Through Ordination

Priesthood is conferred through the rite of ordination. Authority to function is legally given at that time. Ordination involves the laying on of hands and a prayer of blessing and pronouncement which specifies the office of the priesthood conferred.[6] The act of laying on of hands is symbolic and gives a tangible expression of granting the intangible power and authority of priest-

29

hood through the Holy Spirit. In reality, the gift of the Holy Spirit is a divine gift. The scriptures state that one being ordained "is to be ordained by the power of the Holy Ghost which is in the one who ordains."[7]

The law requires that all ordinations in organized jurisdictions of the church shall be approved by the vote of the church. However, in emergencies or in unorganized fields certain priesthood members may receive calls and ordain to some offices of the priesthood without a vote of the church. This is done after their recommendations have been approved by the proper administrative authorities. The church law on this matter states:

> No person is to be ordained to any office in this church, where there is a regularly organized branch of the same, without the vote of that church; but the presiding elders, traveling bishops, high councilors, high priests and elders may have the privilege of ordaining, where there is no branch of the church, that a vote may be called.[8]

> Every president of the high priesthood (or presiding elder), bishop, high councilor, and high priest, is to be ordained by the direction of a high council, or General Conference.[9]

Joseph's Statement on Authority

Joseph Smith III stated the following about priesthood authority:

> The powers of the priesthood . . . are conferred for no other purpose than the salvation of man, and are continued only in the just exercise of them in the pursuit of this object; hence any act of any man called into this calling performed with any other intent, or attended with a different result is not authorized of God, and hence does not bind the powers of heaven.[10]

Likewise, Joseph the Martyr wrote:

> The powers of Heaven cannot be controlled nor handled, only upon the principles of righteousness, that they may be conferred upon us, it is true, but when we undertake to cover our sins, to gratify our pride, vain ambition, or to exercise dominion or compulsion over the

30

souls of the children of men, in any degree of unrighteousness; behold the heavens withdraw themselves, the Spirit of God is grieved, then amen to the priesthood, or to the authority of that man; behold ere he is aware, he is left to kick against the prick; to persecute the saints, and to fight against God.[11]

Priesthood Members under Full-Time Appointment

Some responsibilities in the work of the church require the persons who perform the tasks to give their full time to it. The general officers at headquarters have more than they can do in the work of the church alone and do not have other employment. The traveling and supervising ministers must give full time to their tasks. The church, therefore, appoints or employs some people to work full time for the church. They are authorized representatives of the church according to their assignment or the terms of their employment, but when these persons are also members of the priesthood, their authority as priesthood members is not altered.

NOTES

1. Doctrine and Covenants 83:3a, 3b.
2. Ibid., 25:1b.
3. John 8:3-11.
4. Acts 1:8.
5. II Timothy 2:15.
6. Moroni 3.
7. Doctrine and Covenants 17:12b.
8. Ibid., 17:16.
9. Ibid., 17:17.
10. Joseph Smith III, *Saints' Herald*, Vol. 24, p. 168.
11. Joseph Smith, *Times and Seasons*, Vol. 1, pp. 131, 132.

Chapter 3

GOD'S CONTINUING CONCERN IN PRIESTHOOD

At the World Conference of 1984 President Wallace B. Smith presented to the church an inspired document which was accepted by the Conference "as inspired counsel and directon to the church." The Conference authorized "that the document be included in the Doctrine and Covenants." It is a part of the scriptures of the church as Section 156. The part of that document that addresses the matter of priesthood reads as follows:

Hear, O my people, regarding my holy priesthood. The power of this priesthood was placed in your midst from the earliest days of the rise of this work for the blessing and salvation of humanity. There have been priesthood members over the years, however, who have misunderstood the purpose of their calling. Succumbing to pride, some have used it for personal aggrandizément. Others through disinterest or lack of diligence, have failed to magnify their calling or have become inactive. When this has happened, the church has experienced a loss of spiritual power, and the entire priesthood structure has been diminished. . . .

I have heard the prayers of many, including my servant the prophet, as they have sought to know my will in regard to the question of who shall be called to share the burdens and the responsibilities of priesthood in my church. I say to you now, as I have said in the past, that all are called according to the gifts which have been given them. This applies to priesthood as well as to any other aspects of the work. Therefore, do not wonder that some women of the church are being called to priesthood responsibilities. This is in harmony with my will and where these calls are made known to my servants, they may be processed according to administrative procedures and provisions of the law. Nevertheless, in the ordaining of women to priesthood, let this be done with all deliberateness. Before the actual laying on of hands takes place, let specific guidelines and instructions be provided by the spiritual authorities, that all may be done in order.

Remember, in many places there is still much uncertainty and misunderstanding regarding the principles of calling and giftedness. There are persons whose burden in this regard will require that considerable labor and ministerial support be provided. This should be extended with prayer and tenderness of feeling, that all may be blessed with the full power of my reconciling Spirit.

The Increasing Frustrations of the Growing Church

This inspired counsel calls our attention to the fact that we have in the past often been uncertain about the matter of priesthood calling. We have misunderstood the principles of calling and giftedness. Presiding officers who have sensed the importance of their responsibility in calling persons to priesthood have felt the burden most heavily. The responsibility to exercise wisdom and judgment as well as respond to the promptings of the Holy Spirit have led many to wrestle with their own sense of integrity both in calling and not calling certain persons to priesthood offices. In many places the church developed an attitude that a man who is sincere, devoted to the church, and active in church participation should be called to priesthood and if ordained to the Aaronic priesthood he would, if effective in his office, progress into an office of the Melchisedec priesthood. Some presiding officers in the 1960s and 1970s began to counsel with World Church officers about their awareness of the Holy Spirit prompting them to call certain women to the priesthood. Again the expectations of the members that only men would serve in priesthood put them in a position where the conflict between their own integrity and the expectations of the members, as well as other administrative officers, burdened them.

Questions Come Out in the Open

It was not surprising then that in the World Conference of 1970 a resolution was presented to the Conference which in part read as follows:

Resolved, That the World Conference of 1970 ask the First Presidency to provide a clarifying statement on the ordination of women to priesthood which can serve as a guideline to the church in this matter.

The Conference chose not to deal with the resolution. A motion was made, "to lay the matter on the table indefinitely." This motion to lay on the table carried, but the concerns expressed grew more urgent as time passed.

Soon a few recommendations for the ordination of women were submitted and referred up the administrative line to the First Presidency who ruled that under the then existing policies and Conference actions they were not free to approve the ordination of women.

By the Conference of 1976 the issue had generated enough concern that six resolutions relative to the ordination of women were presented for Conference consideration and a letter from the First Presidency on the matter was ordered printed in the *World Conference Bulletin*. Some of the proposed resolutions indicated a lack of scriptural or prophetic guidance on the matter and a reluctance on the part of the jurisdictions submitting the proposals to move ahead in ordaining women until prophetic direction was given. The resolution passed by the World Conference in part stated:

Resolved, That consideration of the ordination of women be deferred until it appears in the judgment of the First Presidency that the church, by common consent, is ready to accept such ministry.

The Burden Was on the Prophet

It was, therefore, very much in harmony with this background and in response to the urging of the Conferences that President Wallace B. Smith approached the World Conference of 1984 earnestly searching out the mind and will of God on this matter. In the prologue to the inspired document President Smith wrote:

As I have continued to seek for greater understanding of the divine will in my role as prophet of the church, the burdens of that office have not become easier. In seeking to address some of the difficult and potentially divisive issues facing the church today, I have found myself spending much time in prayer and fasting, importuning the Spirit on behalf of the church.

Because of the nature of that which I am now presenting, I have sought over and over for confirmation. Each time the message has been impressed upon me again, consistently and steadily. Therefore, I can do no other than to bring what I have received, in all humility, and leave it in your hands, believing with full assurance that it does truly represent the mind and will of God.

Preparation to Implement the Document

The church through the action of the World Conference did accept the document as inspired counsel and direction and has made it Section 156 of the Doctrine and Covenants. In harmony with the document the First Presidency appointed a committee to study the whole question of priesthood in light of the document and to advise them regarding the implementation of the counsel and direction given. The study was intense, comprehensive, and thorough. The committee's recommendations to the First Presidency were further considered by the Joint Council of First Presidency, Council of Twelve, and Presiding Bishopric. Following this exhaustive study the First Presidency has issued the booklet entitled *Guidelines for Priesthood: Ordination, Preparation, Continuing Commitment.* The booklet contains the most basic information and policy for priesthood members and should be studied thoughtfully by priesthood and members alike. It should be read as a companion to this manual. (See Appendix A.)

Examining Ourselves as Priesthood

Doctrine and Covenants 156:8 calls our attention to our need to reexamine our commitments, activities, growth, and motivation for being members of the priesthood. Priesthood does not exist independently from the persons who exercise the priesthood or the situation in which it is exercised. This is to say that priesthood is not extrinsic like a robe, scepter, or crown which is separate and apart from the one who is ordained. It is intrinsic with the person and a recognition that God who is purposefully at work in creation has endowed us with gifts to minister to each other and the corporate body of the church.

God, loving the human race so much, entered into human history in Jesus Christ. This God, who allowed the destructive powers of sin, prejudice, entrenched interests, and fear to crucify Jesus, has a right to say to us, as did the Apostle Paul to the Romans,

I beseech you therefore, brethren, by the mercies of God, that ye present your bodies a living sacrifice, holy, acceptable unto God,

36

which is your reasonable service. And be not conformed to this world; but be ye transformed by the renewing of your mind, that ye may prove what that good, and acceptable, and perfect will of God is.—Romans 12:1, 2

In the spirit of Paul's instruction Doctrine and Covenants 156 calls us to consider our role in priesthood more seriously by being diligently active in ministry, humble in bearing, not using priesthood for self-interest, honor, or aggrandizement. The value and effectiveness of priesthood is diminished when it is taken lightly and the church as a whole suffers.

Developing a Program

To strengthen priesthood ministry the church has instituted a program of priesthood evaluation in which each priesthood member will meet with the appropriate jurisdictional officer at least once every three years to evaluate the member's ministry including such things as ministerial growth through priesthood education, diligent activity, personal fulfillment, lifestyle, and the needs of the jurisdiction for the kind of ministry given. In such an evaluation the priesthood member and administrative officer might both feel by inspiration that the needs of the church and the priesthood member's gifts suggest a call of God to another office. If this is so, action may be initiated by the administrator. It is hoped, however, that in general the ministry of priesthood members will be of such quality that the interview will be both joyful and helpful as the participants share in their common call as servants of God.

Some priesthood members may be unable because of their other commitments, geographic location, or other circumstances to be active and meet the standards of priesthood. They may choose for a time to be placed in a category of inactive status hoping to work out the circumstances that cause inactivity. When the condition of inactivity becomes permanent or of long duration then the priesthood member will be released.

Some priesthood members who have served long and faithfully may be given the honor of superannuation. In this category under the direction of the administrative officers they may continue to minister according to their abilities but are not any longer under the requirement to meet the standards of activity and growth expected of active priesthood members.

Adjusting to Change

For a time it will be difficult to accept membership in a cateogry other than the active classification without a sense of guilt or inadequacy. It is to be hoped, however, that facing up to circumstances which make the responsibilities of priesthood either unwisely burdensome or impossible and doing something to correct the situation is far preferable to continuing to hold priesthood while being ineffective in ministry or inactive. It is certainly preferable to holding priesthood while living beneath the quality of life expected.

The Ordination of Women

The Doctrine and Covenants (119:8b) calls our attention to the fact that "all are called according to the gifts of God unto them." Women as well as men share gifts of ministry which should be received through priesthood. Because of our past social and religious patterns we sometimes find it difficult to forge new roles and accept each other in relationships which are different from the past. In a sense every young person goes through the turmoil of reestablishing himself or herself as an adult equal with other adults in the family and community of their childhood. As an example a few years ago a young woman from one of our congregations in a Third World country was helped to come to Independence where she studied nursing. She graduated as a capable Licensed Practical Nurse. At the time of graduation a group of church people were going on a health mission to her home congregation but as soon as she arrived the family and neighbors immediately pressed her into the subservient position of the little girl that they had known before she left several years earlier for Independence. The frustrations on the part of everyone were intense but worst of all the community members denied themselves health ministries which meant the difference between life and death to people in great need.

The principles of resistance to change and accepting persons in new roles is a part of being accepted in priesthood ministry as well as in other social roles. Women who are ordained must not expect that they will avoid the need to establish themselves as priesthood members and ministers in the church. They can best do this not by resenting the circumstance but by giving effective ministry and reacting in love. Christ who was humiliated, rejected, and eventually crucified expects his servants to minister with the same love he showed. Whether we be men or women we must know that disciples are called to take up their cross daily and follow him. Their most effective way of establishing themselves is by ministering effectively in Christ's Spirit.

Longer-Time Priesthood Must Help

On the other hand those of us who are longer-time priesthood members can open the way and accept new members both male and female. We are called as disciples to share their burden and support them in their ministry. While women do have some gifts different from men we should guard against thinking of women as called to lesser roles or to a more subservient relationship. Studies show this has happened in some denominations who have accepted women ministers. It is true that Jesus said to his apostles, "Whosoever will be great among you, let him be your minister. And whosoever will be chief among you, let him be your servant" (Matthew 20:26, 27). But the subservient role is no more appropriate to women than to men. Administrative officers will do newly ordained priesthood members a great service if they will provide the kind of priesthood education and support that develops ministers of stature and then opens the ways to significant assignments which challenge the priesthood members to give their best.

In Conclusion

Very importantly we should not let resentment and frustrations which accompany change color our own ministry or reflect a negative attitude. The gospel of Jesus Christ is a proclamation of hope. There is plenty wrong within the world and society, but that is not corrected by pointing people to the darkness and error. It is rather our calling to hold up the light of Christ in the midst of the darkness and call people to the hope of that light. We are not called to be messengers of darkness but witnesses of light.

Chapter 4

PRIESTHOOD OFFICES

Priesthood and the Diversity of Gifts

Each person is different from all others. People are different in capabilities, personality, faith, talents, and personal preferences. When God calls a person into ministerial service these individual characteristics are taken into consideration.

It is generally understood that priesthood members will minister in those areas in which they are best qualified. However, priesthood members should not be satisfied to remain at their current level of achievement. They should increase their abilities and develop their neglected capacities. They should become increasingly proficient in those areas of ministry in which they are gifted. As priesthood members respond to the need for ministry in areas where they have not previously served, they may find that they are blessed with abilities and talents of which they were unaware. The principle of fruitfulness applies here just as it does in other realms of life. Often when faced with difficult situations, ministers find they have abilities which had not been previously recognized. These should be developed and used in the service of Christ.

Since there are many specializations within the priesthood offices, priesthood members should not become frustrated at their inability to minister in all fields. There are always other members of the priesthood who can minister well in these areas. Priesthood allows for division of labor even within offices. This is good, for there is much to be done, and even members of the priesthood within one office may minister to one another because certain gifts may be given to one in more abundance than to another.

Two Priesthoods

There are two priesthoods, the Melchisedec and the Aaronic. The Aaronic Order is an appendage to the Melchisedec Order.[1] There are special functions and ministries which each office should perform.

The Melchisedec priesthood is "the holy priesthood after the order of the Son of God."[2] The Aaronic priesthood includes a Christian form of the Levitical ministries described in the Old Testament. It was named after Aaron who was ordained to this responsibility under the hands of Moses.

Because of its divine origin, priesthood is a stewardship. It involves our human spiritual condition before the throne of God. Stewardship implies accountability because agency is both freedom to make choices, and responsibility for such choices.

Priesthood Offices

Priesthood office is the designation of the position within the church in which the priesthood member acts. To speak of priesthood office is to refer both to the authority to act and the area of labor in which the priesthood member should work.

There is no difference in the importance of various priesthood roles, although there are differences in the offices in which one is to act.[3] In addition to priesthood office, it is also important to note that there are administrative and jurisdictional factors which bear upon the work of the priesthood member. A member of the priesthood functions within an organizational structure and in doing so is responsible to the presiding officer of the jurisdiction. The presiding officer in turn is responsible to the administrative officer of the next higher jurisdiction.

The duties and privileges of the various members of the priesthood are defined in the Doctrine and Covenants. Although the offices may be named in other scriptures and some of the duties and privileges inferred from the context, it is the Doctrine and Covenants that is specific about these matters.

Form of Organization

In its early life the church was small and its organization was simple. As the church grew, provision was made for a more complex organization. From time to time officers have been added to the church in response to the church's need. Even today it would be premature to assume that the church organization is complete.

The First Presidency is the leading quorum of the church and presides over the whole church. The president of the church is the president of the high priesthood. The presidency is made up of three high priests. Besides being president of the high priesthood, the president is the prophet, seer, translator, and revelator of the church. The president bears the responsibility of bringing prophetic instruction to the church. It is the responsibility of the First Presidency to be the chief interpreters of the word of God to the church.[4]

Of this office the scriptures state:

> The burden of the care of the church is laid on him who is called to preside over the high priesthood of the church, and on those who are called to be his counselors; and they shall teach according to the spirit of wisdom and understanding, and as they shall be directed by revelation, from time to time.[5]

The Presidency is assisted in judicial matters and in some areas of policy making by the Standing High Council. The First Presidency preside over the Standing High Council.

Members of the apostolic quorum are called apostles. This quorum is commonly called the Council of Twelve. They are called the Second Presidency.[6] They are the second highest council in the church. When the president of the church dies or is incapacitated it is the responsibility of the Council of Twelve to call the church together and preside while the church selects a new president. The scriptures provide a description of the Twelve:

> The Twelve are a traveling, presiding high council, to officiate in the name of the Lord, under the direction of the Presidency of the church, agreeably to the institution of heaven, to build up the church and regulate all the affairs of the same, in all nations; first unto the Gentiles, and secondly unto the Jews.[7]

The Council of Twelve is the chief missionary quorum in the church. It has a major responsibility in the church's missionary outreach. Members of the Twelve are called to bear their own personal witness of Jesus Christ, but more importantly, they enable the church to bear its witness as the body or fellowship of Christ's followers. To help do this they search out and ordain those who are called to be evangelists and patriarchs to the church. It is in harmony with their calling that members of the Council of Twelve commonly are assigned to administer the work of the church in the field. As the leading missionary council, the Twelve are the natural associates of the seventy. They may call upon the seventy to assist them in missionary work, and they direct the seventy in their ministries.

The office of seventy is a specialized function of the eldership. An elder may be set apart to be a seventy, and therefore be especially directed to labor in the missionary arm of the church. A seventy works closely with the Council of Twelve in missionary expansion. When seventies in good standing are released, they automatically are members of the eldership.

The law provides for seven quorums of seventy, each with special responsibility for carrying on the missionary work of the church. Elders who are called to serve in one of these quorums are directed by the Twelve in their labors.

Each quorum of seventy is presided over by a president. There are seven presidents of seventy. They make up a council of the Presidents of Seventy. One of their number is chosen to preside over them and is called the Senior President of Seventy.

The responsibility of the Council of Presidents of Seventy is to select new members for their quorums from among the elders. Their selection is subject to the approval of the First Presidency and Twelve. The Presidents of Seventy also are to provide an educational ministry to the seventy and to facilitate fellowship, morale, and affirmative commitment to the work of the seventy.

The Presiding Bishopric are general officers of the church composed of the presiding bishop and two counselors. Their responsibility to the church has to do with temporalities. This involves custody and management of the income of the World Church. They act as disbursement officers for the church.

Members of the Presiding Bishopric share the duty of interpreting, teaching, and applying the principles of stewardship in the field of temporalities.

Temporalities have to do with the finances and real property of the church. The bishopric are involved with buying, selling, leasing, and maintaining the properties of the church. Since the laws of the land regulate real property and how it is used, the bishopric must deal with legal matters.

Another area of concern for the bishopric is that of judging transgressors of the law. Bishops in stakes, districts, and branches have similar duties within their local jurisdiction as standing courts of the church.

The bishopric also are charged with the responsibility of teaching the law of stewardship and the godly use of temporalities to the membership of the church.

Common Duties and Responsibilities of Priesthood

There are certain duties and responsibilities which are expected of all priesthood members whether they be Aaronic or Melchisedec. They should be diligent in their work and carry out all their duties as faithfully and as promptly as possible. They are to lead clean lives, free from the use of tobacco and alcoholic drinks. They are all called to minister by teaching, expounding, and preaching the gospel. They are to invite all to come to Christ.

Priesthood members should be an example in their diligent response to the principle of stewardship. On September 17, 1952, the Joint Council of the First Presidency, the Council of Twelve, and the Presiding Bishopric approved a resolution which reads as follows:

Be it resolved, That we request all stake, district, and branch presidents to give honest consideration to the question of a man's attitude toward keeping the law of the church in its entirety, having in mind the observance of the financial law along with other mandates of the gospel before recommending such a one for ordination to the priesthood; and be it further

Resolved, That nothing in this action should be used as a means of compelling a man to keep the law. Such compliance should be voluntary. While the observance of the financial law by a candidate for ordination is not now a prerequisite, nevertheless a man's attitude toward the financial law should have bearing as to whether or not his ordination is consummated. Our educational programs should continually tend toward engendering obedience to all of the law of the church; be it further

Resolved, That each member of the Council of Twelve be requested to move as wisdom may dictate in seeing to it that the intent of this resolution is carried out.

This is but one area in which the member of the priesthood should live an exemplary life, but it is one which needs serious consideration by every member of the priesthood because it is so easy to neglect this aspect of one's commitment to Christ. A priesthood member is expected to be a leader in the observance of all of the laws of the church.

The Melchisedec Priesthood

The Melchisedec priesthood has several offices under the categories of high priest and elder. The office of elder is an appendage to the office of high priest.[8]

The office of high priest is the basic office of the Melchisedec priesthood. Bishops, evangelists, apostles, and presidents are specialized officers of the high priesthood. If any of these specialized officers are released from their quorums or orders they automatically are high priests and serve in that function.

Certain administrative officers who have long-term responsibilities are also set apart by the laying on of hands. Stake presidents and bishops, quorum presidents, and presidents of seventy are set apart in this way.

The government of the church is administered through members of the priesthood. Presiding officers of the World Church in well-developed regions and stakes are chosen from among the high priests. Ideally, the presiding officers of the well-established districts and large branches should be high priests, but in situations where none are available or acceptable to the members, an elder may be chosen. In developing areas of missionary potential, a seventy may appropriately serve as the president of the region, national church, or branch. While the president of a branch should ideally be chosen from among the high priests or elders, in cases where no high priests or elders are available or acceptable, the presiding officer of a branch may be a priest, teacher, or deacon.[9]

We are informed in the scriptures of the rights and responsibilities of the Melchisedec priesthood:

The Melchisedec priesthood holds the right of presidency, and has power and authority over all the offices in the church, in all ages of the world, to administer in spiritual things.

The presidency of the high priesthood, after the order of Melchisedec, have a right to officiate in all the offices in the church.

High priests, after the order of the Melchisedec priesthood, have a right to officiate in their own standing, under the direction of the Presidency, in administering spiritual things, and also in the office of an elder, priest (of the Levitical order), teacher, deacon, and member.

An elder has a right to officiate in his stead when the high priest is not present.

The high priest and elder are to administer in spiritual things, agreeably to the covenants and commandments of the church; and they have a right to officiate in all these offices of the church when there are no higher authorities present.

The power and authority of the higher, or Melchisedec priesthood, is to hold the keys of all the spiritual blessings of the church; to have the privilege of receiving the mysteries of the kingdom of heaven; to have the heavens opened unto them; to commune with the general assembly and church of the Firstborn; and to enjoy the communion and presence of God the Father, and Jesus the Mediator of the new covenant.[10]

In a very real sense the nature and responsibility of Melchisedec priesthood require that those ordained to function in this ministry be persons of godly character. Their quality of life should be on such a spiritual level that they may be led by the Holy Spirit. One of the major responsibilities of Melchisedec priesthood members is to administer in spiritual things. This is to be experienced as they function in the ordinances, especially those involving the laying on of hands for spiritual blessings. These include such ministries as the laying on of hands in confirmation for the baptism of the Holy Spirit, administration for the sick, ordination, and for conferring special blessings. They should be spiritually sensitive to the needs of the people to whom they minister as they preach, teach, counsel, and comfort them. They are called to be alert to discern the gifts exercised by persons as they function within the church. These gifts include the word of wisdom, the word of knowledge, faith, the gifts of healing, the working of miracles, prophecy, discerning of spirits, tongues and the interpretation of tongues.[11] There are, of course, other gifts such as preaching, writing, teaching, financial administration, counseling, and artistic gifts which are also quickened by the Holy Spirit. Melchisedec priesthood members should be sensitive to these, and presiding officers should be especially discerning of such gifts in the calling and assigning of persons to responsibility.

The faith and godly character of members of the Melchisedec priesthood should be evidenced by an affirmative and cheerful heart and countenance, and cleanliness of spirit, body, and clothing. They should avoid the appearance of evil, being "without blame in word and deed."[12] Jealousy should have no part in their lives.[13]

Members of the Melchisedec priesthood should observe the covenants and church articles.[14] In this way they may be an example to those who follow. They should be diligent in preparation and in the functions of their office.[15]

The Melchisedec priesthood has an important place in the church. Each one is a spiritual leader whose life must be acceptable to God and the people. The Melchisedec priesthood member is an example to the people, and should visit them in their homes, minister to them in their worship, search for the lost, and in all ways be a good shepherd to the flock.

The Duties of an Elder

All members of the Melchisedec priesthood may appropriately be called elders. However, the office of elder is an appendage to the high priesthood and should be recognized as such. The duties of an elder include the following:

1. Winning persons to Christ and baptizing those who are ready to commit their lives to Christ.[16]
2. Ordaining other elders, priests, teachers, and deacons.[17]

3. Administering the communion of the Lord's Supper.[18]
4. Confirming persons by the laying on of hands for the baptism of the Holy Spirit.[19]
5. Teaching, expounding, exhorting, and watching over the church.[20]
6. Conducting and taking the lead of meetings as the elder is led by the Holy Ghost according to the commandments and revelations of God.[21]
7. Blessing little children.[22]
8. Solemnizing and performing marriage ceremonies.[23]
9. Presiding over a branch or district when selected to do so.[24]
10. Serving in the office of seventy when called and ordained for this office.[25]
11. Serving in judiciary matters as a member of an elder's court when appointed to such a responsibility.[26]
12. Praying for and administering to the sick.[27]
13. Visiting the homes of the members to encourage, strengthen, comfort, and teach them.[28]

All ministry grows out of the elder's responsibility to strengthen the faith of the people and to encourage, nurture, and sustain them. Those who are ill need relief. Members are admonished to call upon the elders in times of illness. The poor need the ministry of elders who have a deep concern for their well-being. The elders should visit the members to ascertain and minister to needs of the poor.

The value of the Holy Spirit for nurture and sustenance goes beyond that of temporal needs. The elder is called upon to preach faith, repentance, remission of sins, and reception of the Holy Spirit among the people. The elder is to be an evangelist, calling all to come to Christ and teaching them the gospel. An elder may also be asked to travel as a missionary. Elders are to call people to a sense of their destiny as a new humanity and as citizens of the kingdom of God. This requires the utmost in elders' consecration and diligence if they are to realize the accomplishments which are a part of the stewardship of Melchisedec priesthood.

The Aaronic Priesthood

The Aaronic priesthood functions in ministries assigned by God. It has spiritual significance. Through the ministry of the Aaronic priesthood spiritual power is introduced to humankind. Therefore, the scriptures tell us the Aaronic priesthood is called to a preparatory ministry. It is a standing ministry, and this makes for stable and permanent growth.

Aaronic priesthood members are constantly concerned with the spiritual achievement of the Saints. This achievement rests on a foundation of good, basic habits. These include the practical expression of Christian love and ministry to the poor, regular worship, diligence in living by the principles of the financial law, maintenance of family worship, and a constant self-evaluation of their Christian discipleship. Aaronic priesthood members should help us live by the principles of repentance and regular practices in godly endeavor. God who creates, sustains, and acts in our behalf has granted the ministry of Aaronic priesthood to provide for our most basic needs.

From very early times God has participated in the

choosing and setting apart of priesthood members for ministry to people. This divinely chosen priesthood body has been commanded to teach and expound the value of right choices, and to exhort, persuade, and lead people to a godly way of life.

We are told the Lord said to Moses, "Take thou unto thee Aaron thy brother, and his sons with him, from among the children of Israel, that he may minister unto me in the priest's office, even Aaron, Nadab and Abihu, Eleazar and Ithamar, Aaron's sons."[29] These men were consecrated for an "everlasting priesthood throughout their generations."[30] The Aaronic priesthood traces its beginning to this divine event. Even when the Melchisedec priesthood was not present upon the earth, the Levitical or Aaronic priesthood remained. From the time when God took Moses and the higher priesthood out of the midst of the children of Israel, the Aaronic priesthood was charged with a "schoolmaster" ministry,[31] to teach the law of physical and material commandments, striving with infinite patience through the centuries to train the people in making right choices and living with those habits and patterns of life which are godly.

Under John the Baptist, the preparation for the coming of the Messiah gave greater emphasis to the spiritual values of reconciliation, repentance, and baptism for the remission of sins. Thus the way was prepared for the coming of Christ.

Jesus followed the pattern established by the preparatory ministry of his time, adding the richness, power, and depth of his own spiritual insight to what had been done. He received the ministry of an Aaronic priest; he was baptized in water by an Aaronic priest.

With the coming of Jesus, however, the ministry of the Aaronic priesthood was further transformed. It continued as a potent factor in the ministry of the church through the early decades of the Christian Era. The work was directly associated with the ministry of the Melchisedec order and adjusted to the new dispensation. Diligent ministry in this priesthood contributed greatly to the expansion of the work.

One of the important events in the Restoration movement was the appearance in 1829 of the angelic minister, John the Baptist. He instructed Joseph Smith and Oliver Cowdery regarding the Aaronic priesthood for the ministry of "repentance and baptism, and the remission of sins."

The Doctrine and Covenants has given to the church a clear and a more specific definition of the office and mission of the Aaronic priesthood. The deep significance and importance of its ministry in performing the outward ordinances was emphasized. The value of temporalities in developing spirituality is revealed throughout the Doctrine and Covenants.

The bishopric preside over the Aaronic priesthood. They are concerned with the education and teaching of the Aaronic priesthood. The temporalities of the church have the special attention of the bishopric, and the Aaronic priesthood associated with the bishopric also have concerns in the matters of tithing, surplus, free-will offerings, consecrations, and in the social ministries.

The offices of the Aaronic priesthood represent three different callings. These include the priest, teacher, and deacon. Each of these offices has certain distinctive areas of ministry even as they have also some callings in common with all members of the priesthood.

The Duties of the Priest

The duties of the priest are given in the Doctrine and Covenants and in Conference *Rules and Resolutions.* The work of the priest includes these responsibilities:

1. To preach, teach, expound, and exhort the church.[32]
2. To baptize.[33]
3. To administer the Lord's Supper.[34]
4. To solemnize and perform marriages where the laws of the land allow.[35]
5. To ordain other priests, teachers, and deacons.[36]
6. To preside over a branch when elected by the people.[37]
7. To travel as a missionary and take the lead in meetings when no elder is present or when delegated that responsibility by those in charge.[38]
8. Ministry to families is a basic responsibility of the priest. The Aaronic priest is to share the duty of presenting the gospel of Christ, visiting the homes of members, encouraging them to pray vocally and in secret and to attend to their family duties.[39] He or she shares with the elder in the responsibility for expounding all things concerning the church to those who have been baptized, but not yet confirmed. In all of their ministry they may expect the direction of the Holy Spirit.

The priest holds the keys of angelic ministry. This means that in those cases where elders are not available and where there are needs which are beyond the priest's authority to provide, he or she may ask that God provide those ministries. The priests administer in outward ordinances as they are agreeable to the covenants and commandments of God to the church.[40]

Priests are called to live clean lives, avoiding the appearance of evil, and being free from the use of tobacco, drugs, and strong drinks. They are to walk in holiness before the Lord and to observe the church articles and covenants exercising the prayer of faith. Their garments are to be free of excess ornamentation. Their countenances should be cheerful, reflecting an affirmative attitude.[41]

By the nature of the priest's concern for the well-being of the Saints and the call to preach, teach, expound, and exhort, the priest carries a concern for the corporate worship of the church. The priest may be called upon to take the lead in meetings. This responsibility is not to be excercised indiscriminately. The priest is not, for example, to displace another minister of any office who may have been assigned to lead the service by the presiding officer. Priests may speak through the voice of warning, but their preaching should be in mildness and meekness and should clearly be the word of God to the people.

The Duties of the Teacher

The duties of the teacher are given in the Doctrine and Covenants and in Conference *Rules and Resolutions*. The teacher's calling includes the following responsibilities:

1. To watch over the church and be with and strengthen the membership.[42]
2. To see that the church meets often and that all members do their duty.[43]
3. To take the lead of meetings in the absence of the elder or priest.[44]
4. To preach, teach, and exhort the church.[45]

5. To be a peacemaker giving ministry which will reconcile those who have taken offense either at another person or the church.[46]
6. To counsel and lead people into paths of righteousness before iniquity can work upon them.[47]

The teacher is a standing minister to the congregation and does not travel for the purposes of ministry.[48] Teachers will visit the Saints in their homes and at such other times as is reasonable and needful. Teachers are to watch over the branch always and be with the members and help strengthen them. In this manner teachers will be able to see that the members are taught their duties.

They are to see that there is no iniquity in the church. This is a shepherding function. They should be closely associated with the flock and recognize the life problems which the members face every day. Through example and good counsel teachers are able to help the Saints avoid the temptations of iniquity. Their relationship to the Saints is one of redemptive love and concern especially for those who have unusual need for personal, spiritual support.

When a family moves into the area in which a teacher has a special concern, that teacher may be the first church contact they receive. Also when a church family is planning to leave and move into another area, the teacher seeks to insure that ministry to them continues so there is no gap in their religious experience. The teacher visits in the home to prepare a transfer of membership report to return to the church recorder.

The teacher should cultivate close contact with the members and sense when they have needs beyond the teacher's ability to supply. This information should be communicated to the presiding officer of the congregation. It may be that the need for professional counseling, for administration in times of illness, or for financial help is required. Some of these persons may be referred for professional help. Church members can be kept informed of the local and general church activities by verbal report and the use of appropriate literature for teachers. The key to adequate functioning as a teacher is the ability to cultivate a friendship, knowledge of the families, and enough concern to open up the homes to the ministry of the church on every level. The teacher is counselor, friend, minister of the word, and one whose empathy lends strength through understanding and service to the members of the church.

The Duties of the Deacon

The deacon is a member of the Aaronic priesthood. Deacons are ordained according to the gifts and callings of God to them by the power of the Holy Spirit. They, like the teacher, are not required to travel. Deacons are appointed to watch over the church and to be standing ministers to the church. The duties of the deacon include the following:

1. To watch over the church. In this capacity the deacon must know how to listen and understand other people. A deacon shares with the people in the life of the church and encourages them in regular attendance. He or she responds to their questions clearly and helpfully, and encourages the members to grow in personal understanding through study of the church's literature.

2. To visit in the homes of the Saints, especially being concerned for their physical well-being. The deacon should try to help persons when

needs are discovered and report such needs to the proper officials when additional help is required.

3. To warn, expound, exhort, teach, and preach as assigned.

4. To maintain order in the church and to care for the physical and social well-being of the corporate body. In fulfilling this responsibility the deacon is to greet the people who come to church gatherings, usher them to an appropriate seat, see that they have necessary materials such as church bulletins and hymnals, and provide for their health and comfort in such ways as adjusting the heat or air-conditioning, ventilation, and lighting. He or she should always leave the people feeling that they are appreciated, and that the church is glad to receive them.

5. To maintain the church properties. The deacon attends to their repair, cleanliness, and appropriate decor. The deacon may have custodial responsibility over the church properties and be responsible for opening the church and seeing that it is properly prepared before each service.

6. To serve the congregation in taking the offering at church services. A deacon may appropriately be selected as treasurer. In this capacity the deacon has custody of the funds of the church and will carry out the wishes of the congregation under the direction of the presiding officers. He or she will need to understand the functions of budgeting, the programs of the church, and the relationship of the budget to these programs.

7. To teach and advise the people regarding the principles of stewardship and financial manage-

ment. Deacons may assist the people in their annual accounting. To qualify as good counselors and advisers deacons should become well acquainted with the procedures and forms used in accounting. The home and family relationships involving finances are confidential and often involve the emotions as well as the intellect of the individual. They are so personal and private that the deacon needs to be tactful and understanding. A deacon's spiritual tone must be affirmative. Every visit should be made in the spirit of courtesy and kindness. The deacon is a representative of Christ.

The work of the deacon is very important in maintaining both spiritual and physical health within the church. Deacons are concerned both with the formal worship of the church and with its individual members. They provide for the sense of comfort, social ease, beauty, and physical well-being which is so important to the effective functioning of the church as the body of Christ. They care for the properties of the church and help insure the financial well-being of both the church as a corporate body and of its members as stewards. Occasionally deacons have thought of their ministry as being less important than that of other priesthood offices. This is an erroneous notion. All offices of the priesthood are equally important and the work of the deacon is especially valuable in the development of the church as the body of Christ.

NOTES

1. Doctrine and Covenants 104:8b.
2. Ibid., 104:1b.
3. Ibid., 129:7.
4. GCR No. 386, paragraph 9.
5. Doctrine and Covenants 122:2.
6. Ibid., 122:9c; 148:10b.
7. Ibid., 104:12.
8. Ibid., 83:5a.
9. Ibid., 120:2.
10. Ibid., 104:3b; 7; 9.
11. I Corinthians 12:8-10.
12. Doctrine and Covenants 119:3.
13. Ibid., 121:4.
14. Ibid., 42:5b.
15. Ibid., 38:9c; 104:44.
16. Ibid., 17:8b.
17. Ibid., 17:8b.
18. Ibid., 17:8b.
19. Ibid., 17:8c.
20. Ibid., 17:8d.
21. Ibid., 17:8f; 9.
22. Ibid., 17:19.
23. Ibid., 111:1c.
24. Ibid., 120:2a.
25. Ibid., 107:44; 143:3a.
26. Ibid., 42:22a.
27. Ibid., 42:12c, d; James 5:14-15.
28. Doctrine and Covenants 120:3c.
29. Exodus 28:1.
30. Ibid., 40:15.
31. Galatians 3:24.
32. Doctrine and Covenants 17:10a.
33. Ibid., 17:10a.
34. Ibid., 17:10a.
35. Ibid., 111:1c.
36. Ibid., 17:10c.
37. Ibid., 120:2a.
38. Ibid., 17:10d.
39. Ibid., 17:10d.
40. Ibid., 104:10.
41. Ibid., 38:9e; 119:3a, c, d; 42:5b; 17:18c.
42. Ibid., 17:11a.
43. Ibid., 17:11b.
44. Ibid., 17:11c.
45. Ibid., 17:11f.
46. Ibid., 17:11a.
47. Ibid., 17:11a.
48. Ibid., 83:22.

Chapter 5

MINISTERIAL ETHICS

Ethical Concerns of the Minister

Leading people into the presence of God is the primary work of a priesthood member. This is done through worship. The Christian way of life is centered in the worship of God. Therefore, sound ethics result from insights gained through worship. Under the impress of the Holy Spirit one is led to understand life as God views it. The priesthood member will always be deeply concerned with the moral actions, motives, and principles which grow out of a knowledge of God's nature and purpose. This understanding helps us be aware of those patterns of life which are in harmony with the will of God. Society refers to these actions and principles in terms of right and wrong.

The standards of right and wrong are ethical standards. The ethics of sainthood are the application of the fundamental principles of the gospel. Ethics grow out of the spirit and way of life taught by Jesus. The foundation of Christian ethics is found in the words of Jesus who said, "Thou shalt love the Lord thy God with all thy heart, and with all thy soul, and with all thy mind.... Thou shalt love thy neighbor as thyself."[1] Jesus said, "On these two commandments hang all the law and the prophets."[2] On another occasion Jesus said, "And as ye would that men should do to you, do ye also to them likewise."[3] This so-called golden rule is expressed in slightly different words by many religions. Such values have formed the foundations for the ethical rules of most societies. The ethical codes and laws of society are helpful. They make the standards of conduct more understandable and easily applied.

The Character of the Ordained

It is the calling of Saints to live their religion at all times. Ethical righteousness is not so much the result of avoiding wrong, but the consistent, affirmative action toward worthy ends. A life full of goodness has no room for badness.

The Apostle Paul supports this view when he says, "Be not overcome of evil, but overcome evil with good."[4] In this way the minister teaches by example the precepts of God.

Very early every priesthood member becomes aware of the high standards expected. These standards involve such areas as honesty, work patterns, business affairs, family life, trustworthiness, and cleanliness of speech and body, as well as the quality of ministry given. A priesthood member must live by the standards which are understood to be right and good.

A priesthood member is called to teach Christian ethical standards to the people both by word and example.

Priesthood is concerned with such things as the development of talents, attitudes toward temporal things, use of time, consideration of family, relationship with the church, association with other ministers, and the obligation to humankind.

The priesthood member should inspire confidence and respect, and build close relationships with people, but must establish certain reserves which prevent over-familiarity. In the midst of all these relationships priesthood members must determine to keep sacred the trust placed in them by the church, the people, and God. As they are led by the Spirit of God they can be particularly sensitive to right and wrong, appreciative of the value of goodwill, and aware of the sacredness of personality.

Christian love, purity, humility, fidelity, hope, joy, and peace are among the qualities of the Lord's ministers. According to scripture "No one can assist in this work, except he shall be humble and full of love, having faith, hope, and charity, being temperate in all things whatsoever shall be intrusted to his care."[5]

Ordained persons are called at all times to take their place within the actual social environment of the people whom they serve. They are called to work with people where they are, thus promoting a better personal life and through it a better social order.

Ethics in the Home

Priesthood members usually find their first opportunity to express wholesome Christian ethical relationships in their homes. Love is more than an inner feeling. It is to act lovingly. Personal unity and wholeness in the Spirit of God is a corporate matter and involves one's relationships with other people. The exercise of integrity, patience, loyalty, self-sacrifice, truth, honesty, thrift, industry, temperance, and justice involves these relationships.

Spiritual qualities and social graces cultivated under the Spirit of God provide the most affirmative foundation for happy families. Here honor, chastity, tolerance, and humor become essential parts of a wholesome Christian home. The spirit of a priesthood member's calling will be reflected in her or his home. In some measure, this is an important element in priesthood lineage. Children who grow up in the home where the spirit of ministry from a priesthood member exists will tend to develop those qualities and sensitivities involved in that priesthood office. The priesthood member's home will be an example to others whether or not it is intended to be. Maturity, love, a sense of permanence, and mutual exercise of personal agency are qualities looked for. At the same time, such homes will exclude things which are detrimental to spiritual development.

The home is the foundation stone of citizenship. The best citizens are those who actively participate in creative living. Conformity to Christian standards is a choice, not an invasion of privilege. It is a choice based upon recognition of the values to be found through Jesus Christ.

The Community and Ethical Concerns

A priesthood member should take an active interest in the community. God works through priesthood to participate in the life of the world. The choice of a person's point of service will depend on one's awareness of the opportunities and needs of the community.

The priesthood member's desire to infuse the ministries of redemption into the general life of the community results from an appreciation of his or her redemption through Jesus Christ. The minister ought to touch the life of the community in a way which lifts people up and gives them hope. Much of priesthood ministry is to the church. Success requires cooperation with other priesthood members, acceptance of one's place on the team, and compassion for every member. Priesthood members should, however, recognize that ministry is not alone to the church, but to the world which God is trying to redeem. They need to participate affirmatively in those good causes which uplift and enrich community life. In more recent times God has emphasized this need for community outreach: "You who are my disciples must be found continuing in the forefront of those organizations and movements which are recognizing the worth of persons and are committed to bringing the ministry of my Son to bear on their lives."[6] While this instruction is not limited to the priesthood, it certainly does apply to them. Priesthood members should lead the church as they personally respond to this instruction.

Puritanism

Disciplined lives, concerned hearts, and firm beliefs are affirmative. When efforts toward righteousness become negative rather than affirmative, they are often destructive.

A good person can become the victim of his or her own prejudices. The severe conscience which demands self-denial and obedience to stifling rules may do more harm than good. Such an attitude denies the innocent and wholesome pleasures of life through which recreation becomes re-creational.

Extremism is evidenced by the person with these characteristics of conscience:

1. The meddlesome conscience which cannot mind its own business but tries to make everyone's business its own.

2. The anxious conscience which finds it difficult to believe the best about anyone.
3. The dogmatic conscience which refuses to really listen to chords played on the heartstrings of its associates. That person's life is a group of cliche's which do not require thought, only repetition.

Such puritanistic approaches are usually more destructive than helpful.

Liberalism and Conservatism

"Liberalism" and "conservatism" are two greatly abused terms. Frequently they are used in the most extreme sense by persons who wish to discredit someone else. A liberal is sometimes erroneously thought to be without any guiding principles or moral sense. On the other hand, a conservative is sometimes erroneously described as a reactionary who clings to the familiar and rejects change without regard to reason or intelligence.

No doubt there are extremists to whom these distorted definitions apply. It is obvious, however, that there is a very real sense in which such labels do violence to most persons.

There is a wide variety of definitions for the term *liberal*, but in its affirmative sense it usually means, when applied to persons, that they more readily accept progress or reform than others, that they are tolerant, favoring giving others freedom of action and personal belief, or that they are relatively free from prejudice or bigotry. Liberal persons tend not to be bound as tightly to traditional ideas or practices as other people.

By comparison when we describe persons as *conservative* we generally mean that they want to preserve existing conditions or institutions. Such persons prefer gradual change rather than abrupt shifts in society. They are more cautious in accepting the new or different.

Few persons are either liberal or conservative. Most of us are mixtures, especially in practice, striving to produce changes where the existing situation is undesirable and to preserve those values and conditions which are attractive, useful, and which we believe to be right.

As ordained ministers, our calling is to be neither liberal or conservative in the extreme sense, but to encourage change as required by the spirit of repentance, and to preserve continuity so that enduring values are not discarded.

Ethics in Church Administration

There are certain ethical standards and procedures which are considered basic to good church administration. These promote good ministerial relationships. Many of the policies and procedures of the church have grown out of these ethical standards. For example, a wise and cooperative minister secures the approval of administrative officers in any jurisdiction before performing baptisms or weddings. Such a priesthood member makes proper arrangements before going into an area to minister, and always recognizes the administrative leadership. Priesthood assignments should be fulfilled promptly. Priesthood should make adequate preparation for the ministry which they perform. It is wise to avoid frontal attacks on the members' beliefs. Priesthood should acquaint themselves with administrative policies and procedures and be careful to follow them. This means that the minister with the new life in

Christ is concerned with doing the divine will and reflecting divine attributes. She or he tries to live by the ethics of the kingdom of God.

Every ordained minister should seek to become skillful in performing the work of the office and should study diligently and regularly and cultivate the Christian graces.

Ethics and One's Devotional Life

Every priesthood member should maintain a living faith in God and in Jesus Christ. Priesthood members should maintain faith in the divine mission of the church. Such a living faith is maintained through personal devotion and group worship. Worship experiences which include attention to the church's world mission will strengthen the minister by putting local needs and conditions in a context of world vision.

Convictions of the divine call to minister are strengthened and enhanced through prayer, study, and service. Such convictions will strengthen the faith of those served.

Ethics and Good Character and Habits

Priesthood members must maintain a good reputation, fine character, and cleanliness of mind, body, and habits. The proper basis for a sound reputation is a sound character.

The World Conference has produced guidelines on several occasions with reference to the use of intoxicating beverages and tobacco.

This conference deprecates the use of intoxicating drinks (as beverages), and the use of tobacco, and recommends, to all officers of the church, total abstinence.—GCR 92

This body declares that the use of tobacco is expensive, injurious and filthy, and that it should be discouraged by the ministry.—GCR 217

Whereas, The addiction to tobacco is clearly a detriment to the physical and spiritual life of a Christian steward, although such addiction of itself is not a test of membership in the church, therefore be it

Resolved, That the Church of Jesus Christ urges its members and all men to live physically and morally in a manner that reflects the image of Christ our Savior, and further be it

Resolved, That the church reaffirms in the context of 1964 the counsel given to the church in 1833 that tobacco is not for the body and is not good for man, but is an herb to be used with judgment and skill, and further be it

Resolved, That this Conference inform the appropriate officials of our concern about the support for suitable controls over the advertising and use of tobacco and tobacco products.—GCR 1046

It is in this light that addiction to the use of tobacco or of intoxicating beverages is sufficient grounds for deferring approval of an ordination to any office of the priesthood. It also is a basis for silencing a member of the priesthood where such use persists.

While traditionally the use of tobacco and intoxicating beverages has been among the most common addictions which, ethically, are inappropriate for priesthood, in the present day these vices have expanded. Today the use of drugs, sexual promiscuity, wanton living, greed, carelessness, and irresponsibility are among those vices which commonly destroy persons. In more recent times we have been asked to repent from these. The scriptures say "You are further admonished to covenant with me anew that you may again be clean men and women and find peace."[7]

The Ethics of Preparation

The divine call and ordination of priesthood members

is not an award for achievement. Priesthood members are called by God and accepted by the church because there is a divine work for them to do. It is important that all who accept such a call make the very best preparation to serve God and humankind effectively. Ordained persons will maintain a desire to honor their priesthood through study. Basic study includes the three standard books of the church, but this is only the beginning. Joseph Smith, Jr., was told to "study and learn, and become acquainted with all good books, and with languages, tongues, and people."[8] In our time it is probably not possible to read all of the good books available. As a result the church has tried to give some help in directing studies. The Temple School provides education and training programs for priesthood members who are wanting to develop the basic skills of ministry. Courses are available through individual home study or in the field schools. These courses are offered periodically in many locations throughout the church. In this way the Temple School attempts to introduce ministers to the broad variety of study materials available, and to assist each person in developing an effective program.

Herald House lists books for study and worship which should be in every priesthood member's library. The church periodicals and magazines provide information about the church. Especially important is the *Saints Herald*, which is the church's basic communication piece with every home.

Church Attendance

Priesthood leadership requires regular attendance at church services. One's own faith and spiritual vitality are kept alive and strengthened through worship with

71

the congregation and sharing with them the ministry of the Holy Spirit.

Regular attendance helps provide the spiritual resources out of which the priesthood member ministers to the people. By worshiping with the people one shares with them the recognition of their common needs. In this as in other things a priesthood member leads the people in their response to the love of God, and becomes their mediator, example, and companion.

It was in the recognition of both the minister's need and mission to others that the writer of the Hebrew letter wrote,

For every high priest taken from among men is ordained for men in things pertaining to God, that he may offer both gifts and sacrifices for sins; who can have compassion on the ignorant, and on them that are out of the way; for that he himself also is compassed with infirmity. And by reason thereof he ought, as for the people, so also for himself to offer for sins.[9]

The Ethics of Financial Responsibility

Every minister is called to support the church through the annual filing of the tithing statement, regular payment of tithes, and contributions to the local church. Through stewardship priesthood members demonstrate their response to the purposes of God, their accountability in temporal things, their integrity, and their responsibility toward funding the budget which supports the ministries of the church.

Since members of the priesthood are called upon to teach the law of the church, it is ethical and fitting that they observe that law in their own lives.

In all financial affairs the ministers of Christ observe the most scrupulous honesty and integrity. This involves their personal, family, and business financial dealings.

Prompt payment of financial obligations is expected of everyone. Unreasonable debt is to be avoided. Management of financial affairs is based on the principles of productivity, repression of unnecessary wants, prompt payment of obligations when due, accountability, and church support through tithes, offerings, and consecrations.

On October 15, 1964, the Standing High Council approved a resolution which has served as a guide for those in the priesthood as they are involved in the promotion of private business interests. This is a highly important ethical concern to both the church and the integrity of the priesthood involved. The resolution reads in part as follows:

Resolved, That it is the opinion of this council that under no circumstances should the name of the church or the names of its officers, its seals, its institutions, pictures of its building or personnel, or other aspects of the church life be used to indicate or to imply in any way that any business is Zionic in character or endorsed by the church unless it is officially authorized; and be it also

Resolved, That it is the opinion of this council that no member of the priesthood should use the fact of his priesthood as a means of encouraging anyone to participate in any way in any business ventures; and be it further

Resolved, That in the opinion of this council, and in harmony with the Conference resolution cited, members of the church should make all reasonable investigations of business enterprises before patronizing or engaging in them, and should not become involved in such enterprises on the basis of the ministerial standing of those who administer or in any way promote the business concerned. (Approved by the Standing High Council, October 15, 1964.)

NOTES

1. Matthew 22:36, 38.
2. Ibid., 22:39.
3. Luke 6:32.
4. Romans 12:21.
5. Doctrine and Covenants 11:4b.

6. Ibid., 151:9.
7. Ibid., 152:4c.
8. Ibid., 87:5b.
9. Hebrews 5:1-3.

Chapter 6

ADMINISTRATIVE FUNCTIONS AND PROCEDURES

The Administrative Role of Priesthood

The right of presidency is inherent in the Melchisedec priesthood.[1] This becomes operative through the consent of the governed. The principle of common consent implies the consent to be governed through common understanding of the divine will.

There are levels of official prerogative and responsibility involving priesthood. At the same time, protection against the abuse of administrative authority is provided in the law.[2] In any ordered government it is important that administrative rights and duties be assigned, accepted, and recognized. In the church the right of calling priesthood involves God who makes the will known to those responsible for receiving the call and to the people who approve it. The call sometimes involves assignment, i.e., Presidency, Twelve, Seventy, etc.

There are other calls which are general, with specific assignments being made by the body from among those called to a certain group. For example, branch presidents are elected by the people from among the priesthood and should be selected from among the elders if there are elders available who can serve.

The Standing Ministry

Early Christian history indicates that the itinerate

missionaries who established groups of believers in various places left the work in the care of local ministers and pushed into new fields. They revisited these fields from time to time and sent instructions in writing to those who were called to continue the church's ministries in the areas where congregations developed.

The term "standing ministry" is peculiar to the Restoration and has come to be used to indicate those members of the priesthood functioning locally in their various offices. The scriptures state:

. . . the standing ministry, the Presidency, second, the high priests; third, the elders, then priests, teachers, and deacons in their order.[3]

The high priests and elders holding the same priesthood are the standing ministers of the church, having the watchcare of the membership and nurturing and sustaining them, under the direction and instruction of the Presidency and the Twelve.[4]

The basic work of the church is done by the standing ministry. Most of these ministers sustain themselves by gainful employment and pay their own expenses in ministering to the church and its people. An example of this can be found in the Book of Mormon where Alma "commanded them that the priests whom he had ordained should labor with their own hands for their support."[5] Without these consecrated self-sustaining workers the tasks of the church could not be carried on effectively. The standing ministry is indispensable.

Priesthood Serving the Church Full Time

Not all of the work of the church can be performed by self-sustaining ministers. For some positions the work is so time-consuming that the persons doing it have no time left over for other employment. The general officers at church headquarters have more than they can do in church work alone. The traveling and supervising ministers must give full time to their tasks. These are sustained financially by the church. They serve harmoniously together with the self-sustaining ministers. Both full-time ministers and self-sustaining ministers are of equal importance to the work of the church and to building the kingdom of God.

Priesthood members who are selected by the Joint Council of the First Presidency, Council of Twelve, and Presiding Bishopric to devote full time to ministerial activities are called appointee ministers. The specific nature of the work they do is defined by their assignments. The following are some of the terms used in these assignments:

Field: An area assigned to an apostle such as the Orient Field.

Mission: An area over which a mission president is selected to preside, such as the British Isles Mission.

Region: An area over which a regional administrator or regional president presides—usually comprising several districts.

_____ Stake or District: The appointee minister is available for general ministerial work as determined by the general minister in charge. In a district the appointee may be elected as president or serve as missionary or in other work.

_____ Stake or District (president, bishop, missionary, etc.): Specialized ministry as indicated.

Assistant to or Assigned to: The minister is to function as the responsible officers direct within the general area of those officers' responsibility.

Director of _____: The minister will function in the division level or as an office head.

Commissioner of _____: The minister is to work in a specialized function under the leadership of a division director and may supervise one or more departments. That person presides over an advisory commission in relation to the assignment.

Supervisor of _____: The minister has some administrative duties but the work is not to be considered as being on the departmental level.

_____ Consultant: the minister has advisory responsibility.

The family allowance is supplied from tithes and offerings. "Elder's expense" (contributions for the minister's official support) should come from those who receive the ministry in the field except in the case of general church officers and headquarters personnel as well as regional administrators, regional bishops, stake presidents, and stake bishops. In regard to these latter church officers an action was taken by the World Conference in 1972 which reads as follows:

As a general policy the elder's expense of regional administrators and regional bishops, as well as elder's expenses for stake presidents, stake bishops, and the members of presiding quorums and their staff assistants, will be met from the tithes and general offerings of the church.

When these officers are giving ministry in the field, voluntary contributions toward their elder's expense will be accepted from field jurisdictions and individuals. This is in harmony with tradition and the provisions in the revelations that "whoso receiveth you receiveth me, and the same will feed you, and clothe you, and give you money" (Doctrine and Covenants 83:16a). Such offerings are accounted for through the monthly elder's expense reports to the Presiding Bishopric.[6]

It is always appropriate for the jurisdiction which receives a person's ministry to contribute to the official expense necessary for the church to provide that ministry. However, the amount of those contributions should be governed by the area's ability to give rather than on the basis of the costs involved. Some areas which are distant from church headquarters need the ministry of World Church leaders. Often they would be denied such help if they were required to meet all of the costs of providing the ministry. To meet this problem the World Church has taken the action quoted above.

The World Church and its jurisdictions also employ priesthood members who serve as executive ministers. The work of an executive minister is usually much more specialized than is the work of the World Church appointee and of necessity the tenure of employment is related to the church's need for this specific ministry. Executive ministers are not subject to assignment by the Joint Council of First Presidency, Council of Twelve, and Presiding Bishopric as are appointee ministers.

Procedure for Appointment

The ministerial policy of the church states: "The total number . . . under appointment and supported by the World Church budget should not exceed the ratio of one appointee per 1,000 members." This necessitates that selection of persons to serve as World Church appointee ministers be limited to those who have had considerable ministerial experience and who with the necessary basic orientation can immediately assume a major leadership responsibility. The procedure for selecting these appointees is as follows:

1. Recommendations may be initiated by members of the First Presidency, Council of Twelve, Presiding Bishopric, and responsible administrative officers in the field. It is also in order for persons desiring to give their full time to the service of the church to express this desire to any of the general officers with whom they may have contact and, most particularly, to the apostle in the field. Such recommendations are screened by the Ministerial Personnel Commissioner and the Director of Administrative Services.

2. The First Presidency, Council of Twelve, and Presiding Bishopric receive detailed information pertaining to each candidate recommended for appointment by the Ministerial Personnel Com-

missioner and the Director of the Division of Administrative Services, after which they make all appointments and assignments. Once a decision has been made, the Ministerial Personnel Commissioner notifies the candidate of the Joint Council's action. Thereafter, those appointed work out with the Presiding Bishopric satisfactory arrangements concerning family allowance and other financial matters.

3. Candidates for appointments are specifically counseled not to sever their business connections until they have been informed by the Ministerial Personnel Commissioner that they have been appointed.

Those interested in serving the church as World Church appointee ministers after the age of forty-five are appointed as Retired Person Contractual Assignees. Each person is appointed in the same manner, and serves the church with the same authority and responsibility as the other appointed ministers, and it is understood that the church's financial responsibility is the same with the exception that the church's financial responsibility for the support of the Retired Person Contractual Assignee and family is limited by contract to the time the minister is an active appointee.

Qualifications of those being considered for appointment should include the following:

1. Convictions of the divinity of the church's work
2. Experience in priesthood service
3. Evident desire to serve in ministry to people
4. Demonstrated capacity to minister
5. Sound character worthy of emulation

6. Initiative with ability to plan work and cooperative endeavor
7. Satisfactory intelligence and judgment
8. Evidence as to his or her probable place in the church
9. Education
10. Age
11. Sound health of prospective appointee and family
12. A winning personality capable of giving leadership
13. No undue financial obligation
14. A reasonable background in family and traditional Latter Day Saint experience
15. An understanding of the beliefs of the church
16. Ability in public expression involving organization and presentation
17. Reasonable compliance with the financial law

CONTRACTUAL ASSIGNEES PROGRAMS

Two-year Contractual Assignees

The Young Adult Two-year Contractual Assignee Program is for persons approximately eighteen to twenty-five years of age. Those selected for this program must have adequate educational qualifications, satisfactory communication skills, and be willing to consecrate two years of their lives to full-time church service.

These two-year assignees are placed in field jurisdictions and report to the administrative officer of the field jurisdiction to which they are assigned. The cost of the program is borne by the field jurisdiction and the World Church.

The arrangements for this kind of service are on a contractual basis.

Specified Term Contractual Assignee

1. The specified Term Contractual Assignee Program grew out of specific needs in which the church contracts with available persons who have developed the required skills to fulfill particular tasks. The usual age range is from twenty to seventy years. Conditions of the assignee's service and the form of remuneration is by contract for a definite period of time.

2. Those selected for this program must have adequate spiritual maturity, educational qualifications, and other skills necessary for the responsibility for which they are considered.

General Principles of Good Administration

Each part of the body of the church should be respected as to personality and office—the Saints, priesthood, appointees, general officers.

The principle of common consent is not satisfied with the perfunctory acquiescence of the Saints. The principle of two-way communication must prevail. Information and explanation need to be shared so there can be an interchange of thought. That is one of the purposes of discussion from the floor at a business meeting. But a business meeting is not the only place where this should be done. As a part of the home ministry program, the visiting minister goes to learn as well as to teach.

There is an urgency about the work of the church. It

must be under control. Time must be given for the maturing of opinion lest "snap judgment" lead to action that may embarrass or destroy. At the same time, by planning ahead, undue delays can be avoided and the work may move forward at a steady pace.

Experience shows that much of the work of the church is of routine nature: bills must be paid, Sunday worship is a recurring event, etc. In order to provide for unity of understanding and to prevent discrimination, so that detailed decisions may be made as close as possible to the point of application, and so that procedures do not get in the way of the "business at hand," standardized routine procedures should be established.

Types and Authority of Legislative Assemblies

Legislative rights at any level pertain to the work of that level. A legislative assembly may make recommendations to a conference at the next higher level.

Branch business meetings are held at least annually. Special business meetings may be held upon call. The dates for business meetings are set in consultation with the district president.

District conferences generally are open to all the church membership of the district. However, district conferences may be organized on a delegate basis. When this is done the district may determine the basis of delegate representation.

Stake conferences are held at least annually. Most stakes, however, hold conferences quarterly. There is no provision for delegate stake conferences. All members of the stake in good standing have voice and vote.

Regional, national, or tribal church conferences are

held at the call of the regional president, or regional administrator. Usually they are held annually. They do not supersede branch, district, or stake assemblies where these exist. They may be delegate conferences. If so, the basis of representation is determined by the region or church concerned.

The World Conference is constituted according to the rules of representation. It enacts legislation on behalf of the entire church.

The representative presiding officers for districts, stakes, missions, or the World Church may call special conferences when necessary.

In general, the presiding officers of the area holding a conference should preside by virtue of their office. It is appropriate for the presiding officer to yield the chair to the person next in authority when the business before the conference deals with matters in which the presiding officer is a party in interest.

In national conferences the minister in charge should preside with the consent of the conference.

In the World Conference the First Presidency presides on a motion from the floor. This establishes the principle that the body selects its president.

Participation

In the branch, district, and stake all members in good standing may participate with the possible exception of a district conference which is organized on a delegate basis. In that case, the branch delegates participate in the district conference.

In the World Conference participation is determined by the Rules of Representation (Rules of Order IV).

Conferences are held for the purpose of conferring

and transacting the business of the church. Each person participating in a conference should try to implement principles of Christian conduct and the willingness to yield to the decision of the majority even though he or she may have personal preferences which the conference does not accept.

The business of a conference should be conducted in the spirit of worship. It is hoped that the Holy Spirit's presence will bring light and the conviction of God's participation in the decisions made in a conference.

Often the decision made is less important to the work of the church than what happens to the development of the people in making the decision. Few decisions are good if the people become estranged from one another in the process. As priesthood members we are called to bring a ministry which unites and encourages the people. We should avoid becoming leaders of factions that divide. A poor decision which leaves the people united and anxious to work in the church for Christ is better than a right decision which creates conflict and division in the body.

Initiating Legislation

In any assembly legislation may be initiated by members of that assembly. Legislation may also be initiated by reference from a lesser legislative organization or from administrative officers having jurisdiction.

Enactments of legislation on the part of any assembly must not be counter to that which has been enacted by an assembly of higher level having jurisdiction. This goes back to the general principle that the actions of a legislative body must pertain to the work in the jurisdiction for which it functions.

Judicial Procedures

Judicial procedure is initiated when the law of the church requires. It is called upon when decisions must be made concerning a member's status and rights. Though such decisions sometimes result in suspension or expulsion, the primary purpose is to bring about repentance, forgiveness, and restitution.

In fairness to everyone, ministers who are called upon to act in judicial capacity must not be personally involved in the case. They are there to minister and must cultivate Christian attitudes.

Courts of the Church

Elders' Courts: Appointed by the appropriate presiding officer, this court is a temporary one, created to hear only the specific case referred to it. It is a court of original jurisdiction where no bishop's court exists. Elders' courts are not held when bishop's courts are possible.

Bishop's Courts: In areas where there is a bishop assigned, the bishop's court is a standing court of original jurisdiction. A bishop's court from another area may also be requested to hear a case in a jurisdiction where no standing court exists if the charges are such that expulsion may be the result. It also may be an appellate court.

Stake High Councils: The stake high council is a permanent stake court. It is an appellate court, hearing appeals from the stake bishop's courts.

Standing High Council: The Standing High Council is a permanent court of final appeal. It is a court of original jurisdiction in cases involving general officers and high priests. It supervises lesser courts and hears appeals from lesser courts that the Presidency determines should be heard by them. The right of the Presidency to determine those cases which it shall hear is for the purpose of protection against abuse of appeal rights.

Court Actions

Charges brought before courts of the church must be specific in nature and show that ministerial labor has been attempted. Ministerial labor should exhaust all possibilities of redemptive ministry before a decision is made to submit the matter to a court.

When the offense is such that the court's decision is expulsion the statement of the decision must not involve discussion of the merits of the case. Decisions requiring expulsion are presented to the appropriate business meeting for acknowledgment, "and the church shall lift up their hands."[7]

Appeals must be within the time prescribed except in those cases in which the appellate court grants additional time.

For further reading see *Administrative Policies and Procedures, Ministry of Reconciliation,* and *Responsibilities in Church Court Procedures* (Herald House).

STAKES

STAKE ORGANIZATION

Ideally a stake is a well-integrated organization of related congregations formed in major centers of gathering for more complete systemizing and honoring of the law of Christ in both spiritual and temporal affairs. A stake is the basic unit of church organization directly related to Zionic mission.[8]

The organization of stakes is recommended by the First Presidency and approved by the Joint Council of the First Presidency, Council of Twelve, and Presiding Bishopric, then by World Conference and by the members of the proposed stakes.[9]

A fully organized stake has a stake presidency, a high council, and a stake bishopric.[10]

The Stake Presidency

The stake presidency presides over the stake and has immediate charge and oversight of all spiritual activities within the stake and is responsible for the welfare and spiritual discipline of all church members within the confines of the stake, subject to the advice and direction of the general spiritual authorities of the church.[11]

In filling the office of stake president the First Presidency presents to the Joint Council of the First Presidency, Council of Twelve, and Presiding Bishopric their recommendation and, upon approval by the council, this recommendation is presented to the stake conference for consideration and approval.[12]

Counselors to the stake president are chosen from among the high priests[13] by the stake president subject to approval of the stake conference, after which they are set apart.

The stake presidency is sustained by vote at the annual conference of the stake.

The Stake High Council

The stake high council is composed of at least seven, and when full, twelve, high priests chosen on recommendation of the stake presidency and approval of the stake conference. High council members are sustained annually at a stake conference.

Vacancies are filled by recommendation of the stake presidency with the approval of the apostle in charge, the director of Field Ministries, the First Presidency, the council, and stake conference.

When organizing a new stake, the First Presidency, in consultation with appropriate supervising and presiding officers, nominates at least seven members of the high council. The stake presidency fill the remaining vacancies.

The high council functions at the call of the stake presidency as an advisory board in both spiritual and temporal matters within the stake. The council has no independent administrative function, but may be consulted on any matters deemed of sufficient importance. Major policy changes or new policies are matters for consultation with the stake high council. Final decision remains with the administrative officers concerned.

The stake high council constitutes the highest judicial council in the stake, having both original and appellate jurisdiction.

The ordination of high priests, elders, and members of the Aaronic priesthood within the stake and the setting apart of stake high councilors require the approval of the stake high council.[14]

Seventy

When seventies are assigned to stakes their principal labor is specified by the apostle in charge in consultation with the stake president. In discharging the duties of their assignments they are responsible to the stake president.

The Stake Bishopric

The stake bishop is the chief financial officer within the stake. In the area of general church finances, the stake bishop has immediate charge and oversight of general church funds and properties within the stake and is responsible to the Presiding Bishopric in this capacity.

The stake bishop has oversight and responsibility for stake properties within the stake and in this regard is responsible to the stake president and stake conference. The bishop is in charge of stake finances. It being understood that the finances of the congregational units of the stake are an integral part of stake finances. The stake bishop is responsible to members of the stake presidency, in their presiding role, and to the stake conference for the administration of such finances as trustee in accordance with budgetary provisions and special funds objectives. However, regarding specific trustee responsibility the bishop is directly responsible to the stake conference.[15]

To carry out responsibilities effectively pertaining both to general church finances and properties and to local finances and properties, the stake bishop is represented in the congregational units of the stake by duly appointed and approved bishop's agents and solicitors.

The stake bishopric also has judicial responsibilities as the standing court of original jurisdiction within the stake.

In filling the office of stake bishop, the First Presidency presents a recommendation to the Joint Council of the First Presidency, Council of Twelve, and Presiding Bishopric, and "upon approval by the council, this recommendation is presented to the stake conference for consideration and approval."[16]

The bishop chooses counselors from among the high priests or elders in consultation with the stake presidency and subject to the approval of the stake conference, after which they are set apart.

The stake bishop is sustained by vote at the annual conference of the stake. The responsibilities of stake bishops ("other bishops") are parallel on the stake level to the responsibilities of the Presiding Bishop on the World Church level.[17] A stake bishop does not receive authority from the Presiding Bishop but by virtue of divine call through the First Presidency and subsequent ordination and appointment. It is with the authority of this procedure that a person assumes the responsibilities of a bishop, as outlined in the law, to be expressed in ministry on the stake level. A bishop is not elected to this area of ministry, for by call, ordination, and appointment, and with the acceptance of the people, the bishop lawfully becomes administrator of temporalities in the assigned stake.

The stake bishop is the representative of the Presiding Bishop in the stake in areas of ministry for which the Presiding Bishop is responsible to the church as a whole such as collecting, receipting, and accounting for tithing, general church offerings and surplus; in receiving and processing tithing statements; as title custodian of houses of worship; in the management of general church properties; in the administration of oblation funds in caring for the poor; in representing the Presiding Bishop as president of the Aaronic priesthood; and in teaching the law of temporalities. The stake bishop is directly responsible to the Presiding Bishop in these areas; that is, the stake bishop reports regularly, accounts for, and transmits general church funds to the Presiding Bishop at regular intervals.

These duties, even though they are World Church oriented, are to be carried out within the framework of a ministerial program for which the stake president has primary concern. In local responsibilities, the stake bishop by right of ordination and stake appointment assumes the same relationship with the stake presidency as the Presiding Bishop has with the First Presidency and has the same trustee relationship to the stake conference on the stake level that the Presiding Bishopric has to the World Conference on the general church level.

The Congregational Bishop's Agent

The congregational bishop's agent is appointed by the stake bishopric with the concurrence of the stake presidency, after such consultation as the stake presidency may desire. The appointment should then be approved by the congregation. In large congregations the bishop's agent will recommend solicitors, with the concurrence of the presiding elder, who will be appointed by the stake bishopric to assist the bishop's agent with the work within the congregational unit. These solicitors, who handle both local and general church funds, should be approved by the congregation at the regular annual business meeting.

The bishop's agent represents the stake bishopric in caring for both general and local finances and properties within the congregational unit. These financial agency functions, however, will be carried out within the framework of a ministerial program for which the stake president and presiding elder have primary concern.[18]

Congregation

The organized subdivision within a stake is the congregation. It is formed by the stake presidency after consultation with the stake high council, the apostle in charge, or the First Presidency, and with the concurrence of the stake conference.

The presiding officers of the congregations are assistants to the stake presidency. They are selected at stake conferences with right of nomination resting concurrently with the stake presidency and the people.[19]

Other full-time ministers in the stakes are assigned on the recommendation of the director of Administrative Services to the Joint Council of First Presidency, Council of Twelve, and Presiding Bishopric.

Disorganization of a Congregation

The disorganization of a congregation may be considered when any one or combination of the following circumstances prevail:

A. Reorganization of an area within a stake
B. Movement of members out of a given area to the extent that it is economically unwise to maintain the congregation
C. Declining leadership potential to the point that undue pressure exists on the stake to provide leadership in the face of limited return
D. Repeated and consistent conditions of disorder within the congregation

When the decision to disorganize has been made by the stake presidency, in consultation with the high council and stake bishopric and with the approval of the apostle to the stake, the director of Field Ministries, or First Presidency, the matter should be presented to the stake conference. The stake conference should share in the responsibility of supporting the major decisions of the administrative officers which affect church growth and outreach. The right of the conference in this matter is limited only to action on that which is proposed by the stake officers. There should be no consideration by the conference of such matters as boundary lines. Neither may the conference propose an alternative action with respect to the recommendation for disorganization.

General Information Concerning Conferences

Stake conferences and congregational business meetings are authorized to transact business relating to the maintenance and spread of the work within their respective boundaries, but subject always to the rules and resolutions of World Conference and to the advice of the general authorities in matters committed to them under the law. Business meetings and conferences should be held as often as needed to transact the necessary business. At least one should be held each year.

Notice of stake conferences should be sent to the First Presidency, the apostle in the field, and to such other general church officers as might be concerned with the business to be transacted.[20]

Congregational business meetings shall be scheduled in consultation with the stake presidency.

Presiding over Stake Conferences

The stake president presides over the stake conference. At the request, or absence, of the stake president one of the counselors may preside. Members of the First Presidency or Council of Twelve, or their authorized representative, may be asked to preside as a courtesy or in view of special circumstances. Congregational business meetings are presided over by the stake president or a representative.

Recommended Order of Proceedings

Opening worship

Reading and approval of the minutes

Reports, communications, and suggestions from the presiding officer

Communications or reports from the First Presidency, the minister in charge or assistant, the Presiding Bishopric, or other general church officers (with precedence in the order named)

Reports of the officers of the stake or congregation other than the presiding officer

Reports of standing and special committees

Right to Vote

The only qualification for participation is membership and good standing.[21]

All members of the church enrolled within a congregation or stake are entitled to voice and vote in the legislative assemblies of that congregation or stake. Members should not attempt to vote in the legislative assemblies of congregations or stakes to which they do not belong. A member who has changed place of residency, but whose transfer has not yet been processed by the Department of Statistics, may be given the right of voice and vote by action of the assembly. This right of voice and vote may also be extended as a courtesy to church members who may have special information or interest in the matter at issue, but it should be clearly understood that the extension of such privilege is at the discretion of the assembly and is not a right which may be claimed apart from such action.

Nominations in Filling Elective Offices

Nominations may be made by any member within the jurisdiction who is present at the business meeting or conference, or by the First Presidency, the apostle in the field or the apostle's representative, by the stake president or presidency, or by the presiding elder.[22]

The right to nominate from the floor is important to preserve the democratic process and to call attention to those who might otherwise be overlooked.

Appointment of Officers

The appointments of certain officers are approved by vote of the appropriate legislative meeting, such as those requiring special priesthood (stake presidents, stake high councilors, etc.), those which involve trust relationships (bishops, bishop's agents, etc.), or those representing general church departments (historians, recorders, etc.).

Should the business meeting vote not to approve the appointment of an officer, it is the responsibility of the appropriate officials to present another candidate for consideration by the business meeting. Such legislative approval should be sought only after the appropriate official has given approval to the nominee. A person who occupies such an office may be removed from office by vote of the appropriate legislative body or by agreement of the appropriate official who made the appointment.

Department or Functional Officers

Selection of departmental leaders should be made in regular business meetings rather than by the departments.

The departmental or functional officers of the stake are an extension of the stake presidency. Their purpose is to assist in the work of the stake by utilizing the services and abilities of specialists in various fields. The work of these departmental officers is supervised by the stake presidency, who also designate their areas of responsibility. A parallel relationship exists in the congregations between presiding elders and department heads.

The Stake Recorder (Statistician)

The stake recorder (statistician) is appointed by the church statistician with the advice and consent of the stake president. It is the recorder's responsibility to care for the statistical records of the stake as a representative of the Department of Statistics. The recorder is to see that the records are kept up-to-date each month with respect to membership enrollments. He or she reports blessings, baptisms, marriages, divorces, ordinations, deaths, transfers, and all other vital statistics. From time to time, the church statistician asks the stake recorder to make special surveys of various kinds.

Congregational Recorder (Statistician)

The congregational recorder is appointed by the stake

statistician with the advice and consent of the presiding elder and the approval of the congregation. The duties parallel in the congregations the duties of the stake recorder in the stake. The recorder receives all incoming materials from the stake recorder. Included in these materials are some which ought to be delivered to the members. These are enrollment cards, marriage record cards, and certificates of blessings. If the presiding elder is to take direct supervision of these deliveries, they should be delivered to the presiding elder immediately on their receipt by the recorder. If the presiding elder arranges that the recorder should deliver these materials, the recorder should deliver them promptly to the individual at home.

Priesthood and lay members alike should assist the recorder by keeping her or him informed. Information on all members who move into, or away from, a congregation must be made available to the recorder for reporting. Information should be concise, accurate, and thorough.

To carry out the work effectively, the recorder should be as widely acquainted as possible. Whenever possible, the office should be held by an ordained teacher.

Priesthood Education

The stake presidency has general oversight of all priesthood education in the stake. Training courses for the Melchisedec priesthood will be provided under the immediate direction of the stake presidency or through quorum presidents. The program of Aaronic priesthood education is under the immediate direction of the stake bishopric, or under their supervision through quorum presidents, in consultation with the stake presidency.

Reports

All stake officers should report to the stake president and hold themselves subject to the stake president's general direction and counsel.[23]

The stake president should report on the condition of the stake as occasion may require, and in any event not less than once every six months. This report should go to the apostle in the field, the director of field ministries, and to the First Presidency. It should be in sufficient detail to indicate the progress being achieved, areas of special opportunity, areas of special difficulty, points at which help is desired, the work of leaders which should be brought to the attention of the church officers concerned, and similar matters.

Congregational officers and department heads should keep the presiding elder informed on the activities for which they are responsible.

Terminology

Stake President—chief presiding officer over a stake

Stake Presidency—the stake president and counselors

Stake High Council—twelve high priests presided over by one or more members of the stake presidency

Stake Bishop—the administrative bishop in a stake

Stake Bishopric—the stake bishop and counselors

Presiding Elder—the minister who presides over a congregation as administrative assistant to the stake presidency

REGIONS

Definition

A region is an association of districts or other "Level 2" jurisdictions under the ministerial supervision of a regional administrator or regional president.

Regions are organized to provide continuity of administration and coordination of administrative planning in matters of inter-district concern.

Regions are organized on the recommendation of the First Presidency and the approval of the Joint Council of the First Presidency, Council of Twelve, and Presiding Bishopric.

Ideally, each region should have a regional bishop. Where no bishop is available a treasurer is appointed by action of the Joint Council of the First Presidency, Council of Twelve, and Presiding Bishopric.

Missionary and other specialized ministries may be supplied to regions by the assignment of appropriate ministers by the Joint Council of the First Presidency, Council of Twelve, and Presiding Bishopric.

Regional Administrator's or President's Duties

Reporting: The regional administrator or president is responsible to the supervising minister and submits written reports regularly to the supervising minister with copies to the director of field ministries and the First Presidency.

Priesthood and Leadership Education: The regional administrator or president provides for regional institutes in priesthood and leadership education, including such fields as women's work, church school, youth work, and every other type of leadership which is essential to strong branches and districts. The regional administrator or president works with district presidents in setting up district programs, and through them branch programs, for priesthood and leadership education.

Reunions and Camps: The regional administrator or president coordinates all reunions and camps within the region and is responsible, with the appropriate district officers, for setting up a staff, working out the program, and for other aspects of these activities.

Missionary Outreach: The regional administrator or president is responsible for encouraging alert missionary outreach on district, branch, and mission levels. Branches and districts are responsible for their own missionary programs and should recognize this as a major function of the church.

District Conferences: The regional administrator or president coordinates the schedules for district conferences and, when advisable, participates in them as the supervising minister.

Church Buildings and Facilities: The regional administrator or president is concerned with the development of church buildings and facilities, and in cooperation with the other officers, gives leadership in selection of new locations and new buildings or major improvements.

Silencing Priesthood: The regional administrator or president is the first officer beyond the district president for appeals from actions silencing priesthood.

Church Courts: The regional administrator or president may appoint church courts as required.

Recommendations for Ordination: In calls to the

Aaronic priesthood the regional administrator or president gives the final approval, after receiving appropriate information from the First Presidency and Presiding Bishopric and before the contact with the candidate or presentation to the appropriate conferences. In the call of the elder, the regional administrator or president gives the final approval after writing to the First Presidency, the apostle, and the Presiding Bishopric for appropriate information and advice. After the regional officer's approval, the candidate may be contacted and the call presented to the appropriate conferences.

The regional administrator or president may recommend calls to the office of high priest, submitting such to the apostle supervising the field or directly to the First Presidency. Such calls must be approved by the First Presidency and a high council and by a branch or district conference or the World Conference.[24]

The regional administrator or president may chair committees and other groups involving the region or a combination of constituent jurisdictions.

Regional Budgets: In regions which do not have regional conferences the budget is prepared by the regional administrator and the regional bishop (or treasurer). It is then submitted to the apostle in charge and the Presiding Bishopric for consideration and for final action. In regions having regional conferences the budget is prepared by the regional president and regional bishop and approved by action of the conference.

Regional Bishops (Treasurers)

The Joint Council of the First Presidency, the Council of Twelve, and the Presiding Bishopric is moving as rapidly as possible toward the appointment of regional bishops who will be responsible for regional administrative funds. If more than one bishop is assigned within a region, one of them is appointed to handle the regional funds while the other(s) may share ministerial, teaching, and other bishopric responsibilities without having the custodianship of regional funds.

The regional bishop (or treasurer) receives from the districts in the region their contributions to the regional budget. He or she is the custodian of these funds and expends them according to the budget under the general direction of the regional administrator. As occasion requires, the regional bishop may request from the Presiding Bishopric those funds which may be available to the region through World Conference subsidy to the regional budget.

When regional conferences are established, the appointment of all regional bishops (or treasurers) will be subject to the approval of the respective conferences (Joint Council Minutes, September 22, 1966). The program of Aaronic priesthood education is under the immediate direction of the regional bishop.

DISTRICT ORGANIZATION

A district is an association of branches.

As a general rule, districts include three or more stable branches.

District organization should be as simple as possible in view of the ends to be served. These are as follows:

- To relieve the Twelve and Seventy from administration of branches in order to push the work into new fields[25]
- To provide guidance for pastors and mission presidents through district presidents

- To provide helps for branch departmental leaders
- To marshal and direct local forces for saturating the area within the district (The natural missionary area in districts is within reach of branches and among groups of members in communities in which no branch organization yet exists.)
- To provide church association beyond the branch areas: general, priesthood, departmental

Appointee high priests, seventies, and elders may be made available to preside over districts, subject to the approval of the district conference (Joint Council Minutes, September 15, 1952).

District Presidency

The district presidency should consist of one or more members of the Melchisedec priesthood. (The Joint Council of First Presidency, the Twelve, and Bishopric has held that no more than three members should be in the district presidency.)

The district president and counselors should become personally acquainted, through regular visits, with each branch and mission within the district.

Their special concerns are the adequacy and balance of the branch and missionary programs; the preaching and departmental ministry available; the spiritual tone of the branch or mission; programming for the future in such matters as priesthood and departmental personnel; financing and planning for housing needs, and so forth. Their advice should be sought in connection with the location and purchase of church sites, plans and programs for new buildings, improvements, and additions to equipment, prospective sales.[26]

Districts may be presided over by high priests or

elders. Members of the Aaronic priesthood should not be chosen for the district presidency, nor should members of the Melchisedec priesthood who have been set apart as bishops or evangelists. In selecting district presidents first consideration should be given to the available high priests. If no high priests are available, or if the high priests are incapacitated by age or other reasons, consideration should then be given to the elders within the district.[27] When a change in the office of district president occurs, this should be reported immediately to the general church secretary, giving the name and address of the new district president.

District presidents need to be capable of administering the major fields of church life and growth—pastoral, missionary, and teaching.

District President Files

Each district president should maintain files of the following information so that it can be handed to the next district president to assist in maintaining continuity of administration.

1. *District and Branch Officers:* A complete, up-to-date mailing list including addresses, zip numbers, and telephone numbers.
2. *Membership Mailing List:* This list should be current with complete mailing data.
3. *Current Priesthood Roster:* Current mailing list of all priesthood members. Such listing should be by branch, mission (or other) with office, age, and activity indicated.
4. *Annual District Baptismal Report:* Statistical information on baptisms plus descriptive report on branch, mission, or other evangelistic programs.

5. *Calendar of District Activities:* This should contain information on camping programs, retreats, institutes, workshops, or other activities.
6. *District Level—General Church Finances:* Record to contain goal, contributions, number of contributors, and number of accounting stewards.
7. *Current District Boundary Lines:* Suggest suitable road map (folder size 8½ x 11) with boundary lines, branches, missions, and group identification for ready reference.
8. *District Conference Minutes:* Have available copies of minutes of district conference for district president's background information. This should include conference minutes, treasurer's reports, and budgets.
9. *Annual Financial Reports from Branches:* This should include operating and building fund data such as income, expenses, and yearly balance from each branch in the district.

Bishops and Bishop's Agents

District bishops and bishop's agents have trustee responsibility to the Presiding Bishopric in the collecting and handling of general church funds. They also have direct relationship with the Presiding Bishopric in teaching the financial stewardship law, in recommending the training of solicitors, in ministry to the needy through the oblation fund, and in caring for general church properties which may be located within the district area. These responsibilities are carried out within the framework of the total program of the district. On occasion the bishop or bishop's agent also functions as district treasurer and is responsible to the district conference and the district presidency for this trusteeship and financial administration.

Departmental Officers and Their Duties

All district officers should report to the district president and be guided by the district president's general direction and counsel in the implementation of the district program. Departmental officers are administrative and staff assistants to the district presidency to whom they are responsible in their respective activities.[28]

Presiding at District Conference

The district president presides over the district conference. At his request, or in his absence, his counselors may preside. Members of the First Presidency or Council of Twelve, or their authorized representatives, may be asked to preside as a courtesy or in view of special circumstances.[29]

Recommended Order of Proceedings

The order recommended for a district conference and branch business meetings is as follows:

Opening worship

Reading and approval of the minutes

Reports, communications, and suggestions from the presiding officer

Communications or reports from the First Presidency, the minister in charge or assistant, the Presiding Bishopric, or other general church officers (with precedence in the order named)

Reports of the officers of the district other than the presiding officer

Reports of standing and special committees

Special District Conference

A special district conference may be called at the discretion of the district president (or presidency) or in response to the formal or informal request of representative members of the district through the appropriate district officers.[30]

Reasonable care should be taken to see that all those who have a right to participate have sufficient notice of time and place of meeting and of business to be considered.

In emergencies the presiding minister next higher in the administrative line may call and preside over a conference in any of the local organizations which constitute his jurisdiction, subject to the confirming action of the conference when it convenes.[31]

Representation at District Conference

All members in good standing within the district are members of the district conference. Under exceptional circumstances districts may organize their conferences on a delegate basis in harmony with Section IV:29 of the Rules of Order, but this is normally not desirable.

Right to Vote

All members of the church enrolled within a branch or district are entitled to vote in the legislative assemblies of that branch or district. If the district has a delegate conference, only delegates may vote. Members should not attempt to vote in the legislative assemblies of branches or districts to which they do not belong. A member who has changed place of residency but whose transfer has not yet been processed by the Department of Statistics may be given the right of voice and vote by action of the assembly. This right of voice and vote may also be extended as a courtesy to church members who have special information or interest in the matter at issue, but it should be clearly understood that the extension of such privilege is at the discretion of the assembly and is not a right which may be claimed apart from such action.

Information Concerning Conferences

District conferences and branch business meetings are authorized to transact business relating to the maintenance and spread of the work within their respective boundaries, but subject always to the rules and resolutions of World Conference and to the advice of the general authorities in matters committed to them under the law. Business meetings and conferences should be held as often as needed to transact the necessary business. At least one should be held each year.

Notice of district conferences should be sent to the regional administrator, the apostle in the field, and to such other church officers as might be concerned with the business to be transacted.[32]

Nominations in Filling Elective Offices

Nominations may be made by any person who is properly a member of the conference, or by the First Presidency, the director of field ministries, the apostle in the field, the regional administrator or president, or the district president or presidency.[33]

Approving Officers

Certain officers are appointed by World Church leaders and approved by vote of the appropriate business meetings, such as those requiring special priesthood (stake presidents, stake high counselors, etc.), those which involve trust relationships (bishops, bishop's agents, etc.), or those representing World Church departments (historians, recorders, etc.). For further information, concerning organization of branches, branch officers, business meetings, etc., see Rules of Order, paragraphs 44-59.

Should the business meeting vote not to approve such an officer it is the responsibility of the appropriate World Church officials to present another for consideration by the business meeting.

Other District Officers

The number of officers needed in the district depends upon the size and program of the district but the following are the most common:

Secretary: Keeps the minutes of district business meetings and may be called on to prepare official district correspondence.

Treasurer: Handles all district funds and carries responsibility with the district president to keep expenditures within the approved budget pattern. The books are subject to audit at request by proper authorities and should be audited at least once each year for accuracy and the treasurer's protection. When available, it is desirable for a bishop to be selected as district treasurer.

Director of Christian Education: The function of the director of Christian education is to facilitate the work of the church school directors in the branches and missions of the district. The director should keep informed about this work through contact with the World Church Christian Education Office.

District Women's Leader: The district women's leader

assists the branch presidents and their women's leaders in their work and coordinates inter-branch and district programs in consultation with the district president.

District Youth Leader: Assists branch presidents and their youth leaders in their work. Coordinates youth activities of the district, such as youth camps and institutes, in consultation with the district president.

Bishop's Agent: The bishop's agent is appointed by the Presiding Bishopric with the concurrence of the First Presidency, minister in charge, and the district presidency. The bishop's agent receives tithes and general offerings from the solicitors of the branches and other World Church funds received in the district, issues receipts for the money, and forwards it to the Presiding Bishopric. A vote to sustain the bishop's agent in this office is requested at the district conference.

Music Director: The district music director is concerned with assisting branch presidents and the music directors of the branches and district missions in counseling and in providing, through institutes and other meetings, opportunities for education in the use of music in the church.

Historian: The district historian is appointed by the general church historian on the recommendation of the district presidency, and sustained by the district conference. The historian maintains a current history of the district and assists branch historians in their work as they may have need.

Recorder: The district recorder keeps a record of the nonresident membership of the district. The recorder is appointed by the church statistician on the recommendation of the district presidency and sustained by the district conference.

District Departmental Leaders

District departmental leaders may be elected to advise presiding officers and departmental workers throughout the district concerning the women's department, Zion's League, children's work, music, young adults, etc. Such district officers, with the approval of the district president, may conduct institutes on the district level. They may be called in for consultation by branch officers, but it should be understood that district departmental officers have no administrative relation to branch departmental officers.

Selection of Departmental Leaders

In branch and district business meetings and conferences, the presiding officer may make nominations or nominations may be made from the floor.

Selection of departmental leaders should be made in regular business meetings rather than by the departments. A department should not commit itself by some independent action in advance in such a fashion as to set up thereby a prior claim on the services of certain persons as against the interest of other departments.

Departmental leaders should be selected not less than a month prior to the date they assume responsibilities.

Basic Departmental Programs and Special Gatherings

Such meetings of the district department of women, church school, young adults, Zion's League, and children's departments should be cleared with the district presidency whose function it is to keep these in balance and pointed forward. All district rallies, retreats, and institutes should receive the prior approval and support of the district presidency.

Boundary Line Changes

Changes in district boundary lines are authorized by the Joint Council of the First Presidency. Council of Twelve, and Presiding Bishopric.[34]

District Budgets

Each district should adopt a budget for its year's activities. Each branch in the district should carry its proportion of the district expenses. The district budget should include a proportionate share of the regional budget.

The budget should be projected by the district president and treasurer after adequate consultations with department heads. In some cases, this responsibility may be performed by a budget committee with the district president and treasurer as ex officio members and with the district president acting as chairman. Budgetary projections should be determined on the basis of the resources of the district, the total program to be implemented, and the balance needed between the ministries of the various departments. The budget must have the approval of the district conference.

District Treasurer

The district treasurer is an elected officer of the district responsible to the conference for the care of the funds belonging to the district and for their disbursement in accordance with the approved budget as the program progresses under the administrative direction of the district presidency.

The treasurer's ministry, as is the case with all district officers, is under the general direction of the district president. The treasurer, therefore, should work in close association with the district president, keeping the district president informed of the trends in response to the financial needs of the district, special problems which may arise, and other matters which will enable the district presidency to give whatever support is possible to the local financial program.

BRANCHES

Branch Organization

Branches may be organized by the authority of the First Presidency or of any member of the Council of Twelve having jurisdiction, or by their direction when circumstances prevent them from being present.

At the date of organization, branches normally should have the following:

A minimum of fifty members

At least three qualified members of the priesthood

Proved congregational stability on a mission basis

Capacity to provide resources for operation and future housing

Promise of further missionary growth (Branches should continue to be the concern of missionary authorities until they have achieved sufficient strength to be stable.)

Sufficient area for missionary expansion whether they be established in rural or urban areas

When necessary, branches may be disorganized by the authority of the apostle in charge.

In all matters of mission or branch organization or disorganization the district president should be consulted and the conferences concerned and the World Church statistician informed.

Branch and Mission Names

Branches and missions should be known by the names of the towns, cities, or communities where meetings are held. Apostolic approval should be obtained before any changes of names are made.

Bylaws

No branch or district should set up bylaws but should follow the rules given in the World Church Rules of Order, as recorded in *Rules and Resolutions* (Herald House).

It is better to legislate for specific situations as they arise than to try to cover them by adopting a separate set of bylaws.

The Branch President

The branch president must be a member of the priesthood.

The rule is that the one holding the highest office in the priesthood shall preside if there are no good reasons to the contrary, it being understood that evangelists or bishops should not be selected as branch presidents. In selecting a branch president, first consideration should be given to the high priests available. If none are available or if a good reason exists for not selecting an available high priest, consideration should be given to the elders.

If no elders are available, or a good reason exists for failure to select an elder, then the priests, teachers, and deacons may be considered in that order.

Branch presidents should work closely with the district president and should cooperate as fully as possible in district activities.

Change of Address

Any branch president who moves should immediately notify the district president, regional administrator or president, and the World Church Secretary, giving the old and new addresses; and any district president who moves should send such notification of the change of address to the regional administrator and the World Church Secretary.

Change of Branch President

Any change in branch president should be brought to the attention of the regional administrator or president and the World Church Secretary immediately, giving the name and address of the new branch president.

Presiding at Branch Business Meetings

The branch president presides over a branch business meeting. When a member of the First Presidency, Council of Twelve, regional administrator, or district president is present at a branch business meeting, the higher administrative officer may be shown the courtesy of being given the opportunity to preside.[35] "In emergencies the presiding minister next higher in the administrative line may call and preside over a conference [business meeting] in any of the local organizations which constitute the jurisdiction, subject to the confirming action of the conference [business meeting] when it convenes."[36]

Branch Elections of Officers

Branch officers should be elected one to three months prior to the date of taking office. This will permit the departmental leaders to plan programs and the pastor to prepare a branch calendar for the ensuing term of office. Election dates should be discussed with the district president.

Other Branch Officers

Secretary: Keeps minutes of the business meetings and may be called on to handle official branch correspondence.

Treasurer: An elected officer of the branch responsible for the care of the funds belonging to the branch.

The treasurer should issue receipts for all monies received from individual contributors and all other sources and make disbursements of the funds in accordance with the budget approved by the branch and as the program progresses under the administrative direction of the branch presidency.

The treasurer's ministry, as is the case with all branch officers, is under the general direction of the branch president. The treasurer therefore should work in close association with the branch president, keeping the branch president informed of trends in response to the financial needs of the branch, special problems which may arise, and other matters which will enable the branch presidency to give whatever support is possible to the local financial program.

The *Local Treasurer's Record Book* has been prepared by the Presiding Bishopric, and is available through the book stewards. It contains sufficient sheets for one year's branch accounting. A major feature is a complete manual of instruction which is illustrated by a sample budget, monthly accounting sheets, bank reconciliation, and treasurer's reports.

This record book will aid in bringing uniformity and accuracy in the collection, administration, and accounting for funds in branches.

Church School Director: It is the responsibility of the director to plan and administer the educational program of the church school and work in harmony with the Department of Christian Education. Specialized education within the departmental framework or in priesthood and leadership education may be handled separately.

If it is the intent of the branch membership that the director's duties cover a broader field of Christian education than that of the church school, the title should be Director of Christian Education.

Branch Women's Leader: The women's leader participates on the branch leadership team bringing the hopes, concerns, and resources of women into the planning and implementation process. The women's leader serves the branch as a consultant on women's ministries. Where there is an organized women's department, the women's leader serves as its director, assisting the department to accomplish its goals which have been derived from the branch goals.

Youth Director: The youth leader supervises the youth programs of the branch, such as Zion's League, Zioneers, Orioles, Skylarks, and Boy Scouts.

Music Director: The music director supervises the musical aspects of worship and culture within the branch. This includes appointing choir directors, maintaining close counseling relationship with the branch president concerning music used in orders of worship, and planning special musical programs.

There are other officers who are appointed by World Church departments and some by the branch president. Following the principle of common consent, these appointments are subject to a vote of the body.

Solicitor: The solicitor is appointed by the Presiding Bishopric on recommendation of the bishop or bishop's agent having jurisdiction and with the concurrence of the branch president. Obviously, the solicitor should be one who keeps the financial law. Out of experience comes more effective teaching, and response is stimulated toward financial stewardship principles and procedures. This appointment should be sustained at the branch business meeting.

The solicitor collects and accounts for all contributions to general church funds. The solicitor writes and delivers official receipts to all contributors to such funds and reports monthly to the district bishop or bishop's agent. The solicitor may be called on by the branch president, bishop, or bishop's agent to investigate situations of need and make recommendations for oblation fund assistance.

The solicitor is not given the responsibility of disbursing general church funds except those incidental to making remittances such as postage, stationery, etc.

For further details regarding the work of the solicitor, see the *Solicitor's Manual* prepared by the Presiding Bishopric.

Branch Recorder (Statistician): This officer is an assistant who is appointed by the church statistician, with the advice and consent of the branch president and the concurrence of the branch, and acts as the direct representative of the Department of Statistics. It is his or her responsibility to care for the branch records. The branch recorder is to see that the records are kept up-to-date each month with respect to membership enrollment, and report blessings, baptisms, marriages, divorces, ordinations, deaths, transfers, and all other vital statistics to the Department of Statistics. The branch recorder receives all incoming materials from the Department of Statistics. Priesthood and lay members alike should keep the recorder informed. Information on all members who move into, or away from, a branch must be made available to the recorder for reporting. This should be concise, accurate, and thorough.

Included in these materials are some which ought to be delivered to the members. These are enrollment cards, marriage record cards, and certificates of blessing. If the branch president is to take direct supervision of these deliveries, then immediately on their receipt the recorder should deliver them to the branch president. Otherwise, the recorder should deliver these promptly to the individual at home.

From time to time, the church statistician asks the recorder to make special surveys of various kinds.

To carry out the work effectively, the recorder should be as widely acquainted as possible. Whenever possible, the office should be held by an ordained teacher.

Historian: Appointed by the World Church historian, the historian keeps record of the events of historical interest concerning the branch, in harmony with procedures established by the church historian.

Deacon in Charge: Appointed by the pastor, the deacon in charge supervises the work of the deacons with reference to the physical comfort of the membership during meetings, selects ushers, and oversees the details of the operation of the church plant. The deacon in charge should supervise the work of the custodian of the building, if such is required, or should make satisfactory arrangements for keeping the church buildings clean and in good repair.

Publicity Agent: Appointed by the pastor, the publicity agent maintains good relationships with the various news media and other potential publicity outlets. She or he prepares newsworthy items for local newspapers and for the church publications.

Group

A group is an informal association of people for church purposes, in a district or unorganized territory, who do not have sufficient strength to be a branch. Membership may not be transferred to a group but must be retained on the appropriate branch or nonresident list.

Mission Organization

Standards for mission organization are intended to be enlightening rather than restrictive since the types of mission organization vary widely.

Missions are dependent pastoral units. They may be organized under regional, district, or national/tribal church supervision.

All missions shall be organized with the knowledge and consent of the regional administrator/president or apostle in the field. This consent should be indicated to the Department of Statistics at the beginning of the organization process so that the organization may be of record.

Membership should be transferred into the mission as soon thereafter as possible. The organization is completed when all transfers are sent to the Department of Statistics.

Ordinations among mission personnel shall be on the initiation of the district president, or general church officers concerned. Approval should be secured from the district and not by a vote of the mission.

Pastors of missions shall be appointed by the district president, regional administrator/president, or apostle concerned. Approval may be secured from the district but not by vote of the mission. The pastor should feel free to make recommendations to the appointing officer regarding calls to the priesthood, reinstatements of silenced priesthood, and other administrative matters.

Priesthood Education

A branch president should conduct priesthood training courses within the branch. The district presidency is also responsible for planning and administering priesthood training courses supplemental to those within the branches. While the program of priesthood education is the responsibility of the administrative officers concerned, these officers can find valuable assistance through the Temple School.

World Church Funds

Early in the year each pastor receives a statement of World Church contributions made by the branch as a whole during the preceding year. It will include loose-change contributions for all general church funds such as the oblation fund, Graceland College Day fund, or other funds.

The statement to the pastor will not include a record of tithes and offerings receipted to individuals. Each individual contributor in the branch will receive a statement covering his or her receipted contributions of tithing and offerings.

Branch Budget

Being the coordinator of the entire branch program, the branch president needs to consult with the various department heads to formulate the total branch program for the year. After this has been done, the branch treasurer and branch president determine together the amount of money needed to implement the proposed program. The branch program will need to be within the limits of potential financing. Program planning nevertheless should be the first and basic step of budget preparation and should serve as the reason and stimulus for maximum income effort.

After the branch president and treasurer have prepared an estimated budget it is submitted to the branch for final consideration and approval. The branch has a right to make such changes as the majority wish; the budget is not valid until it is approved by formal action of the branch.

Some branches may want a large number of expense items in their budgets, but it is best to keep these to a minimum.

NOTES

1. Doctrine and Covenants 104:3-7.
2. GCR Nos. 849, 861.
3. Doctrine and Covenants 122:9.
4. Ibid., 120:3c.
5. Mosiah 9:57.

6. GCR No. 1101.
7. Doctrine and Covenants 42:22c.
8. Ibid., 98:4; Rules of Order, paragraphs 35, 36.
9. Rules of Order, paragraph 37.
10. Doctrine and Covenants 125:10.
11. Rules of Order, paragraph 39.
12. Ibid., paragraph 42.
13. Ibid., paragraph 38.
14. Doctrine and Covenants 17:17; 99:1, 4-10, 14; 104:14, 35; 122:6; GCR No. 988.
15. Rules of Order, paragraph 41.
16. Ibid., paragraph 42.
17. Doctrine and Covenants 68:2b.
18. Ibid., 149A:1-3.
19. Rules of Order, paragraph 35.
20. Ibid., paragraphs 43 and 46.
21. Doctrine and Covenants 125:9.
22. Rules of Order, pargraph 13.
23. Ibid., paragraph 39.
24. GCR No. 1051.
25. Doctrine and Covenants 120:1b; 122:7c; 141:6a.
26. Rules of Order, paragraph 45.
27. Doctrine and Covenants 120:2b; Rules of Order, paragraph 45.
28. Rules of Order, paragraph 45.
29. Ibid., paragraph 47.
30. Ibid., paragraph 20.
31. GCR No. 1097:3.
32. Rules of Order 46.
33. Ibid., paragraph 13.
34. Ibid., paragraph 44.
35. Ibid., paragraph 53.
36. GCR No. 1097.

Chapter 7

PRIESTHOOD CALLS

Principles and Procedures in Considering Priesthood Calls

Jesus personally chose his apostles from among his disciples. The scriptures tell us that Jesus spent all night in prayer prior to choosing his apostles.[1] When they were chosen he charged them with particular duties on behalf of the people. The spirit of their ministry was service. They were warned not to think of their ministry as a means of personal aggrandizement.

Jesus showed his love and sense of responsibility for the people when he quoted from Isaiah to explain his own ministry. In this quotation the needs of the people were recited as the justification for his divine anointment by the Holy Spirit.[2] Not only are priesthood members called to minister to the people in need, the people also share with God in calling and authorizing those who will serve. The church formally recognizes this principle in its procedure for calling and ordaining those in the priesthood.

The law of the church provides for a procedure in considering calls to the priesthood in organized jurisdictions. This includes the discernment that God is calling, through the spirit of wisdom and revelation in those who act officially for the church,[3] and the authorization for ordination by a vote of the members in a conference or business meeting of the appropriate church jurisdiction.[4] Thus both God and the church share in the calling, ordination, and authorization of a priesthood member.

The calling and ordination of a priesthood member is a formal procedure of the church. In actual practice the pastor or other administrative officer always carries a concern for those persons who are called. When the administrative officer is prayerfully seeking divine guidance it is expected that the Holy Spirit will indicate those whom God is calling into various priesthood offices. After presenting the call to those other administrative officers and councils concerned, and receiving their approval, the initiating officer then informs the one called. The presiding officer should discuss the nature of the call with the candidate for ordination. When the person being called is willing to serve, the whole matter is presented to a legislative conference or business meeting for the approval of the people. By such approval the members indicate their belief that the candidate is called and that they are willing to receive and support that person as a minister. After the legislative conference approves the call, the administrative officer provides for the ordination.

We have described the methods which the church has instituted for carrying out its corporate functions. This does not prevent God from working in and through anyone. It does mean that God recognizes those who are called to administer the work of the church. God honors the church in decisions regarding those from whom the church will receive ministry as well as the willingness of the person who is called to give ministry. The church does authorize an ordination and grants the authority for legal acts, but it is the Spirit of God which gives the priesthood member the power of redemptive ministry.

125

Calls to the priesthood come through those who are ordained to priesthood office and in administrative authority.[5] In some instances calls to specific orders of the priesthood originate with particular quorums. Bishops are called through the First Presidency; evangelists are called through the apostolic council; seventies are called through the Council of Presidents of Seventy.

High Priest

Nominations for ordinations to the high priesthood may be made by members of the First Presidency or the Council of Twelve, stake presidents, regional administrators or other high priests having administrative jurisdiction. Inasmuch as high priests are especially designated as standing ministers to the church under the direct oversight of the First Presidency (Doctrine and Covenants 122:8, 9), all such nominations should be presented to the First Presidency directly or through other administrative officers for consideration and presentation to the General Conference or appropriate high council. If council approval is given, further approval should be secured from the stake or district conference or—in unorganized areas—from the branch concerned.[6]

All such calls must have the approval of the First Presidency before being presented to the individual for that person's consent. These calls must have the approval of a high council and of the appropriate conference. Thus, the principle of common consent is expressed.

Persons serving in certain official functions must be high priests. The initiation of calls to those responsibilities follow a prescribed protocol:

1. Calls to the First Presidency, the Twelve, and the Presiding Bishopric generally come through the president of the church in a revelation to the entire church, and are approved by World Conference.

2. Counselors to the Presiding Bishop may be desig-

nated by revelation through the president of the church, or they may be chosen by the bishop and approved by the church.

3. Calls to the office of bishop come through the First Presidency.

   Ordinations to the Bishopric, which are recommended by the First Presidency, shall be presented to the General Conference or to the appropriate high council and to the stake or district conference or branch business meeting concerned.[7]

4. Calls to the office of evangelist come through the Twelve.

   Ordinations to the evangelical order, after having been recommended by the Council of Twelve and approved by the First Presidency, shall be submitted to the General Conference or to the appropriate stake, district or branch conference.[8]

5. The Seventy are selected by the Council of Presidents of Seventy and upon approval by the First Presidency and Council of Twelve, their ordination may be ordered.[9]

Unorganized Area

Calls in unorganized areas where no branch exists must be endorsed by the minister in charge. Calls to the Aaronic priesthood or eldership in branches which are not included in a district must be approved by the administrative officers of the branch and the regional administrator or minister in charge and the branch business meeting. Calls to the office of high priest are initiated by the regional administrator and/or minister in charge and recommended to the First Presidency. If a call receives the Presidency's approval, they will arrange for it to be presented to a proper high council and conference for action. Calls to all other Melchisedec priesthood offices in such branches are usually initiated by the regional administrator and/or the minister in charge, and presented to the appropriate quorum for approval and conference action.

The Regional Administrator or Regional President

A regional administrator or regional president assigned to an administrative area, will process all recommendations for ordination to Aaronic priesthood and to the office of elder. Before the recommendations are considered to be in order, the regional administrator will check the records in the offices of the First Presidency and Presiding Bishopric. In the case of elders, this information is sent to the apostle concerned.

In Stakes

The congregational presiding elder normally initiates calls to the eldership and the Aaronic priesthood. The stake presidency may also recommend calls to the priesthood in any of the congregations in a stake at their discretion.[10] The calls are not to be discussed with the candidate or with the membership until administrative approval is received. After the candidate has accepted the call, public announcement and provision for conference action is made.

All calls to the priesthood in stakes must be approved by the stake presidencies, the stake high councils, and the stake conferences.

Calls to the office of high priest are initiated by the stake presidency and must be approved by the apostle concerned, the director of Field Ministries, the First Presidency, the stake high council, and the stake conference.[11]

In Districts

The district president initiates calls to the eldership and the Aaronic priesthood in district missions. In emergencies the district presidency also may recommend calls to the priesthood in any of the branches of the district. However, the normal responsibility for calls within a branch is that of the branch president.[12] The calls are not to be discussed with the candidate or with the membership until administrative approval as indicated hereafter is received. After the candidate has accepted the call, public announcement can be made.

Forms used for submitting priesthood calls are available through Herald House.

Recommendations for ordinations for those enrolled in branches should be approved by vote of the branch and, if in a district, by the district conference. For those in district missions or enrolled on the "nonresident" list, calls should be approved by vote of the district conference. These approvals should be given by the branch and district where the candidate is enrolled, even though the place of enrollment differs from the place of attendance.

In organized regions calls to the Aaronic priesthood and to the office of elder in the Melchisedec priesthood shall be the responsibility of the branch president, the district president, and regional administrator. In calls to the Aaronic priesthood the regional administrator should give the final approval, after clearance has been made with the First Presidency and the Presiding Bishopric and before the contact with the candidate or presentation to the appropriate conferences. In the call of the elder, the regional administrator or president should give the final approval after writing to the First Presidency, the apostle, and the Presiding Bishopric for appropriate information and advice. After the regional administrator's approval, the candidate should be contacted and the call presented to the appropriate conferences.[13]

Calls to the office of high priest must be approved by the First Presidency and a high council and a district conference or World Conference or branch business meeting.[14]

Should an ordinand decline the ordination for a period of one year, the ordination should not be consummated until it has been reprocessed.

Emergency Measures

In case of emergencies, within branches and districts, ordinations may be provided by the minister in charge. In stakes, ordinations may be provided by the stake presidency in consultation with the stake high council and the First Presidency.

Approaching the Candidate

All official consultation and approval of priesthood calls should be completed before the candidate is notified. Experience indicates that the utmost tact, patience, and sympathetic understanding are required in approaching the prospective minister with regard to ordination. The final choice in every case must rest with the candidate. The candidate must not be unduly urged and certainly must not be coerced. After the candidate has been contacted opportunity should be given to attend a series of classes which provide preordination instruction.

At a branch, district, or stake gathering held to consider the approval of calls to priesthood, the ones called should be given ample opportunity to express their feelings, and others should be allowed to speak regarding the ordinations if they so desire before the vote of the body is taken. On favorable action of the branch the candidate is presented to the district conference for action.

After approval has been received from the stake or district conference, arrangements for the ordinations should be made by the pastor in consultation with the candidates and any others legitimately concerned.

NOTES

1. Luke 6:12, 13.
2. Luke 4:18, 19.
3. Doctrine and Covenants 8:2; 120:9; 124:3, 125:14.
4. Ibid., 17:16.
5. Ibid., 125:14.
6. GCR No. 1051.
7. Ibid.
8. Ibid.
9. GCR No. 966.
10. GCR No. 988.
11. GCR Nos. 386, 638; Doctrine and Covenants 17:7; GCR No. 1051; *Administrative Policies and Procedures*, 1971.
12. GCR No. 988.
13. Joint Council Minutes, March 3, 1967.
14. GCR Nos. 386, 638; Doctrine and Covenants 17:7; GCR No. 122; *Administrative Policies and Procedures*, 1971, p. 33.

Chapter 8

PRIESTHOOD STATUS AND ACCOUNTABILITY

On many occasions the church has been informed through prophetic instruction that "All are called according to the gifts of God unto them." We again were reminded of this in Doctrine and Covenants 156:9 given in 1984. While it is recognized that God has endowed us with gifts for ministry and as stewards we all are accountable for the use of those gifts, we often are in situations which either hinder or prohibit that ministry. These limiting factors may be such circumstances as the opposition of spouse and family, the unwillingness of the people to accept the ministry, lack of preparation which makes the ministry ineffective, attitudes of jealousy, negative criticism, or uncooperativeness which renders our ministry destructive, and other obligations which leave us without time or energy to give in ministry. Sometimes age or health limits our ability and sometimes we are just negligent or, for personal reasons, become inactive.

Priesthood is not an honor or possession to be held for personal aggrandizement or benefit. It is a responsibility accepted by a person to perform certain ministries after having been called by God and the church and officially designated through ordination. When an ordained person is no longer willing or able to fulfill that responsibility, then the church and the person need to recognize that condition and make appropriate adjustments in the priesthood status of that person.

To implement the performance and determine the status of priesthood members the church has made provision for a periodic review when the priesthood member and the appropriate administrative officer may evaluate the circumstances in which the priesthood member works and the effectiveness of the ministry given. This review can take place as often as needed and requested but is regularly provided every three years. The evaluation and review will, it is hoped, lead the priesthood member to the most appropriate category of priesthood status and relieve priesthood members from unwanted responsibility.

The categories of priesthood are as follows:

1. Active status

    This category is composed of the priesthood who actively provide ministry according to their ability, life's circumstances, and the needs of the people.

2. Superannuated status

    This status is extended to older priesthood members who have served long and faithfully but who have reached the age when limitations prohibit full functioning in the priesthood. They may labor under the direction of the administrative officers as health and age permit.

3. Inactive status

    This status is available to priesthood who because of personal reasons or circumstances are, for a time, unable to serve in active ministry. This status does not carry any pejorative connotation and is not given in cases where moral or ethical conduct has broken the standards set by the church for priesthood members. It is expected that persons on inactive status will work toward reinstatement to active status and if the inactivity extends beyond two triennial reviews the priesthood member will then be released from priesthood.

4. Released status

A member of the priesthood may choose to be released from priesthood responsibility. If no cause for a priesthood silence exists the priesthood member may be granted release from priesthood through the same administrative process for approval to the office to which the person has been ordained. Release is required when a priesthood member has been in inactive status for two triennial reviews and the member is still unable to resume priesthood activity.

5. Suspension status

Suspension is the status given primarily to priesthood members involved in divorce from their spouse. It is appropriate for the priesthood to accept suspension of priesthood activity until the problems surrounding the circumstances of the divorce are resolved.

6. Priesthood silence

Priesthood silence is of long standing status in church procedure.

The church may withdraw priesthood authority for

cause. The procedure for such withdrawal is called "silencing." When a "silence" is imposed upon a priesthood member it is an official recognition of conditions which have nullified the capacity of the minister to function in the calling.

The silencing of a priesthood member is "an administrative action which does not affect membership status and is not within the jurisdiction of the civil or church courts."* Silences are officially imposed by the presiding officer of the jurisdiction in which the minister lives or functions. When a priesthood member travels outside that jurisdiction he or she is subject in ministry to the direction of the presiding officers in the area.

A minister who is silenced must be given a written notice of the silence which includes the grounds for the silencing action, the facts or evidence supporting each ground, a written statement of the minister's rights of appeal including the name and address of the next higher administrative officer who is the proper appellate officer. Silenced ministers who wish to appeal must do so within sixty days after the silence is imposed.

A copy of the letter of silence with such supporting information as is available should be sent to the First Presidency. A notice of the silence should be sent to each administrative officer having jurisdiction.

Appeal from Silences

When a silenced minister feels unjustly silenced, an appeal should be made within sixty days to the next higher administrative officer having jurisdiction.

An appeal should be in writing and should give the

---

* General Conference Resolution 1158

reasons for the appeal, stating what injustice has been done and the supporting evidence.

While an appeal is pending the minister affected is still under silence.

If the silence is sustained the minister has another sixty-day period from the date of notification that the silence was sustained to file an appeal with the next higher administrative officer in the administrative line.

In the event that an appeal is filed, the officer receiving the appeal should notify the First Presidency, who will refer to the officer the record and evidence in the case. If the silence is upheld, the silenced minister has the right to continue the appeal to successive administrative levels (district president, regional administrator, apostle, director of field ministries, First Presidency; or stake president, apostle, director of field ministries, First Presidency), with final appeal to the First Presidency. After each review of such appeal if the silence is upheld the decision should be communicated to the silenced minister and to the First Presidency.

The Restoration of Priesthood Authority

Priesthood licenses are restored only by the First Presidency. It is appropriate for the presiding officer of a jurisdiction where a silenced priesthood member resides to recommend the restoration of the priesthood license when the reasons for silencing a minister have been corrected and that person's ministry will be beneficial to the church. The silenced priesthood member may initiate a request for the restoration of the license through the presiding officer. Recommendations for the restoration of priesthood licenses are made in writing and sent up the administrative line. Each administrator may concur in the recommendation or register objection giving reasons, but he should not unduly delay sending the recommendation on to the next higher administrative officer. No administrator has the right to "pocket veto" a recommendation for the restoration of a priesthood license. The administrative officer has the right only to register his or her reaction and forward it on. When the recommendation reaches the First Presidency all reactions will be considered and the First Presidency will render the judgment regarding whether or not the priesthood license will be restored.

Additional information regarding priesthood review and status will be found in the "Guidelines for Priesthood: Ordination, Preparation, Continuing Commitment." (See Appendix A.)

PART TWO
WORSHIP

Chapter 1

WORSHIP IN THE LIFE OF THE CHURCH

The Experience of Worship

Worship can be understood in many different ways. Moments of worship can be identified in every part of life's experience. Human beings differ in their understanding and approaches to life. They attach a wide variety of meanings to the term *worship.* Furthermore, worship can be an intentional act or it can be an unexpected moment identified only after it happens. Worship can be something one experiences in isolation from others. Yet it also occurs in community, among the fellowship of other people. In any event, worship is intensely personal and as such is difficult or impossible to describe in a way that is acceptable and meaningful to everyone.

Characteristics of Corporate Worship

Rather than attempt one or more *definitions* of corporate worship we will instead identify some characteristics or ideas that we hope may be found in our worship experiences.

1. *In worship, we encounter God.* The experience of corporate worship is one of interaction between God and humanity and between one person and others. We receive God's self-revelation through all of our senses—our whole selves—and we also give our whole selves to God in response. Worship, then, is an occasion for meeting God.

2. *In worship, we celebrate and share the gospel.* A central focus of our worship is the redeeming and reconciling activity of God who sent us the Son through whom we can receive salvation. Underlying our worship and finding expression in its focus and language is the reality of Jesus Christ who is present with us today. Furthermore, our worship is an expression of our faith and our beliefs, or in other words that which is important to us.

3. *In worship, we find meaning in life's experience.* We live in God's world. The church exists as part of the world which God desires to redeem. Although some of the forms of language that we use in worship are different from those we use in everyday life, there is an essential continuity between our worship and all other experience. In worship we do *not* come out of the world where God is absent and into the sanctuary where God is present. Rather, in worship we celebrate the presence of God in all of human experience. The forms and language of our worship need to be meaningful to the worshipers. Our worship needs to address and engage the life situations, needs, and desires of all of the people in our congregations however diverse these may be.

4. *In worship, we participate together in community.* The church is the body of Christ, made up of a variety of people brought together in unity. Our worship expresses this unity by calling the entire congregation together and by providing for the participation of all people—old and young, male and female. In worship we come together to share and be involved, not to watch a few leaders perform for us. True community makes possible the giving and receiving of the varied gifts and ministries of all people.[1]

5. *In worship, we remember and rehearse our story.* As a church we have a rich heritage. This includes the last one hundred and fifty years (our Latter Day Saint heritage), the last twenty centuries (our Christian heritage), and the last several thousand years (our Judaic heritage). One of the functions of corporate worship is to remind us of who we are as the people of God, to strengthen and sustain us in this knowledge, and to send us out again to be God's servants in a world full of needy people. Our scriptures, hymns, testimonies, and other worship forms are the means that we use to remember and retell our story.

The Elements of Worship

There are many moods and expressions in our corporate worship. Of these, four elements are primary; adoration and praise; confession and repentance; proclamation and affirmation; commitment and dedication.

1. Adoration and Praise

Worship begins with the acknowledgment of

141

the presence of God. When we experience God we naturally express thanks and adoration. Praise comes when we recognize a Presence in the world that is divine—One on which we depend and which gives meaning to our lives. We do more than recognize God's presence in the sanctuary; we also express appreciation for those times when we experience God at work in our daily lives and in the world around us. Isaiah expressed it this way, "Holy, holy, holy, is the Lord of hosts; the whole earth is full of his glory."[2]

2. Confession and Repentance

When Isaiah experienced the presence of God he immediately sensed his unworthiness and exclaimed, "Woe is me! for I am undone; because I am a man of unclean lips, and I dwell in the midst of a people of unclean lips; for mine eyes have seen the King, the Lord of hosts."[3] For Isaiah, unclean lips were the symbol of his inadequacy.

Repentance involves seeing ourselves in some part as God sees us. It is acknowledging our shortcomings, our unworthiness, our inadequacy, our sin. The mood of confession is one of humility, and of appreciation of God who cares about human beings. The emphasis is on human action or inaction in the face of God's action. It is characterized by the prayer of the publican: "God, be merciful to me a sinner."[4]

3. Proclamation and affirmation

Our words of confession and repentance are

answered by God's Word of forgiveness. Isaiah experienced this as a live coal from the altar touching his lips—"thine iniquity is taken away, and thy sin purged."[5]

Central to our experience of worship is the proclamation of the Word of God. This proclamation focuses on the gospel, i.e., the good news that "God so loved the world, that he gave his only Begotten Son, that whosoever believeth on him should not perish; but have everlasting life."[6] This is the word of forgiveness extended into the word of salvation. It is the celebration of the whole life, death, and resurrection of Christ as the central revelation of God. The proclamation is the declaration of what God is doing to establish the kingdom on the earth by transforming the persons and structures of society. God's righteousness, power, and love are proclaimed and made real in the community of believers who gather for worship.

Yet proclamation does not stop with the declaration of God's saving activity. It continues by extending the invitation for our participation and response. In the words of Isaiah, "I heard the voice of the Lord, saying, Whom shall I send, and who will go for us?"[7] The call is issued.

4. Commitment and Dedication

The concluding element of this four-part sequence reflects the human action of response. Isaiah's words are simply, "Here am I; send me."[8] Here we offer ourselves in commitment and dedication. By committing ourselves publicly in worship, we take our discipleship seriously. We also recognize that our calling lies not just within the sanctuary but in the world in which God is at work. Our commitment is the vital connecting link between the church and the world. In commitment we give in response to that which God has freely given us—new life in Christ Jesus our Lord.

The Order of Worship

No prescribed order of worship is found in the scriptures, rules and resolutions, or instructions from headquarters. Congregations, therefore, have considerable freedom in ordering services according to their own needs and available resources. There is, however, considerable value in having some form of pattern, rhythm, or order that generally characterizes our services. We might call this a framework or outline into which the forms and expressions appropriate for a particular service can be fitted.

A useful framework for the order of worship is the four elements described in the preceding section. This means that we will begin a service of worship with expressions of praise and adoration, continue with confession and repentance, then move to proclamation and affirmation, and conclude with dedication and commitment. This permits considerable variety and flexibility but retains a familiar sequence.

Forms of Worship

Many worship forms common to our experience today have centuries of tradition behind them. These include hymn singing, scripture reading, drama, prayer, offering, preaching, the sacraments, etc. It is very probable that these forms will continue to be meaningful expressions of worship for years to come. With the advent of electronic media, however, new forms are now available for use in worship. These include films, filmstrips, videotapes, sound records, and tapes. With a growing consciousness that worship involves the whole person, renewed attention is being given to the use of all the senses in worship. Included in this category are movement, gesture, touch, taste, and smell.

When developing the order of service, worship planners should consider the full range of forms available and choose those which contribute best to the intention of the service. We should remain open to the use of newer, less-traditional forms while at the same time remembering not to neglect those valued forms which have centuries of experience behind them.

Participation in Worship

Worship is action or activity in which the entire congregation participates. The forms and order of worship are not themselves worship. Instead they are there to make it possible for persons to worship. People come to worship to be involved. Worship planners should make sure that each service includes opportunity for the entire congregation as well as individuals and groups to participate in significant ways.

Leadership in Worship

Church procedure requires that activities of the local congregations be under the general supervision of the pastor/presiding elder who is a priesthood member. In most cases, a priesthood member will preside over corporate worship services. The presiding officer can be assisted in other leadership responsibilities in worship by other persons ordained or unordained. The only aspect of corporate worship that *requires* priesthood members to officiate is the administration of the sacraments of the church.

In choosing persons to offer leadership in services of worship consideration should be given to what particular ministry is desired and which persons in the congregation can effectively bring this ministry. The statement "All are called according to the gifts of God unto them"[9] is wise counsel to follow. Although traditionally most or all leadership of worship has been done by priesthood members it is well to remember that the call to ordination is not a call to do all the ministry that is needed. Those in the priesthood should draw out the ministries which are inherent in all people.

Planning Services of Worship

The presiding officer will delegate the planning of many services to others in the congregation. Some services may be planned by other priesthood members, some by families, and some by a worship commission or other group. In general, the more people involved in planning services for a congregation over a period of time, the more enthusiasm, creativity, and quality will likely result. It is a good rule to include the presider in the planning team and make sure that all persons making decisions about a given service (e.g., presider, speaker(s), organist, music director, etc.) do so in cooperation with the others. This will ensure maximum continuity, integration, and fewer "surprises."

Resources to Assist Worship Planners

The greatest resource in worship is our people. In each congregation there are generally a number of persons who could assist with worship planning and leadership who are not being used in this way.

In addition there are many printed and audiovisual materials that are very useful. Consult the current Herald House catalog or write to the Worship Office, the Auditorium, Independence, MO 64051 for help.

Informal Worship

People sometimes meet informally. Their purpose in meeting may be fellowship and worship but they do not plan for a formal service. Song fests, fellowship suppers, and work parties are examples of this kind of gathering. Preparation must be made and leadership of such groups is important. The work party may end the day with a campfire. A fellowship supper may easily become a testimony meeting, or a song fest may lead naturally to shared prayers and testimonies. In all of these, worship of the finest kind may take place.

Physical Arrangements

Maurice Draper has given some very helpful comments about the physical arrangements for worship. He wrote as follows:

"Most worship sanctuaries are arranged to facilitate an observer role by the congregation rather than a participant role; rows of fixed pews are arranged so the worshiper sees the minister, the chancel, and, sometimes, the choir. In recent years, there has been an attempt to eliminate the problem of looking at the backs of people's heads by arranging the sanctuary 'in the round,' where the seats complete a full circle around the chancel or altar. There is developed, thereby, a situation where more face-to-face contact is achieved for the members of the congregation.

"Creative planning for worship may call for the worship service to be held in different locations so the seating can fit the need of the occasion. Panels of speakers, especially when in forum discussions, and occasions for films and formal major musical presentations seem to call for the more traditional seating arrangement. Drama, preaching, prayer and testimony, etc., might take a different setting with effective worship.

"These ideas are only illustrative. The physical arrangements should be matched as closely as possible to the purpose of the activity. Flexibility within a stable context is the ideal."[10]

Preparation for Worship

The formal church worship service is usually led by members of the priesthood, one of whom presides. It should be understood, however, that there may be exceptions. The one in charge of the service has the responsibility of directing those who participate. Additional persons may assist by offering prayers, reading scriptures, ushering, and receiving the offering. Last minute appointments to these tasks should be avoided insofar as possible. Each needs to make adequate advance preparation for the service.

The specific duty assigned to each participant does not end his or her responsibility in the service. Each participant should share with the congregation in every part of the order of worship. This includes singing hymns, worshipful attention to the anthem, amd participating in the offering. Each should come prepared to worship as well as to minister.

Preparation for worship is needed on the part of the congregation. Members should come with holiness of purpose, having made personal preparation in their homes and on their way. Group worship is encouraged by a musical prelude, instrumental or vocal. This may be followed by the call to worship and hymns of praise. Undivided attention should continue to the message of solos or choral singing and participation in all of the activities of the service. When there is preaching all should give thoughtful consideration to the sermon.

Helps and Hindrances in Worship

A good setting for worship calls for simple beauty, created by tasteful decoration of the sanctuary, artistic floral arrangements, and the architectural features of the building itself. The setting should create a worshipful atmosphere and should not call attention to itself.

Care should be taken that the seats and other furniture of the meeting place are neatly arranged. Hymnals should be placed in an orderly manner. Unsightly objects such as easels, blackboards, littered tables, piles of music on the piano, unused or odd chairs, distracting pictures and papers that have no significance to the order of worship, and other unnecessary things should be removed.

The room should be clean and comfortably heated and ventilated. Defective equipment should be removed, repaired, or replaced. Noisy doors, creaking floors, glaring lights, and faulty windows should be eliminated.

Attentive participation by the congregation, as well as the ministers, is desirable. Friendly greetings should be exchanged before and after rather than during the service. Parents and deacons should see that children do not run about the room during the service.

Those who arrive late should be ushered in quietly and inconspicuously, preferably to seats reserved in the rear of the sanctuary.

Ushers should move quietly in the aisles and should not make unnecessary noise or distract the congregation.

Cloak racks should be cleared of cluttering materials before the people assemble. In times of inclement weather, mats should be cleaned and in place in advance. Temperature settings and ventilation adjustments should be made prior to the service so there will be a minimum of changes necessary during the service. A room filled with people rapidly becomes warmer. Temperature should be cool at the beginning.

At the opening of the service, an orderly, quiet, and dignified entrance and seating of the worship leaders and choir are in harmony with the spirit of worship. During the service the posture and deportment of the leaders and choir are important. Their eager participation in the service will stimulate similar participation by the congregation.

Here are some practices to avoid:

1. Signaling from the chancel for the attention of the deacon or a member of the congregation is distracting. A vocal request is better, if necessary.
2. Slumping in the seats, crossing of legs, signs of nervousness or boredom, shuffling of feet, dozing, whispering, or other distracting movements of the body are all bad, whether among the ministers, the choir, or the congregation.

3. Obvious looking at the clock or a watch. The worship leaders and choir may assist effectively by being attentive to every part of the order of worship. All eyes should be on the one who is speaking before the congregation.

Ministers participating should cultivate humility and warmth, with sincere and kindly respect for all members of the congregation.

The personal appearance of the minister is important. Simplicity of dress and cleanliness are essential. Casual wear is out of place in the pulpit. A good rule to observe concerning dress and personal appearance is that the minister should not be "the first in nor the last out" in changing styles.

Before a service begins adequate preparation should be made by each participant. One might check off each item of the order of worship to insure that nothing is omitted or forgotten. This should be done unobtrusively.

If adequate preparations are made before the service, there will be no need for a hurried search through books or pockets for a misplaced scripture reference, hymn number, or announcement. It is very helpful to have a printed order of worship to place in the hands of all, including the congregation. It should include most announcements and introductions. If a formal introduction of a priesthood member is necessary, her or his title may be used. For all members of the Melchisedec Order the term *elder* is appropriate, adding after the minister's name an identifying phrase if he or she belongs to a general quorum, e.g., "of the First Presidency" or "of the Council of Twelve." For members of the Aaronic priesthood, the name followed by such a phrase as "deacon (or teacher or priest) of the Aaronic Order" is appropriate.

Analyzing the Services

Although the order of worship is not the worship experience, the experience is enhanced by adequate preplanning. The effectiveness of public services should be evaluated from time to time to guard against the development of slovenly habits and meaningless routine.

People truly worship when the following things happen:

1. Their vision is expanded and their insights are deepened as to the nature and will of God.
2. They are moved to confession of their sins and are converted to the right ways of life.
3. They receive ministry of comfort and renewed courage to face the issues of life.
4. They feel definitely challenged and strengthened to give of their best talents in service to their Master.
5. They are caused to rededicate themselves to Christ.
6. They feel as if they have communed with God and stood in holy places.

A good worship service should create in members of the congregation a spirit of thankfulness for their experience and the feeling that they have moved nearer God and toward a better understanding and appreciation of themselves and others.

NOTES

1. Doctrine and Covenants 119:8b.
2. Isaiah 6:3.
3. Ibid., 6:5.
4. Luke 18:13.
5. Isaiah 6:7.
6. John 3:16.
7. Isaiah 6:8.
8. Ibid.
9. Doctrine and Covenants 119:8b.
10. Adapted from an article titled "Worthscipe" by Maurice L. Draper, *Saints' Herald*, November 1971, p. 36.

Chapter 2

THE MINISTRY OF PREACHING

Essential Elements of Sermon Preparation

Anyone who reads the history of the Christian movement or studies the book of Acts is impressed with the power and effectiveness of preaching in the church. Peter's sermon on the day of Pentecost launched the church and convicted those who heard so that they cried out, "Men and brethren, what shall we do?"[1] This was not a sermon for social courtesies. Nothing led those present to congratulate the speaker and say, "I enjoyed your sermon today" but "there were added unto them about three thousand souls."[2]

The Apostle Paul's sermon on Mars' hill gripped the attention of the Greeks who heard. Some scoffed. Some said, "We will hear thee again of this matter,"[3] but they were concerned and the scriptures report, "Howbeit certain men clave unto him, and believed; among the which was Dionysius the Areopagite, and a woman named Damaris, and others with them."[4]

Examples of the great preaching of the early church are so numerous that we can call attention only to the persuasive power which united the believers, converted the Jews and Gentiles alike, guided the saints and motivated them to change the world.

Few, if any, priesthood members approach their preaching ministry with the expectation that they will move their listeners so greatly as did those mentioned above. Nevertheless, having been called by God priesthood members should bring an effective preaching ministry when representing their Lord. God has promised to priesthood the same power experienced by those called into service in earlier times.

Great preaching results from hard work, deep searching, spiritual agonizing, and by the inspiration of the Holy Spirit. It is only on a rare occasion that worthy sermons come suddenly out of some experience or spontaneous thought. It is important, therefore, to plan for this hard work in preparation for preaching.*

Lest any think that effective preaching is merely a human enterprise, it is important to be reminded that "God gave the increase." Priesthood members have no powers of ministry except as God empowers their efforts.

There are some elements of preaching that are necessary to cultivate to be fruitful ministers for Christ. The following are important:

1. The message of effective preaching is centered in Jesus Christ. Paul said to the Corinthians, "And I, brethren, when I came to you, came not with excellency of speech or of wisdom, declaring unto you the testimony of God.

   "For I determined not to know anything among you, save Jesus Christ, and him crucified."⁵

   The power of the gospel is present in our midst

---

* An excellent resource for sermon preparation and delivery is the book by Barbara McFarlane Higdon. *Good News for Today*, Herald House, 1981.

because God's only begotten Son has come into the world and identified himself with humanity. Through him humans comprehend and have access to God. Through him also is received the "Spirit of adoption" to become "heirs of God, and joint heirs with Christ."[6]

Persons may be interested in social problems, scientific insights, and good causes, but these are not the power or source which causes rejoicing. Human hope and anticipation are centered in God's mighty acts which all culminate in Christ. All that went before or after the advent of Christ are but footnotes to bring depth and understanding of what already is revealed in him. Preachers need to study the scriptures to be thoroughly conversant with Christ's life and message. They are called to become saturated, not with some new fad or the latest theory about Christ, but rather with the central meanings of Christ's revelation as it has been understood and lived out by humble followers through the centuries.

2. The power of effective preaching is in the light and testimony of the Holy Spirit. Paul wrote to the Thessalonians: "For our gospel came not unto you in word only, but also in power, and in the Holy Ghost, and in much assurance; as ye know what manner of men we were among you for your sake."[7] Preaching which is empowered by the Holy Spirit comes out of a life of depth and devotion. Study of the scriptures, fasting, prayer, and thoughtful meditation on the basic meanings of the gospel will help to develop a spiritual reserve out of which one's participation in preach-

ing experiences empowered by the Holy Spirit may take place. A priesthood member should never try to manipulate the Holy Spirit. God grants gifts according to the divine will, but we do know the kind of persons God has called priesthood members to be. God grants the Holy Spirit to those who respond in truth and sincerity.

3. The credibility of effective preaching is largely dependent on the life of the speaker. In the scripture quoted above, Paul reminded the Thessalonians "what manner of men" the missionaries were. Effective preaching seldom comes from shallow or uncommitted persons. The life of the speaker must supplement the spoken word. Hearers believe those who know the subject of their message and whose integrity they trust. This is one reason why persons who have never been seriously ill have difficulty in ministering to the sick. One who has never lost a loved one is unable to adequately comfort those who have; a priesthood member who refuses to tithe does not convincingly present the financial principles of the gospel to others.

The evident way in which the priesthood member lives out in life the meaning of the message will either support or deny it. The life of an effective preacher does not conflict with the message presented. It is for this reason that good, humble priesthood members who are trusted and have earned the love and respect of their people will be able to speak with an authority which the newcomer does not have. In many ways the message is dependent upon the manner of person ministers have become, as well as upon the words which they speak.

4. The accuracy, consistency, simplicity, and persuasiveness necessary for effective preaching are the result of study, observation, and thoughtful scholarship. It is true that many great speakers have had little formal education, but the formal classroom is only one place where one can learn. Many ministers who have little opportunity for experience in school have nevertheless been astute observers of life, avid readers, and bring to their ministry a wealth of experience. Formal education is usually a quicker, easier, and more satisfactory way to achieve the knowledge and skills and procedures a minister needs in great preaching. Furthermore, it introduces one to the breadth of thinking which gives balance to ministry and avoids the blind spots in ministry or from an overemphasis which distorts the message. Both the depth of understanding reflected in the message and the accuracy of the fact and interpretations given are dependent upon study and experience. The degree and confidence which any audience has in the speaker will depend upon his or her command of information about the subject and the evident judgment in evaluating the meaning of the information.

5. The preacher must be godly. Words are empty unless they are winged by the power of the Holy Spirit. A priesthood member does not achieve effective preaching by personal efforts alone. It is the gift of God who empowers and whose spirit bears its testimony of the validity of the message.

A minister will be constantly drawing from the springs of devotional life and will be both sobered and empowered by the knowledge that the message is not of his or her own making, but is rather the message of the Lord, Jesus Christ.

Personal Preparation

In order to achieve those characteristics mentioned above, it will be important where the minister works and studies. This need not be an elaborate place. It will help if it can be reasonably quiet and apart from the bustle of everyday life.

It is preferred that the study be done in the same place each time. In this way much lost motion will be prevented. Books, notes, and such will be near at hand, requiring a minimum of adjustment and arrangement.

A desk or worktable, writing materials (pencils or pens, or typewriter, paper, etc.), a place for a few reference books, a chair, a lamp, files, or notebooks for records and illustrative materials are the tools needed.

The three standard books, a dictionary, a Bible dictionary, a single-volume Bible commentary, Book of Mormon commentary, and Doctrine and Covenants commentary are all helpful. Other books relating to church history, devotional subjects, counseling, theology, world history, and sociology should be selected with care. Books containing sermon outlines, written sermons, prepared sermon illustrations, and the like can be useful as one learns sermon techniques but should be used naturally lest they destroy spontaneity.

The great preaching "reference library" for the priesthood member is that which grows out of concern for the children of God. The minister is with them in corporate worship, in their homes, on the street; the minister is the good shepherd. Through such ministry he or she can arrive at a worthy objective for sermons.

The preacher can arrive at a statement of objectives by asking such questions as these:

1. Who will be present at the service?
2. What is their manner of life?
3. What are their needs?
4. Is there any special day on which this sermon can be preached best?
5. How much of this subject can I cover at this time?

These questions can be answered best when the priesthood member prayerfully reflects upon the needs of those who will be in the congregation. Human needs can be met only by divine grace. Then light, warmth, joy, and peace shine forth to flavor the sermon.

The objectives will vary with the occasion. Usually, however, preaching will relate to one of these purposes:

1. To declare God's love and action for all persons
2. To invite all to Christ
3. To comfort, encourage, and inspire continued loyalty to Christ
4. To help sincere and willing persons build honorable characters through lives of righteousness
5. To teach or impart information, such as explaining the beliefs of the church

Types of Sermons

The Doctrinal Sermon. Doctrinal preaching presents time-tested principles of truth and ways of life. To be effective these must be related to and interpreted in the light of contemporary human needs. This type of sermon is most frequently used in missionary situations. The preacher should avoid questions beyond his or her depth of understanding and present simple concepts in the spirit of testimony.

The Ethical Sermon. In this sermon the preacher points out the moral standards of Christian life. Personal and social sin are seen as the root of immorality, unchristian conduct and relationships, and lack of integrity. Sermons of this nature should emphasize the redemptive ministry of Jesus and the resources of spiritual power in the Holy Spirit. Ethical behavior is not merely response to a list of "do's and don'ts" but the behavior of redeemed persons.

Preparation for the Sermon

Read, study, think, and pray until you are saturated with your subject. Preach what you know; then you can speak with authority. Make notes as you read. Prayer for divine inspiration is indispensable. Prepare the sermon in outline form to assure organization of ideas in the most effective sequence. This will also help you to crystallize in your mind what you wish to present, in case you choose to preach without notes. In preaching from an outline, use only as many notes as are necessary to bring to mind the contents of the sermon.

Mark the texts you plan to use. Colored paper markers will help. If these markers are placed at the bottom of the page, they will not be distracting to the congregation.

Physical and mental rest will enable you to approach this important assignment with a fresh mind and body. When the preaching experience begins never apologize for lack of ability or preparation.

The Creative Approach to Sermon-Building

Have a creative attitude. As you ponder the needs of the congregation; think of their good qualities. Jesus died for them; they must be of worth. Be willing to let God's Spirit guide you in new ways.

Analyze the need so you can concentrate on the appropriate solution. Do not let superficialities blind you to the real problem. It is not too much TV or too little church attendance that is your real concern, but rather a jaded soul in need of a vision of God and a purpose for living.

Seek all the facts you can in the time you have. This is where your references come in handy. This is where your ministry in the home is invaluable. This is hard work, but there is no substitute for it.

Write down ideas, sensible, and "far-out." As you search for facts, write down ideas that may come to you for helping the congregation. The Spirit of God can inspire your mind. Ask questions. Consider answers. Questions raise more questions. Ideas breed ideas.

Let the facts mature in your mind. It takes time to grow corn or acorns and it takes time for facts to sift down in the mind. Let your mind relax and daydream a while.

Evaluate your ideas. Select the best and recheck them until you have settled on the best. Arrange them in their natural order. Simplify them so all can understand. Since God is the creator, you may expect help in such creative endeavor.

The Sermon Outline

A sermon may be developed by the use of a simple outline such as the following.

An Introduction: At the beginning of the sermon state the problem to be discussed, or present a setting for the message of the sermon.

The Main Divisions: Develop each point by subheadings and illustrations. It is usually best to have not more than three or four main divisions arranged in order of most effective artistic or logical development. Use illustrations to clarify each point. Note scripture references to avoid forgetting them.

The Climax: This should be near the end of the sermon. The message comes to climax in a challenge for the congregation to respond to what has been said. If this is well thought out beforehand, it can be forcefully and appealingly presented.

The Conclusion: It is well to summarize the message in a few sentences. Be careful not to prolong the sermon by "tacking on" a few additional thoughts you may have forgotten or neglected to present earlier.

Contents of the Sermon

Make the content worthy of the time occupied and the need of the hour. Don't condemn the congregation; inspire and challenge them to a better life. Avoid unfavorable criticism of other churches. Preach basic principles, ethical standards, and testimonial invitations to discipleship.

Improvement of Delivery

Speak distinctly. Avoid pretentiousness. Modulate your voice. Let it naturally emphasize your own convictions and the value of basic principles. Use correct grammar.

Never apologize for deficiencies or inabilities.

Keep to your subject.

Avoid distracting mannerisms.

Stand erect—don't sprawl over the pulpit.

Vary your gestures.

Be dignified but not stiff.

Look your congregation in the eye.

Avoid sarcasm; it is neither argument nor proof.

Smile occasionally.

Have a friend—maybe one of your family—listen and make notes of mannerisms, suggestions, etc.

Have recordings of your voice made and study them.

Use short sentences and simple language.

Always end on a lofty, encouraging note.

Tests of a Sermon

The test of a good sermon comes after it is ended.

Did it end on time? "A sermon is as long as it seems," but the best length is from thirty to thirty-five minutes.

Can you summarize your own sermons?

Does the congregation leave with certain definite resolutions to more devoted discipleship?

NOTES

1. Acts 2:37.
2. Ibid., 2:41.
3. Ibid., 17:32.
4. Ibid., 17:34.
5. I Corinthians 2:1, 2.
6. Romans 8:15-17.
7. I Thessalonians 1:5.

Chapter 3

CONDUCTING THE PRAYER SERVICE

The Nature and Purpose of the Prayer Service

This service gives opportunity for direct congregational participation in prayer, testimony, and song.

The group expression is that of adoration, praise, mutual support, and dedication.

The purpose of the service is to help us understand the nature and purpose of God in the spirit of repentance. It provides opportunity to seek forgiveness and reconciliation with God and other people. It gives us a chance to pray with others. It helps to satisfy our need and hunger for spiritual enlightenment. It affords opportunity for clear thinking and deep feeling regarding the purposes of God.

This service provides the spiritual fellowship all of us need. Testimonies and prayers become as strength to all.

Members of the congregation do not meet in the prayer service to offer private prayers and bear private testimonies while others listen. Rather the congregation meets as a corporate body. Each person who prays should attempt to express for the people the desires and needs of the group. Those who listen should feel they are praying with the one who speaks, so that in a sense they can say silently, "God, that's my prayer, too." Participants should also be aware under the impress of the Holy Spirit what God wants the group to pray about and express those prayers for the group. As this is done each speaker brings new insights to the people and the spirit of intelligence and commitment builds throughout the service. Each one contributes in ministry to everyone else.

The same principle applies to testimonies. Often the most helpful testimony is not one of some unique experience, but rather one similar to the common experience of others. The congregation can silently say, "That's my experience too, but I never thought of it that way before."

Priesthood members who understand these principles of congregational worship will be better able to lead and participate in the prayer and testimony service.

Occasionally someone who is out of touch with the group will offer a prayer or bear a testimony so unrelated to the congregation's interests or needs that the good spirit of the meeting is dampened. When this occurs priesthood members present should be ready to participate in ways that will restore the thrust of the meeting to those concerns of the corporate body.

Elements and Procedures

There are no hard and fast rules for directing the prayer service. Experience has proven that this service should be flexible enough to allow for a liberal amount of expression and participation. However, certain principles and procedures help create the worship experience.

Preliminary Song Servcice

The purposeless visiting that often occurs before the meeting begins should be transformed into mutual concern. The singing of hymns is an inspiring preparation for prayer and testimony. Hymns draw the people's minds together in accord with the purpose of the meeting. It has been customary for instrumental accompaniment not to be used.* Selection of hymns should be made in harmony with the purpose of the meeting.

Pastoral Welcome

It is good for the minister in charge to welcome those who have come and set the tone of the service. These remarks should be brief and should immediately turn attention to the purpose of the meeting. This greeting often closes with the announcement of the invocation hymn. If the group is to stand for the hymn and prayer, the presiding minister may so state, also giving the name of the person who is to offer the prayer.

Invocation

The invocation should be brief, earnest, and reverent. Habitual, droning, or spiritless prayers should be avoided. The spiritual enthusiasm in the invocation helps set the tone for the whole service.

Hymns

In general, prayer service leaders begin the meeting with a hymn and use hymns to give continuity to the major parts of the service, such as the introductory talk, the period of prayer, and the period of testimony. Hymns may be interspersed with prayers and testimonies. When this is done, the hymns should be selected carefully. The words should speak in harmony with the spirit of the meeting; the tune should be familiar enough so as not to cause strain. Hopeful, encouraging hymns that promote faith and goodwill are best. Those direct-

---

*Doctrine and Covenants 119:6c.

ing the hymns should not allow them to drag along; and conversely, they should not be pounded out in march time nor too rapidly. A good rule on tempo is to sing at the rate at which the group reads naturally together. In practice sessions song leaders can test this procedure and determine comfortable tempos.

The Scripture Reading

It is not always required that a scripture reading be used, but an appropriate one frequently stimulates a line of thought that inspires the people. Every human need can be met by something from the scriptures. The scripture reading should generally be short. Long readings dull the meeting and tire the people. Ministers should read only that which gives the central idea or purpose and leave out preliminaries or unrelated material. It is what is read and how it is used that count.

The Theme Talk

The purpose of the talk is to encourage the people to reflective thought, service, dedication, spirituality, and participation in the meeting. It should help to stimulate thought, prayer, and testimony, but should not cover everything and leave the people nothing to say on the subject.

At the close of the theme talk, it may be good for the speaker to leave some specific questions for the people to answer from their experience.

The Period of Prayer

As the hymn before the period of prayer is announced, the elder in charge may request that while the people are singing, a number of them should make ready to offer prayer. Sometimes it is wise to name someone to lead out in prayer. At the beginning of the period of prayer, the presiding elder may ask if there are any unusual needs which challenge the concern of the people for each other. Prayers should not be long. They should be sincere.

The Period of Testimony

As the presiding elder announces the hymn preceding the testimonies he or she may ask a number of persons to be ready to testify. Testimonies should express gratitude. They should be designed to help others. A good testimony is not the detailed telling of a spiritual experience but the truth learned from the experience.

Closing Time

The prayer service should not be unduly prolonged. Waiting for one more testimony in a meeting which has lacked vitality will probably not provide that vitality. A service in which the response is active and the people are still participating should be closed while the spirit of the service is at a high level. Those who desire to participate but are prevented by lack of time, in circumstances when scheduling is important, should be kindly thanked for their support even though they are unable to speak.

At the end of the meeting, the minister in charge may have some final words of exhortation and appreciation. The presider should not sermonize at length nor attempt to summarize the contributions of others.

Visiting after the service is good, but if the meeting place is a private home, the visiting should not be prolonged and thus create a hardship on the host family.

Related Factors

The purpose of a theme is to provide a central thought or idea about which the minister who leads the worship groups the elements of the service. A theme should be expressed through the total nature of the service. The Saints are likely to direct their prayers and testimonies toward the theme if it is presented in this manner.

The ideas expressed may move from one area of religious experience or truth to another. Prayer meeting leaders should not attempt to prevent this movement but rather to control it and keep it within the proper channels. Choose a hymn, scripture lesson, theme talk, and other features of the service with the theme in mind and so conduct the service as to permit the congregation to discover the theme themselves.

Themes which are most rewarding are those which touch lives at the most vital points, releasing within persons the presence and power of the Spirit of God. Themes should be concerned with spiritual uplift and with things common to God and human beings.

A large attendance is desired, but it is not essential to a good meeting. One of the best ways to build attendance is to have good meetings. If the people respond to thoughtful and vigorous leadership, the spiritual quality of their prayers and testimonies will attract others to the service. Frequent invitations to nonattending members should be part of the regular pastoral ministry.

Participation Encouraged

The talk or opening remarks should leave something for the people to say. If everything is said on the theme, they may say nothing. If problems or questions are raised for discussion which relate to their own experiences, they can contribute to the meeting. The attitude of the minister should let them know that the humblest of them is as important to God as anybody in the world. The strength of one will minister to the weakness of another. Participation may be encouraged by announcing a hymn and asking for volunteers to be ready to pray or testify afterward.

It is necessary to maintain order in every prayer service. The presiding officer should direct the meeting. There is no justification for elders to open the meeting with the usual preliminaries and talk, and then say, "Now the meeting is in your hands." This suggests an abandonment of responsibility. Leaders should seek to make each meeting a fine spiritual experience for the people. They should pray silently for the meeting and for the people and should encourage participation.

In many groups there may be one or more unwise persons who may talk or pray too long, indulge in questionable or false manifestations of the "gifts," go into long and meaningless accounts of experiences, personal history, illness, or operations. These people should be admonished privately at first to avoid causing them embarrassment. If this advice is disregarded, in extreme cases of abuse of time or inappropriate expression the presiding officer can rise to ask the member to be brief and remain standing until the member sits down. Such public reprovals, however, are likely to crush the spirit of the meeting and cause other members to be reluctant to participate; therefore, if possible, public reproof should be avoided.

Chapter 4

HOME MINISTRY

The Role of Home Ministry

There are many references in Latter Day Saint revelation directing priesthood members to minister in the homes of the Saints. Traditionally these visits were made by two priesthood members or on occasion by a priesthod member and an unordained person. Jesus said to his disciples, "Go forth from house to house, teaching the people; and I will go before you."[1] Latter Day Saints accepted that principle and gave home ministry a high priority.

In its larger sense this commission directs us to understand that priesthood members should live close to their people, giving ministry and pastoral care in the full range of life's activities. Therefore, priesthood responsibilities should not be confined to the meetings which take place within the walls of the church building.

172

In more recent years, however, the conditions of society have changed so much that the old-type home ministry offered by priesthood members seems artificial to the homes in many parts of the world. Priesthood members have found themselves increasingly unable to perform ministry adequately in the home. It is difficult to find a time when all members of the family are together and free to visit about their spiritual concerns. Modern attitudes have made home visiting more unnatural to family life. Neighbors do not visit each other in the cities as people formerly visited in rural areas. It may help to look at ministry in the larger sense and to consider giving pastoral ministry to persons in the situations where they live, rather than to try to carry on a certain kind of formalized activity. Often a home ministry program seems artificial both to the ministers and to the families. For better or for worse many of the functions of family ministry have been taken over by peer group ministries.

The Home Is the Basic Unit

Great changes are taking place in family life throughout the world. Many homes today are led by single parents. Often the parents work away from home during part of the day. Priesthood members should not be surprised to find that some homes which need their ministry are led by unmarried parents. The public ministry of the church should recognize that there are special needs in these homes and include timely and necessary ministry. Some of this will be offered through the departments such as the church school or Zion's League. But much of the ministry will be more individual and person-centered. Priesthood members must attempt to interpret the gospel at the personal level.

The Purpose and Importance of Home Ministry

The church is designed by God to minister in every way to perfect the lives of people. God has placed priesthood in the church "for the perfecting of the saints, for the work of the ministry, for the edifying of the body of Christ."[2]

Priesthood ministry encompasses the whole range of human experience. It involves family relations, personal concerns, and social life. It is interesting to note that Jesus in the short time of his ministry was with the people at a wedding in Cana, at their work fishing, on the roads and highways, and in their homes. Wherever people lived, Jesus was there.

Priesthood ministry can stimulate the life of the family and help its members to grow spiritually. Ofttimes through visits in the home members can be encouraged not only to attend regular church services but to plan for those special events where they can participate with the church in its larger gatherings such as conferences, reunions, and youth camps. Through family ministry the members may come to understand better the purposes of God in their lives. Visits in the home can help members see how much the church needs them and encourage consistent attendance. It can guide members in giving their help and money where the need is most apparent and where they feel most fulfilled in keeping the commandments of Christ. Home ministry can promote missionary awareness and stimulate the evangelistic outreach of the family. Through priesthood visits the initiative can often be taken to unite families in the church.

Ministry in the home can be educational, corrective, and inspirational. The church is strengthened as the personal ministries, the ordinances, and the teachings of the church become more relevant to life and increasingly experienced in the life of those who feel an active part of the fellowship.

Ministry in the home often deals with the emotions, habits, and relationships of individuals. It may involve the minister in some very delicate matters. This fact requires that priesthood members be able to keep confidences and be trusted by those whom they visit.

Priesthood home ministry can open doors of opportunity for the expression of individual and team talents within the church. One of the surprising things to many persons is the amount of latent talent that has never been tapped within any congregation. This is due often to the fact that many persons are timid or have never been brought to the attention of those who should know about their abilities. Priesthood members who visit in the home can discover these gifts and can call them to the attention of the pastor.

Every member needs to become involved in some form of Christian service. This can take many forms within the church program and within the community. Christian service requires involvement in the lives of others in a good way. Those who are not involved should be given the opportunities. The discovery of talents unused or latent is a good type of ministry.

Priesthood ministry may be the only tie between the church and some families. The first symptom of problems within a home may be erratic participation in the corporate activities of the congregation.

Those involved in home ministry seek to transmit faith, trust, and knowledge. They discover family situations and individual needs which should have the attention of the pastor or other specialized ministers. They make available advice, direction, and spiritual guidance to those members separated from the worshiping body of the church. This ministry should be of help to the family in building a Zionic homelife.

Family Relationships Affect the Church

The strength of the church lies in the spiritual health of its families. This is true because homes are the primary social units of society.

The family with an affirmative attitude toward the church is usually an asset to the church in mission. Such families will participate in church ministries as individuals and will support one another in such participation. They make a financial contribution to the church because they know it serves as an extension of their own concerns for humanity.

Family Relationships Affect the Inner Family

Interpersonal relationships are reflected in the emotional climate of the home. Good marital relationships and parental attitudes are important if there is to be good communication among family members. Parent-child relationships have much to do with the emotional health of the children. Where there is love and equitable division of labor within the home, mutual companionship can flourish.

Societies all over the world are changing. The roles of individuals vary. Psychological differences between the sexes, disciplinary techniques used with children, and the understanding of self-image are changing. It takes spiritual, emotional, intellectual, and physiological maturity to cope with this change.

Good family relationships tend to condition lives to good living. Harmony in the home, love expressed freely, and respect for individuality should be in every church home. When this does not exist, the home is weakened in its witness before the world, and individuals are deprived of self-identity and security.

Families that worship together find strength, unity, and love that others do not experience. True worship includes the spirit of thankfulness and mutual appreciation. A Zionic family worships God together.

Criteria of Spiritual Health and Outreach

Since the priesthood members are concerned for the spiritual condition of the home some criteria are needed to identify the level of this condition in family life. There may be many more than those here enumerated but the following areas recently set forth seem to be significant.

1. Church attendance is one sign of spiritual well-being. Erratic attendance frequently dwindles to nonattendance. Experience through the years has shown that those who are spiritually healthy desire to commune regularly with the Saints.

2. Financial support of the church is indicative of commitment. Partial or limited support, or support withheld, is indicative of need for ministry. The amount of support must never be compared between families. The criterion rests on the sound principle of financial stewardship, of which tithing and offerings are a part.

3. The family's sense of well-being is an important factor. This involves physical and mental health, financial security, and general mutual concern

for one another. Those who lack adequate food or clothing, whose energies are vitiated by illness, whose self-respect is put down by unemployment, or whose ability to relate with the community is impaired by nonsocial or antisocial attitudes cannot well serve the cause of Christ.

4. Affection and supportive family relationships indicate healthy homes. The interdependence of members of the family should be recognized, along with the personhood of the individual. The fine balance between the two makes for good social adjustment and happiness.

5. An optimistic and hopeful attitude is significant. An affirmative and reasonable attitude toward life is an indication of vitality. Negative attitudes are danger signs. Those who are trained in counseling and psychotherapy tell us that the expressed attitude toward others is a strong clue to the nature of the mind of the individual.

6. The reading literature in the home tells much about it. Every Saint should read church literature regularly. The home where the *Saints Herald* is read regularly, where the standard books of scripture are read and studied, where church school literature is studied, and where other church publications are to be found is one where the ongoing movement of the church has set the pace. Financial factors may limit the amount of such literature, but there should be some there, and it should be used.

7. An evangelistic outreach is to be found in good, saintly homes. The ingrown family or the family that confines its social contacts to church members

is missing a very important asset of sainthood. The joy of sharing is the heart of evangelism.

8. The saintly home is a witnessing home. Christian witness is the breath of fresh air in a world of pollution. The quality of the home in the community should be attractive, and support the good word of testimony.

Thus we hope to develop in homes of the Saints regular church attendance, financial commitment, a sense of well-being, good family relationships, an affirmative attitude, and an evangelistic outreach. We should expect the church literature to assist in this development.

Who Performs Home Ministry?

Home ministry involves a significant aspect of the makeup of the church of Jesus Christ. The fact that there are many offices of priesthood presupposes varying responsibilities, for if all had the same duties there would be but one office. Thus, there is provided a ministry of specialists; a call to a specific office is a call to specialized ministry.

While every elder, priest, teacher, and deacon is to perform a general ministry to "teach, expound, exhort" and "take the lead of meetings" under certain conditions, he or she is also called to a specialized ministry.

"Every elder, priest, teacher, or deacon, is to be ordained according to the gifts and callings of God unto him."[3] The significance of priesthood office is in the specialized duties. Priesthood will magnify their calling when they develop their special gifts while honoring the general priesthood work. Pulpit ministry, administering the ordinances, and administrative leadership are primarily ministries of the Melchisedec priesthood. While the Aaronic priesthood may bring public ministry when necessary, its basic responsibility is related to families and individuals. Home ministry is a significant ministry of the Aaronic priesthood.

All of the ministry extended by the church in a congregation is under the supervision and direction of the presiding officer; however, pastoral or shepherding ministry includes all members of the priesthood and must be shared by them. The presiding elder will help priesthood members to appreciate the specialized characteristics of their callings and counsel with them in preparing to do this specialized work. Particularly the presiding elder will help each priesthood member take his or her place in home ministry according to the office held.

Priesthood Preparation for Home Ministry

Priesthood members need to be spiritually ready. The attributes of godliness must be nurtured constantly. Openness to spiritual guidance and ability to discern right from wrong need to be developed. A genuine love for people is imperative. Spiritual readiness is a growing thing, never static. It is the quality of the shepherd.

All members of the priesthood should know and understand the duties of their calling. They ought to take courses of study related to their office and function. Since home ministry will inevitably bring the priesthood members into counseling situations, they should take at least one fundamental course in ministerial counseling. They should learn where resource helps may be found and how to use them.

The skills of successful home ministry are sharpened

by home visiting. The whole program should offer "on the job" training and provide "feedback" sessions for the benefit of all.

Making the Priesthood Call

Appointments may be made with the family well ahead of the visit. Occasionally people are reluctant to make an appointment, and a brief call sometimes may be made without previous arrangement. All priesthood members will make some general pastoral calls, many of which will be by appointment or by announcement. Frequently the purpose of these calls is to bring some aspect of the general program of the church into the home. Other priesthood calls will be made to present an office-centered ministry.

It is advisable for two members of the priesthood to visit together. Visits by a priest to help with family study or a teacher to discuss church membership responsibilities could well be enhanced if there are teams of two. But it should be understood which one is to take the lead in the discussion. The general pastoral ministry of watching over the church involves a variety of circumstances in which two members of the priesthood are needed to strengthen and support each other. Some priesthood members also need the training gained by association with those more mature and experienced.

Reporting

Reporting must be done for a definite purpose, not for the sake of reporting. The true value of ministry is not indicated in a report but in the kind of reponse the family makes toward the ministry.

The branch president or supervisor of home ministry

ought to encourage each minister to report. Such reporting will help the minister assess the progress of those under his or her care. Further, it presents a better control over the necessary information about families—where they live, new addresses, their needs. Special situations should be reported to the pastor immediately, while routine visits may be reported at the month's end or as the pastor may determine.

An annual or semiannual analysis of the program of home ministry should be helpful to both the pastor and the priesthood. It can serve as a guide in evaluating what has been done and in determining what improvements should be made for the home ministry program to be more effective. Constant mutual encouragement is needed to keep the program alive. A careful analysis will determine those members to be visited first and most often. In most situations more than one contact is needed for adequate ministry. The desirability of a monthly report is a matter which cannot be overemphasized. Every report should be obtained. No month should go by without a report from each minister. The report should be acknowledged, and the minister should be thanked. A report unacknowledged is often unrepeated.

In Summary

Home ministry is a very important part of the work of priesthood members. Perhaps one of the significant understandings that home ministry opens is the awareness that calling reaches beyond the activities officially organized by the church such as formal worship, educational activities, and social gatherings. Those in the priesthood are called to be with the people sharing their burdens, joys, and interests. In a sense it is important to guard against undue formality in these broader ministries. Home ministry may take place within the house where people live; but it may also be taking a boy or girl fishing or out for lunch where his or her concerns can be discussed, or helping a person in a rest home write a letter.

It will perhaps help to realize again that the primary calling of priesthood is to minister to people. The ways in which such ministry is accomplished may vary. The church is a community, and the nature of such a mutual fellowship indicates that ministers, as shepherds, are to be vitally concerned about the welfare of people, and use whatever methods seem most appropriate to meet the needs of each one.

NOTES

1. Matthew 6:26.
2. Ephesians 4:12.
3. Doctrine and Covenants 17:12a.

Chapter 5

VISITING THE ILL

Suggestions for Pastoral Ministry

People visit friends and loved ones when they are ill to show concern for their welfare and to encourage them. Members of the priesthood may feel a responsibility even greater than most others to call on the ill because they feel a pastoral concern for bringing ministry to those confronted with such circumstances. Priesthood members in the Reorganized Church of Jesus Christ of Latter Day Saints should recognize, however, that our situation is somewhat different from that of many other church denominations.

First, the church usually has several ordained priesthood members in each congregation, while most denominations have but one ordained minister in a congregation. Our priesthood members should be very sensitive to this fact when visiting in a hospital and not assume ministerial privileges or prerogatives when circumstances do not justify it. Furthermore we should be sensitive to the sheer numbers of our priesthood members who may visit a sick person. When it has been indicated that a sick person should not have visitors, priesthood members should respect that request unless they are visiting for specific ministerial purpose, such as that of administering to the sick person or responding to a request for pastoral counsel.

Second, the majority of the self-sustaining priesthood members have not had training or experience in pastoral ministry to the sick and should therefore enter into that aspect of their ministry carefully and prayerfully. As priesthood members do go in a ministerial capacity the following suggestions will be helpful.

1. When visiting in a hospital check with the nurse in charge, or her or his representative, before visiting a patient. Such contact is a matter of courtesy which will be appreciated by the medical staff responsible, but it will also help you to know if there have been any changes in the patient's condition, any innovations in the treatment which might affect the patient, or any problems with which you might help.

2. When visiting, respect the privacy of the patient. If the ill person is in a room with the door closed, you should knock, identify yourself, and, if the patient is not acquainted with you, identify the purpose of the call. This will help the ill person know what to expect and to prepare the way for a successful visit. Surprises and uncertainty often distress persons who are ill especially if they are in the unfamiliar surroundings of a hospital. A former chaplain at the Independence Sanitarium and Hospital recently wrote, "While serving as chaplain at the San, I received more complaints from patients about being surprised by a minister or visitors when the door was closed than for any other reason." Anything ministers can do to

make their presence and purpose known will be helpful.

3. Take a position which makes it easy for the sick person to see and talk with you. Generally it is best for the ministers to stand unless asked to sit down. Never sit or stand so the patient has to stare into the light or twist the neck or other parts of the body to face you. If you will observe the situation carefully, you will sense where to stand or sit in relation to the sick person. Under no circumstances should you sit on a patient's bed. The bed covers may keep you from seeing medical equipment of a life saving nature that could be damaged by your weight.

4. Observe carefully the setting and situation in the sickroom. You can learn much from such observation and it will help you not to embarrass the patient. If a woman patient is unkempt or if a man is disheveled and unshaved, it may indicate low morale. If a patient has been ill for some time but there are no "get well" messages or flowers in evidence, it may indicate a reason for loneliness. The hospital equipment in the room may give some clue as to the patient's condition and treatment. This will help the trained observer in understanding the patient's needs.

5. Speak in normal tones to the sick person. Help the ill person be at ease.

6. Say only what you want the sick person to hear. Even if the patient is delirious or too weak to register any knowledge of your presence, say only what you want the patient to hear. Often the sick person's hearing is quite sensitive even to a

faintly whispered comment. Any appearance of talking to others in a way which makes the patient feel that information about his or her condition is being withheld is often distressing because the sick person may already be apprehensive.

7. Don't touch, sit on, or lean against the sick person's bed. The added sensitivity of one who is ill may make this painful or discomforting. The desire to appear at ease or friendly sometimes causes the visitor to forget these unusually delicate feelings of the sick.

8. Make visits brief unless there are circumstances such as pastoral counseling or other ministry requested which require a longer time. Even then the person's ability to tolerate such a call should be carefully observed. Usually five minutes is long enough for a visit. Seldom should any visit to the sick exceed fifteen minutes either in the hospital or the home.

9. Let the person express his or her feelings. A good way to begin a visit with an ill person who wants to talk is simply to ask "How are things going?" The patient can then choose on what level to respond. The sick person may choose to talk about his or her sickness, but may be more concerned about family or religious feelings which often emerge in times of sickness or tragedy. Listen with understanding and accept the person's feelings as he or she states them. Don't respond to the patient's despair or discouragement by contradicting the feelings or with optimistic platitudes. Let the sick person feel and talk honestly about those feelings.

Avoid asking medical questions and above all, don't "play doctor." Let the patient know you are there for a different reason than the medical personnel. The ministerial concerns of priesthood members have to do not with medical advice but rather with helping the sick person understand that God cares. You are there to help the sick person reestablish faith in God and in those persons who are helping, such as the doctor, nurses, and friends. Your ministry helps the person find again the faith to know that no matter what happens, even if it be death, God can and will provide both the resources and the loving presence of the Spirit necessary to deal with it. Ministry develops a spirit of hopefulness and trust which may help the healing processes, but whether or not physical healing takes place, it can heal the soul and bring new strength and peace to the person. This is not to be interpreted as "giving up." It is yielding one's life to God, believing God will do the thing which is good, and finding both peace and assurance in that faith. Healing is improved when a person is free from anxiety, but assurance is more than the patient believing that he or she will get well. It is believing that God in infinite love and power will keep us. Even if physical health is not restored there is still no cause for anxiety.

To help a sick person develop such an assurance you must experience it yourself. Anxious, frightened, or doubting priesthood members can actually do more harm than good. The assurance needed in the sickroom is not "whistling in the dark" nor ignoring the reality of suffering. It is the ability to face the hardest facts with courage and dignity. Such assurance does not come from bluffing, funny jokes, back slapping, or feigned optimism. It is caught from ministers with a deep, well-considered faith and assurance in the ultimate lordship of God. We live in God. We trust God who has promised to do for us all ever so much more than we can ever imagine.

Faith such as we bring to the sickroom is caught more than taught. We rarely communicate such assurance by some logical presentation of ideas. It is sensed and caught from the attitude and actions of priesthood members who themselves have thought through their own attitudes toward suffering, their own faith in God, and their willingness to yield their own lives to God whatever the future may hold.

10. Accept the patient's feelings as they are expressed without rendering judgment. Be permissive in accepting the sick person's feelings with understanding. This does not mean that you must agree with the patient. It is not necessary for you to say "I agree with you." It is important to be able to say, "I understand how you feel." It does mean that sick persons can be honest without feeling that they will jeopardize their personal relationship with the visitors or that they will be condemned for what they reveal. Many people who are ill are burdened by feelings of guilt and regret about their past lives. They need to talk with ministers who understand, love them, and will help them make those changes they want to make

and find forgiveness and reconciliation with God and others whom they may have treated poorly. It is important to hold in confidence those things a patient confides to you as a minister.

11. Pray with the patient only if the person indicates a desire for prayer, or if the spirit of the occasion makes it evident that prayer would be desirable. Do not devalue prayer by using it lightly. This is especially important in the sickroom.

12. If at all possible follow the principle of going two by two when visiting the sick. It will help to have the sensitivity and wisdom which each minister can give the other. In cases where there are needs which one cannot adequately meet, the other may be able to help.

When visiting in a home, especially where the sick person is alone, it is very important for everyone concerned to have two priesthood members, or if that is inconvenient, a priesthood member and an unordained person can go as a team.

Ministry to the ill is one of the common needs encountered. Try to develop understandings and skills to minister to those who are sick. You will find that your own depth of understanding will be increased as you experience personal illness and tragedy. In some ways ministers learn to minister out of their own suffering.

Chapter 6

THE FUNERAL SERVICE

Introduction

The call to officiate at a funeral usually comes without warning and it may be too late to do much planning. Where a minister ordinarily has at least a week or two to prepare for a scheduled service, in a funeral the priesthood member is cast into a very demanding personal ministry within a matter of a few hours, or at most a few days.

There are two elements in most funeral services: the recognition of the deceased, and ministry to the surviving family and friends. In conducting the services the minister should include some features ministering to both aspects of need.

The Significance of the Funeral

A funeral is not a sacramental ordinance. We do not believe that the form of the service has any bearing on the eternal well-being of the deceased. Some feel that the service should include a consecration of the final resting place looking toward that day when the body shall be called forth to be reunited with the spirit in resurrection. If this is done it should be recognized as symbolic. The basic significance lies in the recognition of the principle of eternal life, the undying spirit, and the promise of life after death. The service should bring comfort and assurance of God's love and a living hope of eternal life.

Early Pastoral Ministry

The minister should call at the home as soon as possible after learning of the death. Priesthood should offer their services in an unassuming way. The purpose for being there is to offer comfort in a sad and trying time; therefore, the priesthood should offer guidance in modesty and recognize the reasonable desires of the bereaved in planning the service.

Priesthood should make no suggestions regarding the funeral service until invited to officiate. If asked to officiate, the minister should arrange to return at a later time to discuss the details. This will give time to think through the needs of the family, along with any information available before consulting the family.

The minister should seek to learn the wishes of the family. The following is a list of things to check:

1. The nature of the interment: burial, mausoleum, cremation.
2. Place, time, and date of the service.
3. Is someone else to assist with the service? What part is he or she to take? Who shall invite the other minister?
4. Will there be any special service rendered by any fraternal or military body?
5. What kind of music is desired? Who is to secure the musicians? Is there a preferred hymn?
6. Will there be an obituary read? Who is to prepare it?
7. Did the deceased have a favorite text or scripture passage?
8. Does the family have any suggestions regarding the personal interests or virtues of the deceased that would be helpful in preparing the sermon?

Most of this information can be gleaned without pointed questioning, but if it becomes necessary, the questions should be asked. Experience will dictate whether there are other things which need to be checked.

Cooperate with the funeral director in service arrangements. If in doubt on any point, ask the funeral director who usually is familiar with local customs. The atmosphere must be one of calm understanding sympathy, filled with hope and promise. Innovations which depart radically from the customs of the people should be avoided.

Receiving of Friends

Frequently, the family will receive friends at the funeral home during the evening hours prior to the service to be held the following day. The hours are published in the newspaper. Such arrangement is usually cared for by the funeral director. The minister should arrange to be with the family, if possible, though it is not necessary to take any conspicuous part.

The Bier

One of the customs undergoing careful evaluation today centers around the bier. The custom of viewing the body of the deceased grew out of the Middle Ages when families kept watch lest the body be stolen. This was carried to the extreme in that the family remained until the last earth had been placed on the grave. Through the years sentiment changed, and the custom gained a type of respectability as "paying last respects." The disadvantage of the custom lies in undue emphasis upon the body.

As a result of the reevaluation, there is no set pattern today. In some cases the casket is opened at the family reception for all to view. In some cases, it is opened only for the family. In some services the casket is opened prior to the beginning of the formal service and closed during the service. In other situations, the casket remains closed throughout until the close of the service, then opened for friends and family. It is becoming a more accepted practice not to open the casket at all.

The minister should see to it that the atmosphere and practice be in harmony with the theological implications regarding life and death, and that they bring a ministry of peace and reconciliation with God.

The Service

The funeral service should be a worship service. The duty of the minister is to conduct the service in such a manner as to bring family and friends into the calming and assuring presence of God. The worship experience should give them strength to endure and courage to face life. The minister should avoid any language in prayer, hymn, poetry, or sermon that would open wounds or encourage self-pity. The message and deportment of the minister should give quiet assurance born out of experience with God and the sure knowledge that "all things work for good to them that love God."

It is most fitting that the funeral service be a worship service. In the presence of death, the most wicked are sobered. All are inclined to examine themselves in the light of the Eternal. In these moments of self-inquiry, the minister has a golden opportunity to move them closer to God and the ministry of repentance may be given. This ministry is neither a harangue nor a "missionary sermon." Here, by the declaration of the love of God for persons and the gift of Jesus Christ, reconciliation with God may be effected. The story of the resurrection and the glorious promise held therein will penetrate the confused heart and mind in the spirit of hope and assurance. This is the true ministry of the shepherd of the flock.

Prelude music should consist of music with a tone of hope and peace. Sad, depressing music should be avoided. Musical numbers generally consist of hymns, sacred songs, and instrumental music by organ or piano. Vocal music can be solos, duets, trios, or quartets. The effect of the music should bring hope, peace, acceptance, and understanding and not increase sorrow and grief.

Prayers (invocation, general, closing) should bring the congregation into the presence of God in compassion and understanding. Who better than God can appreciate the moment of grief. Christ wept at the tomb of Lazarus, wept over Jerusalem, and in the moment of his own death thought only of others.

Order of Service

Circumstances may permit the minister to have prayer with the mourners before they leave the home for the funeral chapel or the church. The formal service starts as the ministers take their place at the altar. There is no fixed rule as to the order of the service, but suggestions relative to the procedure of the funeral may be helpful:

1. Music by one or more singers as selected by the family
2. Obituary

3. Invocation
4. Scripture reading (Nos. 2 and 4 may be reversed.)
5. Appropriate music
6. Sermon
7. Appropriate music (if desired)
8. Benediction (This may be omitted, in which case the minister announces, "The service will be concluded at the graveside.")
9. The funeral director then takes charge.
10. The ministers precede the casket to the hearse.

Local and national customs may require other practices of a different procedure. In any case the purpose is to sustain the people in their faith at a time of stress.

Preparing the Obituary

Occasionally the minister is called upon to prepare the obituary, a notice of death which includes a biographical sketch. The minister should be certain that all of the data are correct, names spelled properly, and all surviving members of the family included. The funeral director usually takes care of this matter, and may be asked to help if the minister is called upon to prepare the obituary.

The obituary is usually placed in the newspaper in the town where the deceased lived. Sometimes the notice is also sent to other towns or cities where the family lived for some time.

Occasionally the obituary is read from the pulpit prior to the sermon. This custom is sometimes ignored especially when the obituary has been published, since it serves no truly useful purpose. Sometimes, when the attendance at the service is very large and those who attend do so out of respect to one whom they knew more by reputation than as a person, the obituary may furnish them information they may lack. When read, it should be factual, and care should be exercised that it does not become a eulogy. Remarks which may call to mind the good qualities of the deceased should be left for the minister's message.

Date of birth, marriage, baptism, names of children, places of residence, occupation, and unusual features of personal hobby or public activities might all be included as thought appropriate.

In summary an obituary may contain the following facts:
1. Full name of the departed
2. Names of his or her father and mother
3. Place and date of birth
4. Schools from which he or she graduated
5. Facts about marriage (the last, if more than one)
6. Facts about children
7. Facts about church work
8. Facts about occupation, hobbies, and public life
9. Facts about military service
10. Facts about fraternal affiliations
11. The time and the place of death

If the obituary is read in the funeral service, it may contain (a) the words of the deceased's favorite scripture verse, and (b) the first stanza of his or her favorite hymn.

The Nature of the Sermon

The sermon should offer hope and comfort to the bereaved. The deceased does not need our comfort; the living do. This can be done best by sympathetic, affirmative expounding of the doctrines of redemption, atonement, resurrection, merciful judgment, and the love of God. The sermon should hold up the present and future in expectation. The family and friends should go away feeling that they have the courage to face the future with strength, though they walk without the physical presence of their loved one.

Scripture reading and poems for use in the sermon should be carefully chosen so as to truly express the beliefs of the church.

The Use of Scripture

Some ministers have developed the custom of reading a chain of many scriptures as they begin their sermons. It may not occur to them that scriptural language is difficult to follow for those who are unfamiliar with it and to interpret and apply meaningfully. A few passages significant to the occasion and woven into the message may be more effective. One or more of the following scriptures will set the tone for the sermon (all Bible references are to the Inspired Version): I Corinthians 15:19-23; II Timothy 4:1-8; Mosiah 8:54-60; Psalm 8:4-6; I Thessalonians 4:13-18; Alma 19:42-44; Philippians 1:22-25; Revelation 20:11-13; Hebrews 13:14, 11:10; Job 19:25-29; Doctrine and Covenants 22:23; Revelation 14:13; Job 14:14; II Peter 3:8-13; II Corinthians 5:1-10; Ecclesiastes 12:1-7; II Nephi 6:24-35.

Fraternal and Military Organizations

If the deceased was a member of a fraternal or military organization and the family would like to have the organization participate in the service, arrangements should be made jointly by the funeral director, family, and minister.

When a fraternal order is to have a part in the funeral services this should be a separate function. It may be done prior to or after the religious service or at the graveside, but the fraternal service should not be a part of the worship service.

In most communities the fraternal order is willing to function either in the home or at the funeral chapel, holding the service the evening prior to the religious service. Notice usually appears in the newspaper. This provides two services of distinctly different character.

If the graveside service is turned over to the fraternal body the minister should conclude the religious service with the benediction and then the fraternal service begins.

The minister should learn the nature and extent of this ceremony so as to enhance the beauty of the whole occasion.

The military funeral is encountered occasionally by the minister who should become generally familiar with military funerals. However, the military commanding officer or representative, in coordination with the military superintendent and funeral director makes the funeral arrangements and supervises the conduct of the funeral. But the civilian minister has an important role to perform at certain times in the ceremony.

There are three types of military funerals: (1) a complete military escort from the services held at the chapel, church, or home to the cemetery, (2) services followed by a procession which is formed near the entrance of the cemetery, and (3) services at the graveside.

In the complete procession, military regulations set the order: (1) band, (2) military escort, (3) colors, (4) clergy, (5) caisson or hearse, and casket bearers, (6) caparisoned horse (only for the president of the United States and/or other high-ranking officers), (7) honorary pallbearers, (8) family, (9) patriotic or fraternal organizations, and (10) friends. This is a very impressive service. At the appointed time the band plays and the procession moves into the chapel. The minister leads. When everyone is seated, all is hushed. Then the minister speaks. After the service, the minister leads the procession to the funeral conveyance. At the cemetery the minister leads the procession to the grave. After the casket is deposited the flag is removed. When all is ready, the minister is in charge as in a civilian service. At the conclusion of the words of benediction, the minister steps back or to the side and the bugler sounds taps following the firing of three volleys by the appointed squad. It might be advisable to caution family members at the funeral that the firing of a volley at the cemetery is a very loud and startling sound which may be upsetting to family members.

When the family insists on both the church and the fraternal or military order participating, it may be possible for the minister to arrange for one to be responsible for the church or funeral home service, while the other officiates at the graveside or committal service. Appropriateness and length of the combined services need to be carefully considered.

Graveside Service and Committal

The minister confers early with the funeral director on where to drive in the cortege, or where to ride if the minister does not use his or her own car.

When the funeral procession leaves the church or funeral home, the minister should precede the casket or the hearse then stand to one side as the casket is set in place and the door closed.

When the procession arrives at the cemetery, the minister again precedes the casket to the grave and should stand at the head of the casket. At a signal from the funeral director, the minister conducts the graveside rites. This usually consists of a reading of scripture (not too long) and the benediction.

Appropriate scripture readings are John 14:15; Alma 8:98-104; Revelation 14:13; and Doctrine and Covenants 63:13c-f.

In some communities it is the custom, or the family may request, that there be a committal service. This should come before the prayer.

One type consists of dropping a bit of earth or the petals of a flower and saying: "Out of the ground wast thou taken and unto dust shalt thou return, but the spirit has returned to the God who created it."

Another type consists of a statement of committal, such as, "Into the ground we commit the body of our brother (sister), here to await that glorious day when the call from on high shall sound forth and body and spirit shall be reunited in resurrection and stand before the throne of God."

The benediction ends the formal service. The minister should go immediately to the family and give a friendly handshake and a brief word of comfort to the bereaved.

Whenever it is appropriate some good friend should be at the home to receive the family so that they do not return alone to the emptiness of the house. All of the sympathy and kindness, including a meal brought in, assure them of the tie that binds in Christ.

Follow-up Ministry

The attending physician or funeral director will make necessary reports of the death to civil authorities. The officiating minister is responsible for making a report to the church statistician. It is not enough to assume that the local recorder will take care of the report.

The minister is needed at the funeral service, but the need afterward is far greater. Many people take time out of a busy life to pay respect to family and departed ones by their presence, but the bereaved are often left to themselves afterward. The minister can be helpful by making not one but a number of visits after the services. The frequency of such visits will depend upon the need. They should always be kindly and comforting in their nature. If hardships appear to beset the family, proper reference should be made through the channels of the church to provide help. Such ministry will probably touch the lives of the members of the family more intimately than any sermon ever preached.

Characteristics of the Bereaved

1. Bereavement is a personal loss. It is a loss for which there is never complete compensation. This is a shock, whether the loss was expected or not. The church can offer fellowship, and thereby replace the loss with a type of gain.

2. The bereaved person is lonely. Radical changes should be discouraged lest irreparable mistakes be made. It is not unusual to find that someone who has been happily married and well adjusted to life seeks out another companion shortly after the death of his or her loved one in an attempt to escape loneliness. The task of the church is to

provide help in the adjustment so that another companion will not be chosen on the "rebound." Selecting a life companion requires all of one's intellect. Remarriage should not be considered hastily. This is not only because of appropriate respect to the deceased, but also because of the need to exercise good judgment.

3. Occasionally the bereaved has a guilt feeling concerning the death of a loved one. He or she searches for some sin of self which may have caused the death. The person may feel a sense of failure regarding the loved one because of one's neglect, unkind words, or anger. Small matters may be exaggerated out of proportion in accusing oneself for failures in this regard. This is a very real problem. Such a person should be given the opportunity to fill life with creative thinking and action until perspective is regained.

It is well to suggest that souvenirs be kept to a minimum. Flowers from the grave, pictures of the casket and the funeral service, and other mementos of like nature should not be kept. Before long, all items which tend to recall unhappy thoughts should be put away.

Attending church is a good way to begin moving out from loneliness. Association with people of normal viewpoints is "good medicine."

If there is financial difficulty, the bishop or bishop's representative can be called upon to determine if economic assistance and advice are needed.

Chapter 7

MINISTRY AND THE ARMED FORCES

Serving in the Armed Forces

Service in the armed forces is universally recognized in most countries of the world. Certainly not everyone will be called or will volunteer for military service, but there are few indeed who do not have a relative or friend who has.

Most priesthood members become aware of the type of personal and family problems generated directly or indirectly by the fact of military service. Such things as family separation, duty at remote outposts, and isolation from church friends are representative of these problems. Furthermore, young men and women may request counseling before entering the armed forces, and at times when the military draft is in effect many more will be requesting counseling regarding such service. Priesthood members need additional background and familiarization with the church's stand so that they can provide effective counseling and ministry to members involved in, and those contemplating, military service.

It is not uncommon for priesthood members themselves to be serving in the armed forces. In fact, the church is officially established today in such countries as Japan, Okinawa, and Korea because military church members, many of whom were priesthood members, witnessed to individuals in these lands, telling them of the restored gospel. Apostle Kisuke Sekine was a young Buddhist in Japan until he heard of the church through an American serviceman, and today he is a member of one of the leading quorums of the church.

In addition to providing opportunities for witnessing, duty in the armed forces brings a special obligation to a priesthood member. It is the obligation to espouse and to live by the same Christian virtues that he or she exhibits in civil life. There is always the temptation to "go along with the crowd," or, especially in time of war, to accept an attitude of fatalism and therefore to "live it up" now. One who senses the divinity of priesthood and truly believes that he or she has been chosen by God to serve in a special way as God's representative could never behave in a manner that would betray this trust.

Statement of Theology

One universal truth that most members recognize, is that the church and its members are a part of the society of the country wherein they live. In the countries of the Western world particularly, church members vote in national elections, and therefore help shape the social order in which they are living. When and if the situation of national affairs develops to a condition wherein that society deems that armed conflict is the appropriate course of action, it does appear to be a serious matter at that critical moment in a nation's history to elect to withdraw from the society and refuse to support it during its hour of need. One whose personal philosophy would dictate such action has some responsibility to explain such a stand rationally.

The Church's Stand on Military Service

In 1974 the World Conference adopted a fundamental stand on the subject of military service. The central thought of this resolution (No. 1087) could be summarized as follows:

> The church officially objects to warfare and urges governments throughout the world to seek other ways to settle their differences. At the same time, the church recognizes the need to maintain law and order, and therefore if it bcomes necessary to serve in the armed forces, individual members should be supported according to their own conscience. (The church recognizes each individual's agency.) One who feels it is his or her duty to join the armed forces to protect society and/or the democratic way of life, will be supported in his or her conviction. Likewise, for the member who feels that it is morally wrong to bear arms, the church will support this individual's feelings also.

It is significant that the church took this course of action, for in some countries where the church is established, citizens are not given the right to object to military service or to bearing arms.

Conscientious Objection

Although the military draft in the United States was placed on standby in January 1973, it still remains in many other nations and, as for that matter, could be resumed in the United States. The subject, therefore, is discussed here for general information.

Conscientious objection is defined as the long-standing and deep seated religious and moral conviction opposing military service. Because persons in this category are generally small in number, Selective Service laws in the United States (and comparable laws of some other nations) have allowed persons in this category, under certain circumstances, to be relieved of military duty and/or be given the option of alternate channels of service to society. The burden of proof is up to the individual, and experience has shown that conscientious objection is a very difficult thing to prove to the satisfaction of Selective Service boards.

In addition to individuals who object to military service, there are others whose objection is not to military service per se, but rather, to bearing arms. When such convictions can be proved to the satisfaction of Selective Service boards, such individuals may be given noncombatant military duty, as for example, medical service, or other comparable duties which do not involve bearing arms.

In view of the church's stand in recognizing the right of agency of church members, it would be inappropriate for priesthood members to endeavor to persuade or counsel members, who are contemplating or expecting military service, to become conscientious objectors. Rather, the priesthood member is to assist members in understanding all the facts and alternatives so the individual can reach his or her own decision and feel right in that choice.

Exemption from Military Service

In countries with mandatory military service, persons in certain professions or with specified technical skills may be exempt from military service. In the United States, for example, students of military age have normally been given draft deferments until their education through the baccalaureate degree level (and on occasion, even graduate level) was completed. Also, the Selective Service policy in the United States provided exemptions to full-time clergymen. Under this policy, general officers and appointee ministers readily qualify. For the self-sustaining priesthood member, this is quite another matter. During World War II, the First Presidency established the policy of providing letters petitioning an exemption from military service to self-sustaining presiding elders, if there were no other priesthood members available to replace them. Although there is no occasion for such letters now, the policy stands and would be reinstituted if required.

Serving in the Armed Forces Chaplaincy

The concept of service to humanity through service to the church is basic to the Restoration theology, and through the years it has become so commonplace in the thinking of most church members it could almost be described as an RLDS distinctive. One such avenue of service that sometimes is contemplated by military church members is that of serving as a chaplain in the United States Armed Forces.

Although the church is authorized to have only a limited number of military chaplains* in the Armed Forces of the United States, circumstances could always change and therefore information is given here to assist priesthood members in answering inquiries regarding chaplaincy. At the present time the military is especially anxious to get qualified women chaplains.

Chaplains can serve in the United States Armed Forces only after receiving an "endorsement" from the First Presidency.

---

* The present authorization for four chaplains represents the number authorized to serve on active duty. The number who can serve in the Reserves or National Guard is almost unlimited; however, the First Presidency has ruled that qualification requirements are the same as for those who serve on active duty.

In naming priesthood members to serve as Armed Forces chaplains, the First Presidency uses the same administrative process and psychological testing that is used in selecting persons to become full-time appointee ministers, except that a member must ask to serve in the chaplaincy.

In the United States the Reorganized church is numbered among the approximately thirty-five major denominations which provide the ministers who serve in the armed forces chaplaincies. Denominations are allotted spaces commensurate with membership strength. Each year the chief of chaplains of each of the three armed services sends an official letter to church headquarters advising the First Presidency of the number of chaplains' spaces reserved for this denomination.

There are stringent educational and psychological requirements to be met to become a chaplain. Additionally, not everyone is amenable to a career that requires the family to move frequently and that may entail long periods of separation while on special assignment. As a result of these, and perhaps other circumstances, some chaplaincy positions have gone unfilled through the years.

The educational requirements are a baccalaureate degree plus a graduate degree from an accredited seminary or ninety hours of equivalent graduate training. The church requires additionally that the candidate must hold the priesthood office of elder and must complete some courses at Temple School. And finally, the candidate should have sufficient pastoral or hospital chaplaincy experience to assure the First Presidency of the candidate's demonstrated competency to serve. The question is frequently asked why our ministers must have seminary training to serve in the armed forces chaplaincy. The answer is quite simple. The First Presidency has insisted that our chaplains be fully qualified and equal in every respect to the ministers of other denominations with whom they will be serving. A lack of seminary training might be viewed as a deficiency by some senior military officers and could result in slower promotions or failure to receive the best assignments.

Priesthood members who express interest in the Armed Forces chaplaincy are referred to the Armed Forces Ministry Office at World Headquarters and a temporary file is established for such candidates. After the member actually enters seminary, the First Presidency is kept informed of the individual's progress.

For those willing to make preparation, the chaplaincy offers an opportunity to serve the church in an unusual way. It is a different kind of ministry, but one that offers a lifetime career. It can be tremendously rewarding, while at the same time serve as a fulfillment of one's stewardship commitment.

The Church's Program of Ministry to Armed Forces Personnel

During the Korean War (1950-1953) a dedicated priesthood member serving as an army officer in Korea made it his mission and priesthood duty to visit as many church members as he could during the months he was there. Out of his effort an armed forces newsletter was begun in Korea which proved so successful that after the war the World Church created a committee to continue its publication. Called the Committee on Ministry to Armed Forces Personnel, this agency not only publishes the *Armed Forces Newsletter* but also advises the

First Presidency on all matters regarding military ministry. The committee is composed of a chairperson who serves additionally as an administrative assistant to the First Presidency, and eight or ten men and women who are either serving in the armed forces or are closely associated with it. The committee members are in touch with military problems and their recommendations on this specialized ministry are available to the First Presidency.

The *Armed Forces Newsletter* is now issued four times a year and is sent free of charge to more than 1,000 families around the world whose addresses are on file with the committee. This publication carries the unwritten message that "the church cares about you." It reports good news about the church, includes photographs and articles about service members, and every issue contains new names and addresses to facilitate military members contacting one another, even in remote places of the world. Although a thousand names and addresses are presently on file, there are reliable statistics to indicate that at least 2,000 church members are serving in the armed forces. When spouses and children of these families are included, this represents a congregation of more than 3,000 members.

In addition to the *Armed Forces Newsletter*, each new member entering the service receives a pocket-size booklet titled *The Armed Forces Manual*. This small manual explains something of the history and meaning of the church, explanation of the three standard books, statements of faith and belief, and guidelines and hints on living a clean Christian life while serving in the armed forces.

How You Can Help

There is a continuing task for members to report names and addresses of members entering the service to the military committee at World Church Headquarters. The committee normally recommends that the presiding elder ask someone in the branch or congregation, or requests that the women's leader name someone in the Women's Department to assume this responsibility of sending these names and addresses to the Auditorium. Additionally, certain civilians, such as schoolteachers, students, government employees, business men and women serving in another country and away from a church congregation are entitled to receive the *Newsletter*, and their names should be included, too, and sent to the military committee. Individuals in the service with special personal problems related to their military duty should be encouraged to write the Armed Forces Ministry Office at the Auditorium for specific help in these matters.

PART THREE

ORDINANCES AND SACRAMENTS

Chapter 1

ORDINANCES AND SACRAMENTS

The Nature of the Ordinances and Sacraments

The ordinances and sacraments provide a significant means for worshiping God. In observing them we experience the ever living Christ more vividly and in greater depth than on most other occasions. We are reminded by the scriptures of those who will not heed the commandments of God "for they have strayed from mine ordinances, and have broken mine everlasting covenant; they seek not the Lord to establish his righteousness, but every man walketh in his own way, and after the image of his own God, whose image is in the likeness of the world."[1]

None of us fully understand the implications of this scripture, but we do know that most of us experience no other acts of worship which are so meaningful or so complete as they are in the ordinances. We know that neglecting the ordinances or straying from them leaves us less sensitive to the will of God and more vulnerable to temptation. There is a sense in which we meet God in the ordinances and through them covenant with God most authoritatively and intensely. Our commitments are made effectual and the blessings God grants us are most adequately understood and expressed in the ordinances.

In "A Statement of Belief" drawn up by the Committee on Basic Beliefs the following declaration is made. "We believe that the ordinances witness the continuing life of Christ in the church, providing the experiences in which God and man meet in the sealing of covenant. In the ordinances God uses the common things, even the nature of man, to express the transcendent and sacramental meaning of creation. God thereby provides the continuing means of investing his grace in human life for its renewal and redemption."[2]

The ordinances and sacraments employ all of our faculties to allow God to disclose to us the nature of reality. They allow us to express most fully our devotions and commitment. God who has created us and said, "All things which I had made were very good,"[3] speaks to our whole being in the ordinances. We respond physically, emotionally, intellectually, socially, because our response to God is total. We are involved in physical action, drama, and speech in ways which cause us to understand most accurately what it is that God is requiring of us and what it means to yield our lives to Christ and be a new person.

The sacraments are an extension of the ministry of incarnation in which God uses human nature and material things to express godliness tangibly in humankind. God does this for our salvation. When Christ is understood as the "word . . . made flesh"[4] it is helpful to us in comprehending the sacraments as a continuing means by which Christ extends divine power into the church and the world for giving spiritual life and salvation.

It is unfortunate but true that persons sometimes become enamored with one aspect of human response to the Holy Spirit. In doing this they may overemphasize the emotional side of their response to the Holy Spirit. Others expect their experience with the Holy Spirit to be intellectual and reject the emotions, believing they cloud the objectivity of the experience. Such limitations are unsound and leave persons open to either rejecting truth because it does not fit a self-imposed criteria for validity, or of being deceived by false manifestations and self-generated experiences which are not valid. Such persons are in danger of manipulation by forces that are not the Holy Spirit. Many are carried away by such notions and follow leaders that are not of God.

There is a power in both the form and spirit of the ordinances that keeps bringing those who participate back from rationalized error to the truth of the gospel. The ordinances help persons experience the power to live by the principles revealed in Christ.

One of the real strengths of the Judeo-Christian tradition is the fact that it holds in balance the truth which comes from within as one is moved by the Holy Spirit and the empirical and historical truth that is found in history, the scriptures, and everyday life. One truth does not deny the other.

When church members accept a document which is presented as an expression from divine inspiration they expect that the document will be consistent with former scriptures, history, and experience. They also expect that the inner assurance of the Holy Spirit will confirm the document's divinity. Members may be misled by meditation or emotion or mental exploration into philosophy or theology if they never force that up against the truth of history or the experience of the people of God through the ages. This principle is extended in the balance which the ordinance brings to us.

In this context we can understand the ordinances and sacraments as divinely instituted experiences which involve our total being in response to God. We are involved mentally as we understand the meaning of the sacrament. We respond physically in the acts which dramatize the meaning of our covenants. We respond emotionally and we are linked with the church spiritually and socially in participating with the groups which make up the body.

Preparation for Sacraments

Since the sacraments are sacred, they should be observed with due reverence and preparation. Specific preparation should begin as early as possible after the minister learns of the assignment. Such preparation is undertaken in the spirit of meditation and prayer as expressed by Alma: "O Lord, pour out thy Spirit upon thy servant, that he may do this work with holiness of heart."[5] The minister needs to keep free from concern for details not related to his or her function in the sacrament. This might be done best by arranging for an assistant to be responsible for these details.

Priesthood members should strive to preserve simplicity and spontaneity of feeling and expression, and maintain a dignified manner, though care should be taken not to be artificially formal or excessively ceremonial.

The preparation of the participant involves a personal understanding of the meaning and implications of the

217

sacrament. Giving this information or counsel immediately before administering the sacrament is good, and the minister should not hesitate to give it then if circumstances permit. However, the sooner the individual has an appreciation of the significance of the act the more time there will be to adjust his or her mind and life to its challenges. Therefore, such instruction should be given as early as possible.

Meditation and prayer are essential to prepare one's mind and spirit for these sacred rites. Informing each participant ahead of time of the procedures and his or her part in the performance of the rite is advisable and helpful. A reverent and humble attitude should be encouraged.

Special Directions

The sacraments discussed in this section include baptism, confirmation, the Lord's Supper, blessing of children, ordination, administering to the sick, marriage, and patriarchal blessing.

The performance of ministry in each of these areas should always be with the knowledge and approval of, or at the request of, the presiding elder.

Every minister officiating in them is required to report promptly to the Department of Statistics on the prescribed report form, and marriages must be reported to the proper public official. Administration to the sick and marriage not affecting a church member are exceptions to the reporting requirement to the church.

The ordinances and sacraments employ a greater measure of our whole being to express our devotion, commitment, and covenants with God. In the ordinances we respond most fully to God's love, power, and holiness. We understand more accurately the sacramental nature of creation and the lordship of God over the physical as well as spiritual universe.

NOTES

1. Doctrine and Covenants 1:3d, 3e.
2. Committee on Basic Beliefs, *Exploring the Faith* (Independence, MO: Herald Publishing House), 1970, p. 14.
3. Genesis 1:33.
4. John 1:14.
5. Mosiah 9:43.

Chapter 2

THE BAPTISMAL SERVICE

The Meaning of Baptism

The "doctrine of baptisms"[1] is listed by the writer of Hebrews as one of the principles of the doctrine of Christ. Commonly we have treated baptism as if it were an event, but in the scripture quoted above, we recognize that the principle extends beyond any one act. Therefore when we speak of the principles of repentance from dead works, or of faith toward God, we know these are continuing principles by which the follower of Christ lives. So it is with the other principles including baptism.

In a very real sense baptism emerges out of our human situation. When any of us truly experience the holiness and majesty of God we know we are unrighteous in contrast to God's holiness. We are unable to attain perfection and unfit to be in the divine presence. We are unworthy to be associated in such a holy cause. The scriptures state, "All have sinned, and come short of the glory of God."[2]

It is when we sense this fact but want with all our hearts to be a part of the divine plan that God offers the way. It is by God's grace that it is possible for us to be and do what we could never achieve by ourselves. When those who heard Peter on the day of Pentecost were convinced of the truth of Peter's words and convicted by the

Holy Spirit, they said, "Men and brethren, what shall we do?" Peter replied, "Repent and be baptized every one of you in the name of Jesus Christ for the remission of sins, and ye shall receive the gift of the Holy Ghost."[3]

When we sense God's holiness and want sincerely to be a part of the divine purpose we may take advantage of the grace which God has extended. Through baptism we covenant with God and in that covenant we are forgiven and cleansed. It involves God's gift of the Holy Spirit to empower us to become new persons in Christ, capable of being what we wanted to be but could not by relying on our human effort. This empowerment is symbolized by the laying on of hands. Because of this we often speak of confirmation as the baptism of the Holy Spirit.

It is in this context that we can better understand the scriptures which state, "And this greater priesthood administereth the gospel and holdeth the key of the mysteries of the kingdom, even the key of the knowledge of God. Therefore, in the ordinances thereof the power of godliness is manifest; and without the ordinances thereof, and the authority of the priesthood, the power of godliness is not manifest unto men in the flesh; for without this, no man can see the face of God, even the Father, and live."[4] God takes the initiative in providing through the ordinances and sacraments, and by the authority of the priesthood, what we could not do for ourselves. It is further in this context that we understand the meaning of the Melchisedec priesthood authority which "Administereth the gospel and holdeth the key of the mysteries of the kingdom, even the key of the knowledge of God."

As this is applied to baptism we understand that the

event of baptism by water is a very important moment in the lives of the persons involved. As members of the priesthood we should approach baptism most seriously and earnestly so that this ordinance will minister in the full measure of its significance to those who participate either by being baptized or by sharing the experience as friends and brothers and sisters of the person making the baptismal covenant.

The principle of baptism extends beyond an event or act of immersion in water. The principle involves the continuing activity of covenanting with God to accept and respond affirmatively to the ever enlarging call which comes to us as we grow in our discipleship. Inevitably life's experiences make new demands upon us. An understanding of this will help priesthood members when they are confronted by questions from parents who feel that their eight-year-old children are not mature enough to realize the things God expects of them as new members of the church. Adults sometimes procrastinate because they feel they do not know enough to be baptized.

None of us know all of God's commandments or all that God will expect of us in the future. When we are baptized we accept Christ and covenant to be and do what we understand God is asking of us at that time. A child at eight years of age may not understand at all that he or she may someday be required to face great personal sacrifice or pain in living out his or her discipleship. For instance a person who receives a call to priesthood may not have understood at the time of baptism that such a call would come later. When these new demands come one is confronted with the need to yield one's life to God in these new dimensions. A person may well feel some rebellion, fear, and reluctance to accept God's will. If and when one can accept God's will and yield all of life joyfully in this new responsibility one will experience again the principle of baptism in life.

This kind of recommitment may well be accompanied by a joy and freedom from guilt similar to that experienced in his or her first act of baptism. This renewal is most often accomplished through the ordinances of the church. In fact, the members of the church have been traditioned to understand that one aspect of the sacrament of the Lord's Supper is the renewing of the covenant. In this the principle of baptism is always present.

Baptism in Water

The act of baptism in water is symbolic of the nature of the covenant made in baptism. It recognizes that one does not have power personally to become godly in attitude and character. Therefore, the covenanting person yields to God's authority vested in the priesthood and expressed in the ordinance. That person is immersed in water symbolic of burying the former sinful life and rising to a fresh new beginning with God and the church. It is symbolic of being washed clean in the water to come forth untainted by the past. As the promise of remission of sins is a part of the act, the person is forgiven and free from the guilt and weight of past wrongdoing. Baptism is a public witness before God and the church that one's life is dedicated to Christ. Baptism is symbolic of one's faith in Christ and of the power of the resurrection. As Christ died and rose from the grave immortal, so the baptized one dies to a past of corruption and rises to a new life with the promise of immortality and eternal life.

Priesthood members have a major responsibility in helping persons understand and respond to the call of God to repentance and to the commitment of their lives in baptism. The Melchisedec priesthood members and Aaronic priests are also to conduct persons into the ordinance of baptism by water.

Prerequisites for Baptism

The candidate needs faith and true repentance.[5]

The scriptures state:

All those who humble themselves before God and desire to be baptized, and come forth with broken hearts and contrite spirits, and witness before the church that they have truly repented of all their sins, and are willing to take upon them the name of Jesus Christ, having a determination to serve him to the end, and truly manifest by their works that they have received of the Spirit of Christ unto the remission of their sins, shall be received by baptism into his church.[6]

Baptismal candidates must be at least eight years old.[7]

If the candidate is a child, the consent of the parents is required. In all cases, do not promise baptism or plan for it until the presiding minister of the group or branch has given approval. Ordinarily the presiding minister will plan and conduct the service or arrange for it to be done.

The Mode of Baptism

The only mode of baptism recognized by the Reorganized church is complete immersion.[8] To be valid, both candidate and officiating minister must be in the water.[9]

If baptism is performed in a tank or font, notice any projections, steps, or water pipes which might cause embarrassing situations or even serious accidents. Water should be up to the hips of a child but waist high for adults, to aid in handling the weight of large persons.

The candidate should always be between the minister and the congregation.

If the baptizing is done in a lake, pond, or running stream, examine the bottom for deep holes, ledges, rocks, or tree trunks before the time of the service.

In running streams, the candidate should face downstream so that he or she is immersed with head upstream. The flow of water will then help raise the candidate upright again, and also tend to prevent water entering the mouth or nose, as well as prevent the disarray of a woman's clothing by the current.

Be sure the candidate understands to wear the usual amount of clothing. White clothing is preferred, but in any case it should be as clean and neat as possible.

Both the candidate and minister should be dressed in baptismal clothes before the meeting begins.

Arrangements should be made for clean dressing rooms with proper privacy.

If the baptism is to be held outdoors, a location should be sought that will provide a setting of natural beauty. If the service is indoors, flowers and other simple decorations will help provide the beauty befitting the ordinance.

Instructions for performing the baptism are given in Doctrine and Covenants 17:21b, c, "The person who is called of God and has authority from Jesus Christ to baptize, shall go down into the water with the person who has presented him or herself for baptism." The minister usually raises his or her right hand and makes the statement calling the candidate by name and saying, "Having been commissioned of Jesus Christ, I baptize you in the name of the Father, and of the Son, and of the

Holy Ghost, Amen." Then the minister lowers his or her right hand to the back of the candidate's neck, and makes a full step to the right to be able to sustain the weight of the candidate before the immersion and to raise the candidate to his or her feet.

Immersion should be complete. Failure to achieve complete immersion or to say the words accurately can have a damaging effect on the spiritual quality of the service.

When the candidate is a woman or girl, a sister should be ready with a large loose robe or blanket to be thrown around her as she leaves the stream, tank, or font to prevent embarrassment.

The Order of Service

Circumstances alter the length and arrangement of the baptismal service. Usually, however, it will include these features:

1. Open with appropriate hymn and prayer.
2. Present a scripture reading and/or a short statement about the meaning of the ordinance.
3. Immediately preceding the baptisms announce the names of the candidates and officiating minister.
4. The actual immersion takes place.
5. Conclude with a hymn and prayer.

Circumstances may make it advisable for the outdoor service to be shorter than one in a chapel. If the weather is cold, the service should conclude without undue delay after the immersion has taken place.

NOTES

1. Hebrews 6:2.
2. Romans 3:23.
3. Acts 2:37, 38.
4. Doctrine and Covenants 83:3b, c.
5. Acts 20:21; 2:38-41; Mark 1:13; Mosiah 2:6-16; III Nephi 3:67, 68; Doctrine and Covenants 16:6; 68:1e-h; 76:5a-e; 83:12; 105:11.
6. Doctrine and Covenants 17:7.
7. Doctrine and Covenants 17:20; 68:4b; GCR No. 552.
8. John 3:5; Mark 1:7-9; Romans 6:4, 5; Colossians 2:12; Doctrine and Covenants 17:21.
9. GCR No. 212.

Chapter 3

THE CONFIRMATION SERVICE

The Significance of Confirmation

Confirmation is the ordinance in which God's gift of the Holy Spirit is granted after one has committed himself or herself in baptism by water. It is often considered to be a part of the principle of baptism. Baptism by water is symbolic of the candidate's yielding of his or her life to God and earnestly desiring to become what the candidate senses at that time to be God's will. Confirmation is the baptism of the Holy Spirit. It is God's response to the candidate's commitments in which the Holy Spirit enters into that life to strengthen, comfort, enlighten, teach, and guide the person in fulfilling the commitment. It is the promise of God to be one's constant companion if that person will continue to yield to the highest understandings of God's will. Confirmation is sometimes expressed as the gift of the Holy Spirit to be an abiding comforter.[1]

One of the characteristics of sin is its power to create an estrangement from God which leaves one without the companionship of the Holy Spirit and therefore less sensitive to God's will and insecure in his or her own human brashness. Through repentance and the ordinances one may participate in the reestablishment of unity with God. This sometimes is experienced as God's forgiveness.

The Conduct of the Service

Confirmation is by the laying on of hands by the Melchisedec priesthood.[2] While one Melchisedec priesthood member may confirm the candidate alone, whenever it is possible two or more should place their hands upon the head of the candidate while one of the elders offers the prayer of confirmation. This person is called the "spokesperson."

The newly baptized person or persons should be seated facing the congregation during the confirmation. Candidates are confirmed one at a time, with the officiating minister(s) laying hands upon the head of the one being confirmed.

In laying the hands upon the head, care should be taken not to rest the hands too heavily on the head of the person.

The Prayer of Confirmation

The prayer of confirmation should be brief. Seldom does the prayer need to be longer than three minutes. It is appropriate on occasion to make a short statement to the candidate. Such a statement might be "Having been commissioned by Jesus Christ, we place our hands upon your head to confirm you and ask God to grant the gift of the Holy Spirit. In this act we extend to you membership in the Reorganized Church of Jesus Christ of Latter Day Saints." The prayer should then be addressed to God. The confirmation prayer is seldom an appropriate time to give the candidate a charge, or instructions, or promises. If there is need for any of these they should be a part of the charge to the candidate, or included in other appropriate parts of the service. It is not necessary to address a statement to the candidate at all and the entire prayer of confirmation may be addressed to God, but in no circumstances should the spokesperson alternate back and forth between addressing God and the candidate.

Arranging the Service

Innovations should be used only with great care in this service. Those things that tend to solemnize, beautify, and dignify should be included. Hymns, instumental music, and vocal music of a religious nature may be used.

Scriptures may be read, and a charge to the candidate and congregation may be used with good effect. These should lead up to the prayer of confirmation as the climax of the service.

An appropriate hymn and prayer may conclude the service.

It should be made a special service or, in a small branch, it may be part of a Communion service.

It is well to separate the rites of immersion and laying on of hands sufficiently to enable the candidate to get the full value of each. Both should be moving, dramatic experiences in the life of every church member. Therefore, where possible, they should be performed in separate meetings, and special preparations should be made for each.[3]

The Follow-up Ministry

The officiating minister should make certain that a statistical report is filed after the baptism in water and the confirmation have taken place.

It is the responsibility of the minister to see to it that

the one baptized continues to receive spiritual nurture. The minister should remain a trusted counselor in days to come.

NOTES

1. John 14:16.
2. Doctrine and Covenants 17:8.
3. Ibid., 17:18.

Chapter 4

THE SACRAMENT OF THE LORD'S SUPPER

The Significance of the Sacrament

The Committee on Basic Beliefs wrote in regard to the ordinances:

The ordinances continue from age to age, an ever-present focal point of confrontation, enlivening the memory of those transformed lives which have preceded us, bringing judgment upon the present, and constantly reminding us that we may participate in yesterday and tomorrow by conserving and renewing our heritage.

The ordinances, by casting us up against the plumb line of Christ, give us a necessary and sometimes excruciating experience. We grow accustomed to crookedness and need the frequent reminder of the straightness which is our calling under God.[1]

While the above statement was written about the ordinances in general, it is particularly appropriate to the consideration of the sacrament of the Lord's Supper. Jesus Christ who is our Lord and perfect example instructed his apostles at the first Lord's Supper saying, "This do in remembrance of me."[2]

The sacrament of the Lord's Supper uses the common things of life, the bread and wine to symbolize the divine principles of life. They tell us that life must be sacrificed if we are to sustain life. They speak to us not only of passing from death to life, but of the transcendence in the risen Christ. We dramatize our surrender to the will of the Father remembering that Jesus went forth from that first Lord's Supper to the Garden of Gethsemane and on to Calvary's cross. His command, "This do in remembrance of me," was not some sentimental wish not to be forgotten, but a challenge to go forth in surrender to God's will even as Christ also went forth from that supper.

However, he said further to the Nephites, "And if ye do always remember me, ye shall have my Spirit to be with you."[3] The gift of his Spirit is that precious gift discussed in Chapter 3 regarding confirmation. Paul in his letter to the Romans said, "For as many as are led by the Spirit of God, they are the sons of God."[4] And Jesus relating this same thought to the sacrament of the bread and wine stated to those of his time,

Verily, verily, I say unto you, except ye eat of the flesh of the Son of man and drink his blood, ye have no life in you. Whoso eateth my flesh, and drinketh my blood, hath eternal life; and I will raise him up in the resurrection of the just at the last day.[5]

The promises made in the scriptures do presuppose the sincerity of the persons involved and their willingness to live by the principles of the gospel of Christ. The sacrament of the Lord's Supper therefore participates in those principles of repentance, commitment, and the willingness to exercise the stewardship of life to achieve the call of God. It is in God's granting of the Holy Spirit in the continuing celebration of the sacrament that we receive power to renew and redirect our lives with the growing understanding we have of God's call to us. Through the Holy Spirit God takes our fragmented and misdirected lives and makes them whole again.

Preparation and Precautions

An elder or priest may officiate in administering the emblems. The presiding officer of the service should oversee the planning and direct the service. The presiding officer is also to assign specific tasks to assisting priesthood. Usually an elder presides, and the priests serve the emblems to the members. Officiating ministers should be especially careful that their hands are clean, both symbolically and actually.

The bread and wine should be prepared and in place before the service commences. The plates and cups should be clean. When linens are used they should be spotlessly white and neatly pressed. Before the service begins, the wine is poured into individual cups, and bread may be broken completely or in part before being placed upon the table. The emblems should usually remain covered until ready for the blessing and serving. After the serving the covering may be replaced.

Personal Preparation

Those who are baptized and confirmed members of the church, in good standing, are eligible to partake of the emblems. Members who are in transgression or who are offended toward another should voluntarily refrain from partaking until reconciliation has been made.[6] The final decision must be left to each individual. It is inappropriate to make a public issue of the matter during the course of the service.

Prayers of Blessing and Serving the Bread or Wine

Before the beginning of the service copies of the prayers of blessing over the emblems should be in the possession of the minister who will read them.

The bread is served first after it is blessed with the prayer recorded in the Doctrine and Covenants.[7] The wine is then served after it is blessed.[8]

All who can should kneel during the prayers of blessing.

It is best to *read* the prayers and thus avoid the confusion which may result from forgetting the exact phrasing. Be careful to read them with the proper inflection of voice, distinctly, and loud enough for all to hear.

The Technique of Serving

Except in very small assemblies it is best for *two* priesthood members to remove the linen covering the emblems, fold it carefully, and lay it aside. After the emblems are served the trays may be left with the deacons in a hall or anteroom, but if they are replaced on the table, the linen should be used to cover the vessels again.

Those who serve the emblems should preserve order and quietness in their work, should keep together or abreast in pairs, and return to the altar at the same time.

It is important to take a firm grip on the trays, and to be careful to maintain balance when reaching. Servers should hold the tray *low* enough for members to partake conveniently and serve one person at a time. It is sometimes advisable for those who serve to hand the glass of wine to aged or handicapped members rather than let them fumble for it on the tray.

Arranging the Service

The purpose of the Lord's Supper should always be readily discernible—communion with God. Planning and arrangement of details should lead toward a climax at the time the members receive the emblems and dedicate themselves to God. The service lends itself well to the use of music: organ, piano, choral, and congregational singing.

Elements of the service include a short message, scripture reading, a pastoral exhortation, prayer, and the blessing and serving of the Lord's Supper. It includes an oblation offering for the poor and needy. Sometimes hymns are sung or scriptures may be read during the serving, though at other times meditation is encouraged with quietude or with meditative instrumental music.

When taking the Lord's Supper to the sick and shut-ins, ministers should endeavor to establish an atmosphere of reverence. Since the prayers of blessing are a part of the sacrament itself, they should be repeated. Sometimes a prayer or brief statement of the significance of the sacrament will help to create the proper atmosphere. The same precautions of cleanliness, orderliness, and dignity should be observed as they are in the public service.

NOTES

1. *Exploring the Faith*, pp. 192, 193.
2. Luke 22:19.
3. III Nephi 8:36.
4. Romans 8:14.
5. John 6:53, 54.
6. Doctrine and Covenants 46:1d; 42:23.
7. Ibid., 17:22d; Moroni 4:4.
8. Doctrine and Covenants 17:23b; Moroni 5:3.

Chapter 5

ADMINISTRATION TO THE SICK

What Is Administration to the Sick?

Administration to the sick is a divine ordinance. In emergencies it may be performed by one elder, but usually it is implemented by two or more.[1]

One of the elders will anoint the head of the sick person with consecrated oil. The elders then lay their hands upon the head of the sick person and approach God in prayer for the blessing and healing ministry of the Holy Spirit. One elder acts as spokesperson and expresses verbally the prayer for the elders participating. All of the elders should sincerely join in spirit and prayer with the one chosen to speak. This ordinance was practiced in the times of Christ and the apostles. Examples are to be found in Mark 16:19; Luke 4:40; Acts 28:8; James 5:14, 15. Administration for the sick was also taught and practiced in Book of Mormon times by the Nephites. References to this are to be found in Mormon 4:87; IV Nephi 1:6; Mosiah 1:98. In modern times we have been commanded to teach and practice the ordinance of administration to the sick.[2]

Calling the Elders

The responsibility for calling the elders rests upon the one needing or desiring the administration. This situation is altered in the case of a child or an individual who is not conscious or competent. Administration may then be requested by a relative or a friend.

Preparation

The ordinance should be administered in faith. The essence of that faith was expressed by Jesus when he taught us to pray "Thy will be done."[3] It is inevitable that both the sick person and those who love him or her hope that God will bring a healing blessing and restoration of health. However, the scriptures do not promise that this will be so. James, wrote regarding this ordinance: "And the prayer of faith shall save the sick, and the Lord shall raise him up; and if he has committed sins, they shall be forgiven him."[4] It will be noted here that the promise is that the "prayer of faith shall save the sick." This is in harmony with latter-day instruction which reads, "And the elders of the church, two or more, shall be called, and shall pray for, and lay their hands upon them in my name; and if they die, they shall die unto me, and if they live, they shall live unto me."[5]

These indications from the scriptures point to the fact that God has not promised physical healing, but that if we die, we shall die unto God or if we live, we shall live unto God. All of these promises presuppose that the sick ones, as well as the elders, have come to God in that spirit and with the preparation necessary to yield their lives to God and, in repentance, commit their lives into God's service. In that spirit the principles of forgiveness, salvation, and commitment are a part of the anticipations of those who participate in the ordinance of administration for the sick. This ordinance should be administered in the atmosphere of trust in God.

The Anointing

It is customary for one elder to anoint the head of the sick person. This requires only a drop of oil and should be accompanied by a brief prayer stating the purpose of the anointing and asking God's presence in the administration. The prayer of anointment should be brief, and it should be related to the act of anointing.

The Prayer of Petition

The prayer of petition for blessing should also be a brief prayer and to the point. It should present the sick person to God in simple, clear terms and leave him or her in God's hands. The one speaking in the administration should avoid either open or veiled promises of healing. The Lord has given us instruction: "Prophesying over them that are sick in administering to them has been a fruitful source of trouble among my people."[6]

Priesthood members who go to administer to the sick often are so anxious for the sick person to be healed that they yield to the impulse to promise recovery. Such a promise should not be a part of the administration. God gives the blessings. We are to present the person to God, who understands the needs of the one who is sick.

The Use of Oil

Olive oil is traditionally used for anointing the sick. While there is no specific command to consecrate the oil for this purpose, it is the long established tradition and a reasonable expectation that the oil used in administration should be consecrated.

In the consecration of oil the regular practice of the church is to have one elder, and sometimes two, consecrate the oil to be used in administration to the sick. The container is opened or the cap is removed for this blessing. One elder serves as spokesperson, generally asking God to bless the oil for the purpose of anointing the sick. There is no prescribed wording for this prayer. The elder prays briefly and sincerely as seems appropriate.

Sometimes requests are made to anoint afflicted parts of the body. This is not appropriate and must not be done. The elder should anoint the head only. The anointing is not for medical purposes, but is is a symbol of the anointing of the Spirit of God. One drop of oil is sufficient. Oil should not be taken internally. It is not a medicine.

Use of the Hands

Hands should rest lightly upon the head. Be careful not to cover the eyes, nose, mouth, or face of the one who is ill. It is easy to be careless at this point, and a sick person may be very distressed by such carelessness.

Length of Stay

Terminate your visit as soon as possible after the administration is completed. It is much better to make frequent short visits than a single long and tiring one. Do not sandwich the rite of administration in between periods of small talk or secular conversation. Make it a spiritual experience.

Following the administration when the sick one has

been assured that you will continue to remember him or her in your prayers, leave the person to meditate upon this recent spiritual experience.

Favorite Remedies

Do not encroach on the function of the physician. The physician is the only person authorized to prescribe. The law of the land is strict in its requirement that only doctors give prescriptions. The doctor is the specialist in medicine; the minister functions in relation to the ways of the Spirit.

Cleanliness

The clothing, person, and mind of the elder should be scrupulously clean. To avoid offense, use a toothbrush and a good mouthwash before going to administer. It is always wise to wash the hands before and after an administration.

Contagious Disease

In cases of contagious diseases, the elder should use special care to not become a carrier and spread the disease. Where contagion is a factor, permission of the doctor in charge should be obtained before entering the sickroom. Proper precaution should be used afterward.

Administering to Nonmembers

Sharing this ordinance with nonmember friends is certainly worthwhile and a fine opportunity to give good ministry, provided the nonmember friend has an understanding of our belief and practices.

Conclusion

Administration to the sick is one of the most comforting and fruitful ordinances of the gospel, and for that reason it should be highly regarded and used with restraint and understanding.

NOTES

1. Doctrine and Covenants 42:12d.
2. Ibid., 42:12d.
3. Matthew 6:11.
4. James 5:15.
5. Doctrine and Covenants 42:12d.
6. Ibid., 125:15a.

Chapter 6

THE BLESSING OF CHILDREN

Significance

The blessing of children by the laying on of the hands of the elders is a beautiful sacrament of the church. In this rite the parents or parent bring the baby to the church for blessing, committing themselves to instill into the life of the child the fundamental principles of belief and conduct upon which to build a righteous life. The church also is committed to offer guidance to the child and family.

Eligibility

Children under eight years of age are eligible for blessing. Children who are eight years of age or older are considered eligible for baptism.[1]

Children of nonmembers may be blessed also if their parents understand the purpose of the rite and request the ordinance.

Preparation and Precautions

Parents should be instructed to make advance arrangements with the pastor, allowing adequate time to prepare for the service.

Only members of the Melchisedec priesthood may officiate, preferably two members of this order.[2]

The baby should be held in the arms of the assisting elder who should hold the baby properly and securely, close rather than with extended arms, and with the baby's head slightly raised and facing the congregation. The assisting elder should keep her or his eyes open to be alert to the care of the child.

One of the parents may be instructed to carry the child to the altar on the left arm so the child will be in the proper position for receiving by the assisting elder, who would stand, in this case, on the left of the officiating elder.

If a child is too large to be held, the child may be seated on a chair or in the lap of one of the parents, in which case the elders lay their hands upon his or her head to pronounce the blessing.

The prayers should be brief and loud enough for all to hear.

It is desirable, but not imperative, that the elder use the name of the child in the prayer of blessing. This is facilitated if it is read from a written announcement by the presiding officer, such as "The infant son of Mr. and Mrs. _____ will be blessed by Elders _____ and _____. The child's name is _____."

The practice of the elder kissing the child after the blessing is discouraged.

This ordinance should be performed in a public service, though circumstances and conditions sometimes make that impossible. In such case, it may be performed elsewhere, though still with the same reverence.

Arranging the Service

Arrangement of the service usually includes the following:

Appropriate hymns and vocal music

Short opening and closing prayers

Appropriate scripture readings and explanation of the purpose of the ordinance

A charge to the parents, impressing upon them their duties as parents, and a challenge to the congregation to help bear the responsibility of the parents

The bringing of the child to the altar by the parents and the pronouncement of blessing by the elders

The blessing may be combined with other sacramental ordinances or a preaching service in which the sermon is related appropriately to the ordinance.

The Follow-up Ministry

A statistical report of the blessing must be prepared promptly by the officiating elder. Obtaining this information gives the elder an excellent opportunity for a visit with the parents.

The elder should check later with the parents to see if the certificate of blessing has been received.

A special blessing booklet entitled *Of Such Is the Kingdom* has been prepared by the church for the parents of the baby. It contains a blessing certificate and is a helpful gift. It may be presented during or after the blessing service.

The child should be enrolled in the cradle roll and the parents encouraged to bring the child with them to church school and worship services.

NOTES

1. Doctrine and Covenants 68:4b; GCR No. 701.
2. Ibid., 17:19.

Chapter 7

ORDINATION

Significance

Ordination symbolizes the outstretched hands of God conferring power and authority to represent both God and the church.

It implies acceptance of the responsibility to be a servant and to become a leader in holiness and in all good works.

Precautions and Preparation

The person to be ordained must have been called of God, and the call must have been approved by the proper authorities of the church. Those called within branches must be approved by the vote of the members of the branch and the appropriate conference.[1] In stakes the ordination is approved by the stake conference.

Preordination Orientation

Preordination classes are offered to those who will be ordained. In these classes the candidates are introduced to some of the fundamentals of ministry—the duties of their offices, the use of the scriptures in ministry, fundamental concepts of the church, etc. The classes are for orientation so that priesthood members may begin their ministry with a clearer picture of what they are called to do.

The Act of Ordination

Ordination is by the laying on of hands.[2]

The candidate should be seated facing the congregation.

The officiating ministers should rest their hands lightly on the ordinand's head.

Members of the Melchisedec priesthood may ordain elders, priests, teachers, and deacons. When occasion requires, an Aaronic priest may ordain priests, teachers, or deacons. A teacher or deacon may not ordain.[3] Usually two members of the priesthood participate, one acting as spokesperson.

The officiating minister and the candidate should be informed sufficiently in advance of the actual ordination to allow adequate time and opportunity for spiritual preparation. Seating arrangements and the movements of those who are to ordain and to be ordained should be determined before the service begins.

The Nature of the Prayer of Ordination

Since the object is to confer authority, the prayer should so indicate. It should be specific but well arranged or worded, clear and easily understood by all present.

Repetitions and set phrases should be avoided; simple language should be used.

Arranging the Ordination Service

The ordination should be performed in a service in which the order of worship emphasizes the significance of ordination as a call to service. Ministry is response to human needs. The order of service should be planned and conducted in this spirit.

The service may be opened with a call to worship or an appropriate hymn and prayer. The ministry of music and scripture reading are appropriate, and a sermon or charge concerning the responsibilities and opportunities relating to priesthood is desirable.

The minister in charge of the service should have in hand a list of the names of those to be ordained and the office to which each is called. The name of each ordinand and the office, together with the names of those who are to ordain, may be announced as each is ordained.

Appropriate hymns or special music may be interspersed in the service as wisdom directs. The service might end with an inspiring hymn, such as "Rise Up, O Saints of God," followed by the benediction.

The Follow-up Ministry

The officiating member of the priesthood is required to make a statistical report promptly following the ordination, and should check later to be certain the newly ordained minister has received a certificate of ordination.

The newly ordained member should be given help in the new work and encouragement and guidance where advisable. He or she should be accepted as a member of the priesthood and granted respect and cooperation.

NOTES

1. Doctrine and Covenants 17:16; 42:4; 125:14.
2. Numbers 27:18-20; Acts 13:1-3; Doctrine and Covenants 55:1c; 117:3.
3. Doctrine and Covenants 17:8b, 10a-c.

Chapter 8

SACRAMENT OF MARRIAGE

Marriage in the Saints Church

"Marriage is ordained of God."[1] From the very beginning the state of marriage has been regarded with high esteem and the wedding ceremony featured as one of the important rites of the Saints church.

The basic procedures governing performance of the marriage ceremony were laid down in a document approved unanimously by a General Assembly meeting on August 17, 1835, in Kirtland, Ohio.[2] This document, now known as Section 111 of the Doctrine and Covenants, has appeared in every printing of this book by the Reorganized church since the first edition of 1835.[3] The procedures outlined in this document have never been rescinded or replaced. They continue to serve as the basis for marriage in the church. The basic understandings and provisions of this document are as follows:

1. The church recognizes that marriage is subject to legal provisions established by various nations and states.[4] This aspect of marriage makes it unique among the sacraments of the church.

2. Marriages within the church should be solemnized in a public meeting of some kind.[5] This most usually occurs in the context of a service of worship.

3. Marriages within the church are to be performed by members of the Melchisedec priesthood or by

Aaronic priests.[6] It should be noted that marriage is not included as a duty of the priesthood in Section 17 of the Doctrine and Covenants where other duties are listed. Neither teachers, deacons, nor laity are authorized to officiate at a marriage ceremony in the church.

4. The church recognizes the marriages of persons who choose to be married by authorities outside the church.[7] This may be by civil authorities or ministers of other faiths. Recognition of this kind is based on the understanding that marriage is regulated by provisions of the state as described in No. 1.

5. Doctrine and Covenants, Section 111:1d states:

> We believe that it is not right to prohibit members of this church from marrying out of the church, if it be their determination so to do, but such persons will be considered weak in the faith of our Lord and Savior Jesus Christ.

The phrase "marrying out of the church" has been interpreted to refer to marriage by other authorities as indicated above. This is the logical interpretation when seen in the context of the verses preceding paragraph 1d. Another interpretation, however, is that it refers to marriage between a member of the Saints church and a person who is not a member.[8]

Members are frequently discouraged from marrying nonmembers because of the high probability that they will cease active participation in the church. On the other hand, many members are successful in bringing their nonmember spouses into active participation in the church and even into membership.

6. Certain procedures within the marriage cere-

mony itself are prescribed. Specifically, the minister shall say, calling the man and woman by name, "You both mutually agree to be each other's companion, husband and wife, observing the legal rights belonging to this condition; that is, keeping yourselves wholly for each other, and from all others, during your lives?"[9] When they have answered affirmatively, the minister pronounces them "husband and wife" in the name of Christ and by authority of the state.[10] An additional benedictory statement is often added as follows: "May God add his blessings and keep you to fulfill your covenants from henceforth and forever. Amen."[11]

7. A record of each marriage is kept at church headquarters and also by the local recorder.[12]

8. "All legal contracts of marriage made before a person is baptized into this church, should be held sacred and fulfilled."[13] This again relates to the legal dimensions of marriage referred to in Nos. 1 and 4.

9. Monogamy is the only form of marriage endorsed by the church, and polygamy is denounced.[14]

10. Individuals whose spouses have died are free to remarry.[15] Remarriage in cases of divorce is not dealt with in Doctrine and Covenants 111 and will be discussed later in this chapter.

The Meaning of Marriage

Marriage within the church is considered to be a sacrament. The following understandings establish its sacramental character.

1. The act and state of marriage have their origins

in the scriptures as being instituted by God. In Genesis we read, "And the Lord God said, It is not good that the man should be alone; I will make an help meet for him,"[16] and "Therefore shall a man leave his father and his mother, and shall cleave unto his wife; and they shall be one flesh."[17] The basic statement in the Doctrine and Covenants is "Whoso forbiddeth to marry, is not ordained of God, for marriage is ordained of God unto man; wherefore it is lawful that he should have one wife, and they twain shall be one flesh, and all this that the earth might answer the end of its creation; and that it might be filled with the measure of man, according to his creation before the world was made."[18]

2. Not only is God seen as endorsing marriage in principle; divine action is also evident in each specific union of two persons in the marriage ceremony. Doctrine and Covenants 111 indicates that after vows have been exchanged, the minister "shall pronounce them 'husband and wife' in the name of the Lord Jesus Christ."[19] In the Bible Jesus is recorded as saying in connection with marriage and divorce, "What, therefore, God hath joined together, let no man put asunder."[20] In the marriage ceremony, the minister acts on behalf of God in joining together a man and a woman.

3. Marriage is a covenant. The covenant is made between the two individuals in the presence of God and of the church as witness. The words, "You both mutually agree to be each other's companion...,"[21] indicate the nature of the

marriage covenant. It is a commitment to companionship, mutual support, shared responsibility, and love toward each other. The marriage covenant has as its ideal the depth and integrity which characterize God's covenant relationship with humanity. The sacramental nature of the marriage covenant derives from its relationship to God's covenant with persons. Furthermore, in marriage two individuals embark on a covenant relationship in which they commit themselves to express their best understanding of the demands of Christian discipleship.

Marriage in the church is considered a lifelong commitment as indicated by the phrase "during your lives"[22] which is required as a part of each wedding ceremony in the church. This understanding of marriage as a lifelong commitment is the reason why divorce is to be avoided. Prior to Joseph Smith's death in 1844 speculation regarding the eternal nature of marriage was present within the church. Suffice it to say that the Reorganized church has always rejected the view that marriage covenants are valid after death. One might suppose that speculation about eternal marriage is based in part at least on Jesus' statements that "whatsoever thou shalt bind on earth, shall be bound in heaven"[23] and "in the resurrection, they neither marry, nor are given in marriage."[24]

Additional emphasis in the church's understanding of marriage can be identified as follows:

4. The marriage relationship is unique. Part of the marriage vow reads as follows: "Keeping your-

selves wholly for each other, and from all others, during your lives."[25] This statement suggests that spouses enjoy a depth of relationship with and commitment to each other that surpasses that which characterizes their relationships with other persons. Even though this phrase has usually been interpreted as prohibiting extramarital sexual relationships it is broader than this. It suggests that spouses hold each other's interests and welfare uppermost when they make decisions regarding the use of their time, money, and other resources. Extremely flexible interpretations of the statement run the risk of violating the spirit of the marriage relationship. However, extremely literal interpretations run the same risk. A view of marriage that denies spouses the opportunity for interaction with other persons stunts their growth as individuals seeking fulfillment in all aspects of their lives.

5. The church has always stood adamantly opposed to adultery. In the same spirit as the Ten Commandments,[26] modern day scripture admonishes the church, "Thou shalt not steal; neither commit adultery, nor kill, nor do anything like unto it."[27] Adultery is seen as a flagrant violation of the marriage covenant. It represents one of the few grounds for expulsion from the church. Persons who are guilty of adultery are counseled to repent in which case they are forgiven. But if they commit adultery again they can be expelled from the church.[28]

The Doctrine and Covenants states that "All legal contracts of marriage made before a person is baptized into this church, should be held sacred and fulfilled."[29]

6. The church authorizes remarriage by church authorities following divorce in certain circumstances. The General Conference of 1884 recognized the need for the establishment of criteria under which a divorced member might remarry within the church (i.e., by church ministers). This began a process whereby, following each divorce, a report is filed and a decision made as to the eligibility of the respective parties to be remarried within the church. This process exists to this day. The 1884 statement said, "Resolved. . .in case of separation of husband and wife, one of which is guilty of the crime of fornication, or adultery, the other becomes released from the marriage bond, and if they so desire may obtain a divorce and marry again."[30] Over the years, as the incidence of divorce in society has become more frequent and the grounds for it broader, the church has responded by extending remarriage privileges to a wider range of persons. The 1884 stance was modified in 1896 by addition of a provision relating to "abandonment without cause."[31]

The most recent statement on this matter was passed by the General Conference of 1962 and includes the following:

The church recognizes that the remarriage of an innocent party in a divorce action is permissible when a divorce has been secured for any of the following reasons: adultery, repeated sexual perversion, desertion, such aggravated conditions within the home as render married life unbearable for the party petitioning or for the children of the marriage.[32]

This is in harmony with the basic requirements of the law and also takes note of the fact that circumstances develop and persist in certain marriages for which no remedy within that marriage seems to be discoverable, and which are so harmful in their effects on one or both of the partners to the marriage, and on their children, as to render life under those circumstances humiliating, fraught with suffering, and intolerable.[33]

This resolution continues:

Though the civil court may have accepted proof of lesser indignities as sufficient grounds for divorce, permission for remarriage should be granted only when the conditions complained of were of such an extreme nature as to place the other members of the family in serious and continuing jeopardy.

Persons who have been divorced, even though innocent of wrongdoing, should pay special attention to the admonition not to marry hastily or without due consideration. Ministers asked to officiate at such weddings should assure themselves that sufficient time has elapsed and that due consideration has been had.

Any person who has been divorced, and who desires to be married by a member of the priesthood, should make arrangements with this minister in sufficient time to permit him to make any necessary inquiry concerning the circumstances of the divorce and to secure the approval of the branch president. If the branch president does not feel free to act, he should refer the inquiry to the next higher administrative officer of the church.[34]

Particularly noteworthy are the provisions for approval that are required for a person to be remarried. A divorce report form must be filed before permission to remarry is granted. This form includes space for information regarding grounds for divorce, terms of divorce, and other related matters. This whole area of ministry is quite sensitive and should be performed with prayer, care, and concern for the involved parties. The laws noted should, if at all possible, be observed in a redemptive manner rather than in a punitive manner.

Premarital Counseling

The minister should counsel with the couple several times prior to the marriage ceremony. The purposes of the counseling are to help arrange healthy and happy marriages, and to provide an opportunity to assist the couple who seem to be unwisely entering into a marriage relationship so that they may analyze their particular situation further. Attention may also be given to exploring some of the following areas of married life:

1. Different family backgrounds
2. Relationship of the role of the woman and the man in the home (How will the couple relate in order to fill expected and unexpected roles?)
3. Use of time and developing a routine
4. Vocation of both marriage partners (What are future plans?)
5. Finance and money management
6. Relationship to parents and parents-in-law or children of a previous marriage
7. Religious differences
8. Birth of children and parenting
9. Family medical care
10. Marriage and the law
11. Human sexuality, including sex education

Most ministers in the church are unlikely to be qualified to assist couples in all the matters listed above. Therefore it is extremely important that the minister assist the couple to find qualified counselors or resources which can help them think through these major life concerns.

Postmarital counseling can also be a most helpful aid for the couple. Extreme caution should be taken not to hurry into the marriage ceremony without adequate counseling. If at all possible, the minister should resist "quickie" marriages or other time pressures which may inhibit the possibility of marital success for the couple.

Planning the Wedding Service

All wedding ceremonies are under the supervision of the presiding elder of the pastoral unit where the ceremony is performed, whether it is performed by the presiding elder or by another priesthood member, and whether it takes place in the church building, a home, or another location.

Designing of the wedding ceremony is the responsibility of the minister in consultation with the marriage couple. The formality or informality, the size of the wedding party, the social situation, the physical facilities, and the availability of assisting personnel all affect the design to some degree.

The acceptability of special music, the propriety of specific activities within the building, and the use of photographic flash equipment shall all be under the direction and control of the minister. Spectacular situations or environments should be avoided. The service should be deeply religious in character.

At least one, and preferably more, planning sessions should be held with the candidates for marriage. It is during these sessions that specific details of the order of service will be worked out. Usually the couple has preferences as to musicians, music selections, the use of such phrases as "giving the bride," the nature of the processional and recessional, the selection and instructions to a photographer, etc. Where these preferences can be allowed, they should be. If inappropriate musical selections or activities are suggested, it is at this juncture that the problem can be corrected so that all will be satisfied.

When planning wedding services the following suggestions might be helpful:

1. The bride, groom, and officiating minister play important roles in the wedding service, but the congregation is also important and should be active in the service. Congregational hymns, readings, and prayers make this possible. In addition to participation by the whole congregation, representatives of the congregation could be asked to offer prayer, read scripture, or make brief statements.

2. The bride, groom, and minister can benefit from working together on the planning of the wedding service. This provides the engaged couple the opportunity to include certain favorite scriptures and music in the service and also to compose their own vows if they wish. The minister is able to provide guidance as to what elements would combine to make the occasion dignified and worshipful. No fee should be charged by the minister for weddings. If the couple desires, they may make a gift to help defray some of the extra expenses of the minister, or they may show their appreciation by bestowing an appropriate gift. This, however, should be done completely at the discretion of the couple and should not be solicited.

3. The husband and wife may play different roles in a marriage, but they are equal rather than one being subordinate to the other. Language and actions suggestive of inequality between the marriage partners should be avoided. For ex-

ample the inclusion of the injunction to "obey" one's spouse is no more applicable to the wife than to the husband and is best omitted. After the vows have been exchanged, it is preferable for the minister to pronounce the couple "husband and wife" (See Doctrine and Covenants 111:2c) rather than "man and wife" and to introduce them to the congregation as "John and Jane Doe" rather than "Mr. and Mrs. John Doe."

4. Marriage is a relationship between two persons that creates a joint partnership but also preserves the identity of each spouse. Giving oneself to another in marriage is a commitment to sharing many things in common, but it also includes a recognition that the wife and husband will never, and should never, develop identical interests and capabilities in all things. The statement made by the minister in the wedding service should give attention to both of these dimensions of the relationship. This statement includes remarks directed to the couple and also remarks addressed to the congregation. The statement should be kept fairly brief.

5. Extravagance and luxury in any form are out of place in any service of worship. The wedding service is no exception. Floral arrangements, the dress of the wedding party, and the order of service itself should be dignified and all tendencies toward excess restrained. A congregation usually does not charge for the use of the building for a wedding unless there are exceptional demands on the time of a hired custodian. If the building is

used for a reception, a nominal fee often is charged to cover specific costs. These costs can usually be kept to a minimum if the cleanup and laundry is adequately taken care of by the wedding group.

6. Symbolism is an important aspect of all sacraments. The exchange of rings and the kiss are two acts which symbolize what happens in the wedding ceremony. Other such acts could include the exchange of other gifts, greeting the bride's and groom's parents, and the presentation to the couple of a special gift from the congregation.

Elements of the Ceremony Needing Specal Attention

Printed Order of Worship: A printed order of worship may be used. It is of special help when there is congregational singing. If it is used, copies may be placed in the hands of the guests as they are seated.

The Processional: There is no set rule for the processional. Various methods are used successfully. Traditionally the bridegroom enters with the minister and waits in front for the bride. The bride is last in the processional, being escorted on the arm of her father. If for some reason the father does not escort her, the groom or a close male relative, or a friend of the family may do the honor, or she may walk down the aisle alone. If the groom escorts the bride himself, the processional can be planned so that the groomsman and the best man escort the matron of honor and the bridesmaid. In this case, the minister stands in front alone or with an assistant.

In the less structured ceremony, the bride and groom

may be seated with their families and among the congregation, coming forward at the proper juncture of the service.

The Presentation: Traditionally, the father or other family member "gives the bride." The question is asked by the minister, "Who gives this woman for marriage?" and the father, still standing where he was when the processional had ended, says, "I do," or "Her mother and I."

Sometimes there is reluctance toward "giving away the daughter." The question may be asked, "Who presents this woman for marriage?" The reply would be the same as in the traditional sense.

A different question, which implies proper attention to parental nurture, may be asked by the minister: "Who has prepared this woman for marriage?" Along this same line, a second question could be put, this time to the parents of the groom, asking, "Who has prepared this man for marriage?"

Introductory Statement: As part of the introductory remarks, the minister usually declares by what authority the marriage is performed. This declaration may be quite formal or very simple. It usually states that a proper license has been delivered. Proper diligence should have been exercised prior to the hour of the wedding ceremony. It is the minister's duty to see that the legal requirements are met in every particular.

Music: Music is an important worship resource both in the service and the other events (e.g., rehearsal dinner, reception) which are usually held. Couples who take an active interest in the selection of music should be encouraged to work cooperatively with the officiating minister, the organist, and the leaders of the pastoral unit hosting the service. Sometimes the officiating minister is contacted concurrently with the organist; other situations require the officiating minister to suggest to the couple that musicians be consulted in the planning stages.

Music used in the worship service should be appropriate for worship. The contemporary popular music, frequently requested by the couple, can be played at either the rehearsal dinner or during the reception. A wide range of appropriate service music has been published for keyboard (organ or piano), voice and instruments. Musicians who regularly assist with weddings may be aware of the variety of resources; others may wish to write the Worship Office (P.O. Box 1059, Independence, MO 64051) requesting lists of music suitable for the wedding service. Adequate advance planning is imperative to allow time for the purchase and preparation of musical resources.

Candles: The use of candles at weddings seems traditional. Sometimes they are used solely for decorative effect. Sometimes they are used as part of the symbolism of the ceremony. It is important that this symbolism be in harmony with the doctrine of the church.

Some have used a central white candle to indicate Christ or his church. The couple light individual candles to symbolize their own lives dedicated to Christ or they may light a single candle, following the ceremony, to indicate that their home is to shine with the light of Christ. Some symbolism used needs to be explained to the congregation.

There are some major precautions about the use of candles that should be observed: (1) If candles are carried by members of the wedding party or if they are used as part of the decoration, there should be adequate clearance around the candles in order to prevent accidental fire. Special care should be taken so that, should the candle burn low or tip, it will not catch anything on fire. Be certain that dresses cannot accidentally brush against a flame. (2) In burning, candles run molten wax. This wax can drip. When it falls on carpets and woodwork, it is extremely difficult to remove. Beautiful pieces of church furniture can be ruined by the dripping of candles. Clear plastic can be spread beneath the candles to prevent this without destroying the decorative effect and, where it can be done, small plates may be placed beneath them. (3) It is not recommended that young children be permitted to carry candles.

Seating of Guests: Various seating arrangements are used. Sometimes only the immediate family members are given special seating. In these situations friends and family of the bride and the groom are intermixed together as a symbol of the uniting of the couple.

In other more traditional ceremonies the parents of the groom sit in the first pew on the right facing the front. In reserved pews are the rest of the family and close friends. Guests who are friends of the groom are seated on the same side in unreserved seats. The parents of the bride sit in the first pew on the left facing the front. In the reserved pews are the rest of their family and close friends. Guests who are friends of the bride are seated on the same side in an unreserved area.

Ring and Flower Bearers: Children old enough to understand the ceremony should be used. The use of ring and flower bearers is a matter of choice.

The Covenant: There is one joint covenant that is required to be used by every minister of the church when he conducts a wedding ceremony. That covenant is: "You both mutually agree to be each other's companion, husband and wife, observing the legal right belonging to this condition; that is, keeping yourselves wholly for each other, and from all others, during your lives?" The answer of the bride and groom shall be "yes," or "we do," or another appropriate response.[35]

Traditionally there has been a covenant which accompanies the placing of the wedding rings. There is no set standard for it; it can be adjusted to the type of ceremony. In some ceremonies there is but one ring, that which the groom places on the finger of the bride. Sometimes there is also a ring for the groom. A wedding ring is not necessary, however, and in some cases it may not be used.

When the ring is given, the covenant or covenants may be read by the minister and repeated by the bride or groom, or it is permissible for the bride and groom to compose their own covenants, giving them a sense of spontaneity that the more formal reading lacks. When this is done, however, the content of the covenant should be discussed with the minister before the ceremony.

It may be desired that there be a covenant in the giving and one in the receiving of the ring, the groom saying "(bride's name), I place this ring upon your finger in token of my love for you. I pledge to cherish you, forsaking all others, to cleave to you as long as we both shall live."

She may respond with something like, "(bridegroom's name), I accept this ring as your token of love and will be reminded of it each time I feel it on my hand. This I do because I love you."

In a double-ring ceremony, the procedure is repeated, the bride giving the ring and the groom responding.

Benediction: The benediction is prescribed in Doctrine and Covenants 111:2d: "May God add his blessings and keep you to fulfill your covenants from henceforth and forever. Amen."

The Wedding Rehearsal

All members of the wedding party should attend the wedding rehearsal. The rehearsal should be at a time prior to the wedding when there will be enough time to work out the details smoothly. This usually is the day before the wedding.

Detailed instructions should be given to all those involved in the ceremony. Each usher should know his or her area of responsibility. The head usher should direct other ushers. The musicians should be present. All parts of the ceremony should be rehearsed so the timing can be clear.

Arrangements of the participants in the wedding ceremony vary according to custom, personal likes, and adjustment to the physical facilities. Following are two sample arrangements of participants:

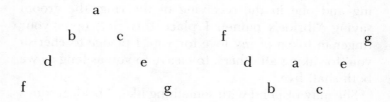

a. The minister, facing the congregation.
b. and c. The bride and bridegroom respectively.

d. and e. The maid of honor and best man respectively.
f. and g. The bridesmaid and groomsman respectively.

A word of advice: The bride and groom will have their backs to the congregation and the minister will be quite close to the wedding party. As a result, voices may be muffled. Each should speak loudly so that those in the congregation will be able to hear. If there is a public address system, this may be used, but it is best not to make the microphone stands conspicuous. A suspended microphone is preferred.

Sample Ceremonies

Following are two brief marriage ceremonies presented as examples. They may be altered according to local customs and the desires of the minister and parties concerned. Other suggestions can be found in *The Sacraments* by Peter Judd, available from Herald House. Other marriage manuals may also be available from libraries and bookstores.

Sample Ceremony A

Honored Friends: Into my hands has been delivered a license, issued according to law, which authorizes me to unite in marriage (bridegroom's full name) and (bride's full name). For this purpose we are now assembled here. (Where a civil ceremony has already been conducted, a simple statement of the purpose of the service, mentioning names of the couple, will suffice.)

Let us ask the blessing of God. (brief prayer)

Address. The holy state of wedlock is ordained of God to promote the spiritual, social, and material well-being of the human family and the home. There-fore its obligations should be entered into with deep devotion, unselfish love, and upright purpose, its bonds being assumed in the sight of God with reverence and sober consideration. (The length of the ceremony is decided by the length of this address, which can include further comments as the minister deems appropriate. Usually the first portion of this address can be directed to the congregation and the second part to the bride and bridegroom.)

To the bridegroom: Do you take this woman to be your lawful wife, to love, honor, and cherish her both in sickness and in health, whether in prosperity or ad-versity, and to be virtuous and faithful as long as you live? (Bridegroom answers "I do.")

To the bride: Do you take this man to be your lawful husband, to love, honor, and cherish him both in sickness and in health, whether in prosperity or ad-versity, and to be virtuous and faithful as long as you live? (Bride answers "I do.")

Marriage pledge: In token of your mutual purpose to unite in this sacred bond and to faithfully observe its duties, you will now join your right hands.

Do you both mutually agree to be each other's com-panion, husband and wife, observing the legal rights belonging to this condition; that is, keeping your-selves wholly for each other and from all others as long as you both shall live? (Bridegroom and bride may answer in unison "Yes" or "We do," or answer may be consecutively, first the bridegroom, then the bride "I do.")

Ring ceremony: (Ring is handed to minister.) As a token of the endless and pure love which the marriage bond requires of you and of the bride, you may place this ring upon the third finger of her left hand. (Minister hands ring to bridegroom to be placed on the bride's finger. Local customs should be observed regarding the finger or hand upon which the ring is placed.)

If a double-ring ceremony is desired, adapt this instruction for the bride's guidance.

Bridegroom and bride rejoin right hands.

Pronouncement by minister: Whereas you have mutually pledged yourselves to each other in the holy bonds of marriage, I now, as a minister of the gospel and by the authority vested in me by the laws of (the state), pronounce you husband and wife. (This may be adapted to local custom.)

Benediction: May God add his blessing and keep you to fulfill your covenant from this day henceforth. (Prayer for divine sanction and grace.)

Each order should be prepared afresh. In this way the ceremony will not become stereotyped but will be meaningful to each couple because it has a part of their own planning in it.

Sample Ceremony B

Prelude

Welcome: Officiating minister welcomes family and friends of the couple.

Congregation Hymn

Processional: Bride and groom walk in the processional together.

Meaning of Community: Officating minister makes a statement about the importance of family and friends who love the wedding couple. Emphasis is placed on past community nurture and on the couple's need for support in the future.

Solo

Readings: Two or three close friends and/or immediate family members read poetry or passages that are meaningful to the couple.

Meaning of Relationship: Officiating minister makes a personal statement to the couple about what each brings to the marriage and how these gifts can be magnified as a couple.

Sharing of Vows: Minister asks the couple to join hands and states, "Do you both mutually agree to be each other's companion, husband and wife, observing the legal rights belonging to this condition; that is, keeping yourselves wholly for each other and from all others as long as you both shall live? (Bride and bridegroom then answer "Yes," "We do," or a similar response.)

Support of Community: At the leading of the officiating minister, various members of the congregation stand in their places to state publicly their love and support for the couple. Some persons should be preselected for this honor so that proper responses are assured.

Exchange of Rings: Personal statements by the bride and groom to each other. These statements can be developed creatively with the aid of the minister.

Pronouncement of Minister: "Whereas you have mutually pledged yourselves to each other in the sacrament of marriage, I now, as a minister of Jesus Christ and by the authority vested in me by the laws of (State, or County), pronounce you husband and wife." (This may be adapted to local custom.) "May

God add his blessing and keep you to fulfill your covenant from this day henceforth and forever. Amen."

Solo

Pastoral Prayer: Officiating minister prays a pastoral prayer on behalf of the couple and the supporting congregation.

Recessional

Congregational Hymn

Sending Forth: Officiating minister states to the congregation, "And now may you go forth in the support and love of (bride and groom). May the grace and love of God go with you all. Amen."

NOTES

1. Doctrine and Covenants 49:3a, March 31, 1831.
2. Ibid., 108A:13.
3. Doctrine and Covenants, 1835 edition, Section CI, pp. 251, 252.
4. Doctrine and Covenants 111:1a.
5. Ibid., 111:1b.
6. Ibid., 111:1c.
7. Ibid., 111:1c.
8. See F. H. Edwards, *A New Commentary on the Doctrine and Covenants*, Herald House, 1977, pp. 397, 398.
9. Doctrine and Covenants 111:2a, b.
10. Ibid., 111:2c.
11. Ibid., 111:2d.
12. Ibid., 111:3.
13. Ibid., 111:4a.
14. Ibid., 111:4b. See also 49:3b and 150:10a.
15. Ibid., 111:4b.
16. Genesis 2:18, KJV. The Inspired Version equivalent reads, "And I, the Lord God, said unto mine Only Begotten, that it was not good that the man should be alone; wherefore I will make an help meet for him" (Genesis 2:23, 24).
17. Genesis 2:24 (2:30, I.V.)
18. Doctrine and Covenants 49:3a-c.
19. Ibid., 111:2c.
20. Matthew 19:6; Mark 10:9 (10:7, I.V.)

21. Doctrine and Covenants 111:2b.
22. Ibid., 111:2b.
23. Matthew 16:19 (16:20, I.V.). See also 18:18.
24. Matthew 22:30 (22:29, I.V.). See also Mark 12:25 (12:29, I.V.) and Luke 20:35.
25. Doctrine and Covenants 111:2b. See also 42:7d.
26. Exodus 20, particularly verses 13-15.
27. Doctrine and Covenants 59:2c. See also 63:5a and 66:5e.
28. Ibid., 42:7e; 22a, b.
29. Ibid., 111:4a.
30. G.C.R. No. 272, adopted April 9, 1884.
31. G.C.R. No. 412, adopted April 11, 1896.
32. G.C.R. No. 1034, adopted April 6, 1962.
33. Ibid.
34. Ibid.
35. Doctrine and Covenants 111:2b.

Chapter 9

MARRIAGE COUNSELING

Introduction

The church is deeply involved in marriage. It is common for couples in love to confirm their commitment to each other by celebrating their covenant in a church ceremony. Often the minister performing the ceremony knows one or both members of the couple planning marriage. Premarital counseling sessions are an important part of preparing for marriage. The caring and responsibility of the minister continues beyond the ceremony with another dimension. Added to the concern for the two individuals is one for the marriage itself.

Marriage as a loving, enduring relationship is important to the couple, their family, the church, and society. A married person can receive acceptance, encouragement, and love in a good marriage relationship. It provides an environment of safety and nurture.

Ministers have a responsibility for the couple and the marriage. It can be helpful to examine how a member of the priesthood may minister to a married couple. It is important to be with the couple "at the best of times and at the worst of times." This simple statement implies a number of things.

In our society today the minister is one of the few people in the helping services who can take the initiative.

Another way of saying it is that they are able and expected to make house calls. It is appropriate for the priesthood member to visit a newlywed couple shortly after the marriage and to continue to do so. The minister should not underestimate the importance and opportunity for taking the initiative to visit people, and does not have to wait until problems occur before making a visit. Ministry may be greatly hampered if members of the priesthood stay away until they receive a call for help. Establishing a relationship which is a genuine friendship provides opportunity for the couple to share achievements with the minister who becomes their friend. Building a treasury of experiences provides resources which can be drawn upon in times of trouble.

Pastoral Care

Sharing the best of times is at the heart of pastoral care, which is a responsibility of the priesthood and the pastoral unit. One definition of pastoral care is, "The mutual concern of Christians for each other and for those in the world for whom Christ died."* Mutual concern cannot be effectively expressed without close continuing communication between the minister and the couple.

Most of our pastoral units are served by more than one self-sustaining minister. Some distribution of responsibility needs to be arranged to permit each minister to be assigned a list of families with whom she or he can establish long-term relationships. Ideally a minister should begin visiting newlyweds in their newly established home and continue to share and be informed

---

* C. W. Brister, *Pastoral Care in the Church* (New York: Harper and Row), 1964.

about the important events of their lives. Birthdays, anniversaries, promotions, and all kinds of achievements should be a part of their continuing interaction. Many contacts will be brief and informal, including phone calls and casual greetings at church. The couple needs to know that what happens to them is important to the minister.

Through the years the minister should have a rather accurate perception of the condition of the marriage. A friend will always know about the quality of the relationship between the couple. It is significant to remember that pastoral care symbolizes God's concern for them and their marriage. Although the couple may mention it infrequently or never, they are aware that the minister by virtue of ordination and role is a servant of God. Several influences may occur. One is the expectation that the couple will live out their lives loving and caring for each other, called to be the best that they can be. Another is a reminder of the grace of God who promises forgiveness when we need and seek it and gives us the opportunity to begin again. Intrinsic to this is the good news of the gospel expressed through Jesus Christ.

The experience of pastoral care can be very rich for the couple and the minister. They affirm each other's worth and develop in experience and understanding. Each will remember and value the best of times which they share. Being able to share concerns may prevent stress situations from developing into more serious problems.

Crisis

Accidents, illness, loss of employment, or death of a loved one may become crises for a married couple. The minister must be alert to such occurrences in the lives of those people with whom he or she is involved in pastoral care.

When something occurs in the life of a couple which they have difficulty coping with through their normal problem-solving methods, they may rather quickly be in the midst of a crisis. The minister who knows people well and maintains regular contact with them should recognize symptoms of stress which are greater than normal. Such symptoms as depression, anxiety, severe or continual headaches, or even a bleeding ulcer may indicate crises which grow out of life adjustments such as leaving home, adjusting to a new marriage, or pregnancy.

Loss of a job, loss of savings, unexpected illness, a natural disaster such as fire or a flood are more quickly identified as crises. The rapid onslaught of such events may overwhelm a couple so that they are unable to cope with the immediate situation. They may panic, be defeated, or resort to ineffective behavior.

On learning of a crisis the minister may take the initiative and intervene. The minister should begin by making contact with the person or couple in the crisis, boil the problem down to its essentials, and help the person or couple to do what needs to be done immediately to relieve the stress of the situation. The one in a ministerial role must take the immediate practical steps possible to help the persons cope with the crisis situation. Once the critical danger is past there is time to review what has occurred and how the couple were able, with help, to cope. Being with and working through is the essential task of the minister in crisis events.

Sometimes a minister will be contacted to help people he or she barely knows; a minister must begin by establishing a relationship. This is much more difficult and tenuous than with people with whom there are years of pastoral care as a foundation for trust and confidence. If a crisis is complex and extends over a period of time, the minister can be a bridge with others in the pastoral unit—helping to provide a support group.

Continuing Marriage Counseling

Good judgment, confidentiality, and discretion are qualities which should be developed and used by a minister. Broad pastoral care and crisis intervention are two of the strongest needs for marriage counseling by the self-sustaining minister. Those who have clinical training in counseling are best prepared to engage in therapeutic counseling with a couple who are having problems with their marriage. Priesthood members should have a realistic understanding of their qualifications and limitations. It is best for ministers without clinical counseling training to make referrals to qualified people. Information of a personal nature should be recognized and kept confidential.

Referral

Some knowledge of local referral agencies will be particularly helpful in crisis situations. Look up information on such referral sources as the following:

A. *Health*
   1. Medical and dental personnel
   2. Hospitals and clinics
   3. Public health services

4. Volunteer health organizations
5. Mental health facilities
6. Alcoholics Anonymous

B. Social Services

1. Public assistance
2. Children's services
3. Handicapped
4. Senior citizens
5. Voluntary organizations
6. Church-sponsored programs

C. Legal Services

1. Consumer protection groups
2. Legal Aid societies
3. Public defender offices
4. Juvenile court
5. Law enforcement agencies

D. Employment Services

1. Employment agencies (public and private)
2. Job-training programs
3. Institutional placement offices

E. Educational Programs

1. Adult education programs
2. Higher education, junior colleges, colleges, and universities
3. Trade and technical schools
4. Business schools
5. Local schools—special programs

It is far better to have some knowledge and even previous contact with referral agencies not commonly used. Refer those who can be helped more effectively by someone else. This will include those who need medical or institutional care, those whose needs are obviously beyond your available time or training, those who need intensive psychotherapy or who are severely depressed and/or suicidal, those with severe chronic financial needs.

Effective referral must be handled carefully so that the person or couple will not feel rejected or abandoned. Mention the possibility of referral as early as possible, indicating why specialized help may be needed. Try to communicate that your concern and care as a minister will continue undiminished after the referral. Help them to work through their feelings about referral so that they will be open to the professional help they need. Allow them to make their own appointment. Follow up with continuing pastoral care, giving encouragement and support. A successful referral can be rewarding to the couple and the minister.

The Pastoral Care Office has developed a number of resources.

A. *Up with Marriage* by James Mayfield, Herald House

B. *Counseling Skills for Church Leadership* by Hyrum H. Husky, Jr., Herald House

C. *"Planning" to Stay Together* by Terry and Anne Armstrong

D. The Pamphlet Series, Herald House
   1. *Dying, Death and Grief*
   2. *Alcoholism*
   3. *Dealing with Divorce*
   4. *Loneliness*

5. *Aging*
6. *Life After Youth*
7. *Parenting Together*
8. *Parenting Alone*
9. *Coping with Stress*
10. *Ministry with the Confined*
11. *Child Abuse*
12. *Children of Divorce*
13. *Human Sexuality*
14. *Multiple Faith Relationships*

Several additional resources (also available from Herald House):

A. *Intimate Partners* by Clifford Sages and Bernice Hunt, McGraw Hill
B. *Peoplemaking* by Virginia Satir, Science and Behavior Books
C. *Passages* by Gail Sheehy, Bantam Books
D. Creative Pastoral Care and Counseling Series, edited by Howard J. Clinebell, Jr., Fortress Press
   1. *Growth Counseling for Marriage Enrichment* by Howard J. Clinebell, Jr.
   2. *Growth Counseling for Mid-Years Couples* by Howard J. Clinebell, Jr.
   3. *Pastoral Care Counseling in Grief and Separation* by Wayne E. Oates
   4. *New Approaches to Family Pastoral Care* by Douglas A. Anderson
   5. *Pastor and Parish: A Systems Approach* by E. Marsell Pattison
E. *The Minister as Crisis Counselor* by David K. Switzer, Abingdon Press

Chapter 10

PATRIARCHAL BLESSING

The Meaning of Patriarchal Blessing

The patriarchal blessing is an occasion of worship in which persons come to the patriarch of their choice to receive the laying on of hands. In tradition and purpose it is as old as Abraham, Isaac, and Jacob blessing their offspring[1] and Alma discerning his sons' needs and gifts, and offering them counsel and motivation.[2] In purpose it is related to the loving concern of Paul for Timothy as he urged him to stir up the gifts of God within him.[3]

The patriarchal blessing is given to persons who are fifteen years of age or older at their request. Only one such blessing is given to each person. Bringing life into focus within the divine purpose, and stimulating enlarged faith in God and commitment to Christ are inherent in blessings. Persons receiving their patriarchal blessings have testified to their benefits in sensing their potential, pulling the strands of life together, and lending through the years a steadying influence.

There is assurance of God's love and concern for the individual. There may be certain promises of God appropriate to that person's life and conditioned on the candidate's faithfulness. Patriarchs testify that their own powers of observation are generally heightened in discernment. People are cautioned not to expect the future course of life to be foretold nor decisions to be made for them. Rather they are counseled to live wisely, making decisions appropriate to their covenant with Christ.

The patriachal blessing is intended to provide lifelong guidance and support. A typed copy of the blessing is provided so that the recipient can refer to it when in need of strength and guidance.

An individual desiring a patriarchal blessing approaches one of the more than 300 evangelist-patriarchs in the church. The candidate is advised to make preparation for the blessing by prayer, meditation, and the reading of a pamphlet prepared for the purpose of explaining the nature and intent of patriarchal blessings. The latest edition of this pamphlet, *Your Patriarchal Blessing* by Patriarch Reed M. Holmes,[4] includes some suggested scriptures and other resources for preparation.

At the time scheduled for the blessing, the candidate and the minister meet in a private room such as an office or chapel, or in a home. Sometimes a place of natural beauty and quietness outdoors is chosen. The setting is one of worship, and includes scripture and prayer. Due to the intensely personal nature of the experience no other individual is present, with the possible exception of a stenographer who records the blessing.

The significance of the patriarchal blessing has been suggested by the fact that a copy is kept on file and available in case the original is lost. Persons may receive a copy of their blessing by writing to the presiding patriarch.

NOTES

1. Genesis 27, 48, 49; Doctrine and Covenants 83:2e.
2. Alma 17, 18, 19.
3. II Timothy 1:6.
4. Herald House, 1975.

PART FOUR
STEWARDSHIP OF
TEMPORALITIES

STEWARDSHIP OF TEMPORALITIES

Spiritual Enterprise

Stewardship is a spiritual enterprise that involves all of life. It is a principle which is meaningful in the development of each individual life. If followed to the limit of our understanding this principle can help us understand our relationship to our Creator and the purpose of life for each one of us. The manner in which we preside over our lives each day determines how we grow in understanding and helps us realize we are an important part of the world. It helps us appreciate the importance of every person toward making a better world in which to live. Such a concept is inseparably connected or immersed in the establishment of God's kingdom here on earth.

The term *stewardship* was the word used as a metaphor in the English translation of the New Testament to describe the management of the property of another. Theologians and philosophers over the years have expanded the concept of stewardship to mean the management of one's whole life in response to God. The message of Restoration scriptures has given added clarity to this understanding as the principle finds application in every aspect of daily living.

What is stewardship? It impacts every element of our being. It draws upon the heart, mind, and strength of every true steward. It causes us to reorder our sense of values. The true spirit of stewardship will cause those of us who love God to seek to find the challenge of life in the gifts of God to us, and to sense our moral obligation to develop and rightfully employ these gifts.

Basics of Restoration Stewardship

Based on the premise as stated above, the concept of *stewardship* is seen as a principle that is an essential part of the Christian gospel which enables the development of a people who have covenanted to build the kingdom of God. Thus, the principle of temporal stewardship is lived out within the terms of covenant, mangement, periodic accounting, and consecration.

1. *Covenant* is that relationship with Christ which gives birth to a new purpose and direction in life.
2. *Management* is the ordering of priorities so one can be a most productive kingdom-building steward.
3. *Periodic accounting* is essential in the flow of life.
4. Through the spirit of *consecration* stewards give a portion of their increase, as well as their surplus, to the church and manage all life's resources for kingdom-building purposes.

The relationship of God to creation is founded upon love. From Genesis to Revelation, from Nephi to Moroni, from the first page on in the book of contemporary scriptures, the scriptures attest that God is love, above all else. It is the very nature of perfect love to give itself, and this is exactly what God has done in a marvelous creation.

Being holy and loving, God has created a universe that is described in scriptures as "good." The world we inhabit is a prepared place for wonderful and useful things, full of mysteries which people of science and industry are constantly discovering and developing for

the use of humankind. Contemporary scriptures significantly reveal that "The earth is full, and there is enough
and to spare" for all of God's children when the things
of this world are used "in the manner designed of God."

There is a divine plan which helps people in the
process of sharing possessions with the cause of the
kingdom. This is the *spiritual law of temporalities* and is
a plan conceived of God which is designed to help people utilize the temporal aspects of life to achieve spiritual objectives in harmony with God's purposes. It is a
law of spiritual undergirding, primarily intended to assist people in developing spiritually into unselfish beings
expressed in daily lifestyles.

God Is Owner

God is the supreme owner of life and all material
things. Individuals need to come to the realization that
all they are and all they have are the result of God's love
for them.

Persons as Stewards

An individual's relationship to God is that of a steward or trustee over the things which have been entrusted
to one's care and which are normally referred to as
one's possessions. The practice of persons to use their
possessions for their own purposes, where such purposes
run counter to the purposes of God, is inconsistent with
the recognition of God as creator. As stewards under
God, persons are called to dedicate their total selves to
God—personality, time, and possessions. No area of
existence is excluded from the claims of Christ since his
lordship extends over all of life. Because the lordship of
Christ includes everything—both in heaven and in

earth—all of life is sacred. There can be no true distinction between what is commonly called secular and sacred.

The Doctrine of Agency

The stewardship of persons has its roots in the doctrine of agency.

A. A person is permitted to act for oneself, but with the responsibility to choose life or death, good or evil.

B. Wise use of agency brings both an increase in freedom and an increase in responsibility.

1. Individuals are free only in the measure of their response to the accountability imposed upon them by their Creator.

2. A good and faithful steward, who knows the Lord's will, must use initiative, not waiting to be commanded in all things; otherwise one is a slave and not a steward.

The Principle of Accountability

The principle of accountability is inseparably connected with the doctrine of agency. Because God gives people their agency, they become accountable for their stewardship over life. All persons must answer to the Creator for their own pattern of behavior. In the church those who make a covenant to be a witness of Jesus Christ are responsible for their stewardship of life as a consequence of the gift from the one who owns—the Creator.

The belief of the Restoration church that stewards must make an accounting to God in this life through God's authorized servants as well as at the Day of Judgment, is unique among Christian stewardship philosophies.

A. *The Financial Accounting*—The financial accounting is not merely a financial report of one person to another; it is our accounting to God through the church. The tithing statement is (1) a tangible expression of one's willingness to be a steward, (2) a methodical way (in fact, the only way) to determine the tithe accurately, (3) a way of keeping one's self informed of the use being made of financial resources and opportunities, (4) an acknowledgment of one's unity with the church in a cooperative endeavor with other persons and God to build up Zion.

B. *The Presenting of the Tithing Statement* is a spiritually significant act; it is an act of worship. Presentation of the financial accounting is a most fundamental response to a steward who believes that the kingdom is offered to all through the building up of Zion.

The Principle of Increase

The principle of increase is a central characteristic of the Zionic community and enables the development of a people who have covenanted to build the kingdom. Our willingness to share with others the gifts and talents God has given us is essential to experiencing the joy of righteous living. Increase makes it possible to look "outward" to the needs of others and express love and concern in sharing. It is a principle of life in all aspects such as faith, knowledge, service, and opportunities.

In the field of temporalities, increase is that portion of life's tangible resources not needed for basic living needs and which may be shared for the purpose of assisting in the establishment of God's kingdom on earth. This increase is the consequence of (1) wise investment of time and energy in the production of economic income, and (2) only the use of an appropriate share of the income for the basic living needs of those dependent on that income.

A. *Temporal Increase Is Twofold*
   1. At the time of the first temporal accounting, increase is the net worth of the accumulated temporal resources of the steward.
   2. After the first temporal accounting is made, temporal increase is that portion of the steward's managed temporal resources which is beyond that which is used for maintaining physical health and well-being, and for assuming a monetary share of mandatory citizenship responsibility as is required by various levels of government.

B. *Basic Living Needs and Increase*
   1. As a beginning point for a sound understanding of stewardship financial accounting, let it first be said that all expenditures fall into the category of having been made as (a) a necessary living expense, or (b) as a disbursement from the increase.
   2. If an expenditure is not made for a basic living need, it is, by definition, made from *increase*. Basic living needs are those needs which are related to basic physical requirements which all people everywhere have in common. Basic living needs, which are relatively few in number, are those required to maintain physical health

and well-being within a reasonable standard of living, such as food, shelter, medical care, etc. Also included are taxes, since a steward is required to assume a monetary share of citizenship responsibility.

3. A basic distinction between increase and a basic living need may be determined by the words *optional* or *mandatory*.

4. The spending of resources for a vacation trip, gifts, investment and securities, tuition for higher education, etc., would be optional with the individual.

5. The spending of resources for physical health and well-being would be those areas whch are mandatory for attaining physical health and well-being.

C. *Just Wants and Increase*

1. The terminology of *needs* and *just wants* may be understood by knowing that *wants* go beyond *needs*. Simply stated, that portion of the annual income not expended for basic living needs is *increase*. Since wants go beyond needs all expenditures for wants are made from increase.

2. Wants are most clearly distinguished from basic living needs by the fact that expenditures made to satisfy wants are not as mandatory as those made for basic living needs.

3. *Just wants* may be technically described as those wants which can be supplied from the increase after the tithe is paid and reasonable support is given to local church and community need.

4. Needs are never supplied from increase and therefore are not subject to tithing, while wants are provided from increase.

The Law of Tithing

Literally, and primarily, the word *tithe* means a tenth. Restoration teaching emphasizes that it is just, equitable, and scriptural to allow the deduction of basic living needs before the tithe is computed.

Although family needs are given a prime consideration in this interpretation, family needs are not an exclusive or sole consideration. The selection of a standard of living, which provides enough increase to share with the causes of the kingdom, is a matter of deep spiritual significance. The steward who spends so excessively that no increase remains for God's purposes is not excused from financial or spiritual responsibility.

The determination of the tithe due on the increase is accomplished through the avenue of the tithing statement.

A. The First Tithing Statement accounts for the accumulated and tangible increase. The intangible portion of increase is not accounted for on the First Tithing Statement (the Inventory).

B. The Annual Tithing Statement provides for determining the increase (tangible-intangible). The payment of the tithe, which is one-tenth of the increase, is the giving of the scriptural "first fruits" of increase.

Socioeconomic Principles

The social message of the Restoration is unique because it protects and nurtures the divinely given freedom of the individual and at the same time teaches the principles and provides instrumentality through which social righteousness can be achieved. It affirms that a person, as God's highest order of creation, achieves maximum freedom and the most effective power for good in the subordination of self for the cause of the kingdom. It also protects and nurtures individual initiative to secure all that should rightfully accrue as a result of the highest expression of God-given individual talents.

Inheritance. Many of the early revelations to the church gave emphasis and urged the membership to secure an inheritance. In Restoration terminology, *inheritance* means much more than an amount of wealth bequeathed to an individual. In stewardship philosophy it is the apparent intent of God that persons shall have as an inheritance all resources and opportunities that are required to exercise responsible stewardship of self and family, consecrating all beyond this for the benefit of others, and thus using one's total resources in the spirit of the kingdom of God.

Based on the principle of needs and just wants, the steward should justifiably acquire and possess assets to the degree that one can view the immediate and foreseeable future needs for oneself and family with a sense of reasonable security. At the same time, the steward should be acutely aware of the needs of others and share his or her resources accordingly so that similar opportunities may be available to all.

The Gathering. The basic purpose of the *gathering* is to be found in the bringing together of those of like spiritual, social, and economic ideals into one area where such ideas can be implemented in community living. Spiritual values are thus paramount and the development of the individual personalities, as ordained by God, is a primary goal. The basic gathering unit is the branch or congregation. The principle of the gathering provides primary gathering areas, such as the Center Place and the stakes of Zion, and secondary gatherings and development of satellite Zionic communities, not only in the "regions round about," but in distant places. Zionic living is to be expressed in the cultural patterns of people all over the world, providing other nuclei directly related to the central nucleus of the Center Place. The application of the principle of increase makes possible the mobilization of resources for an expanding witness of the Lord Jesus.

The Storehouse. Storehouse organization and operation is the underlying socioeconomic distinctive of the Restoration. It involves a new way of life in which men and women will be so concerned about others that they will retain only for themselves that which is necessary for their needs and just wants (their wants being tempered by an awareness of the needs of the kingdom) with the remainder accruing to them, through the maximum development and use of their talents being dedicated to assist in meeting the unmet needs of society.

The Storehouse is a divinely inspired instrument through which there should flow surplus from economically strong and spiritually motivated individual stewards to the larger community for its enrichment and for the common good of all its citizens.

The Storehouse should not be thought of as simply a

repository for funds but as a fiscally sound structure to care adequately for contingencies which occur, and for a continuous flowing out, uninterrupted by seasonal economic fluctuations, of ministries for the development of the kingdom of God on earth.

The purpose of Storehouse ministries is to be in harmony with revelations given and to assist in the achieving of current objectives of the church under the direction of those who have been called of God, and set apart by the will of the people, to give administrative and prophetic leadership to the church.

The primary sources of income to the Storehouse are *surplus* and *consecrations.*

When used by the ministry of the church, the word *surplus* should mean that part of a steward's increase, whether monies or properties, remaining after the responsibility of tithing and freewill offerings has been met. In addition, provision has been made for the inheritance of the steward.

The giving of surplus is a voluntary act on the part of the steward. It is a significant act of participation in gathering to and perfecting Zionic communities. Because the giving of surplus is a part of divine law, one should approach this act of more complete consecration prayerfully and with deep concern. All factors relative to one's obligation to family, to church, to business associates, and to community should be carefully analyzed. Forms to assist with such an analysis are available from the bishopric.

Doctrine and Covenants 129:8 provides a succinct statement on sources of income to the church. In this section *consecrations* are given the same weight as tithing, surplus, and free-will offerings. Consecrations may be used to finance certain ministries of the church through the Storehouse at the stake and/or general church level. Consecrations are to be given, as is surplus, by stewards who have consistently made a financial accounting and paid the tithe.

Oblation Offering

The oblation offering is received during the Communion service in harmony with the resolution approved at the General Conference of 1917 which reads as follows:

... That every branch should comply with the law by receiving oblations at the Sacrament services, as found in Doctrine and Covenants 59:2, and that the amount so received should be placed with the bishopric in harmony with Doctrine and Covenants 42:8.[1]

The present oblation fund, in manner both of receiving and of disbursing, appears also to be in harmony with Doctrine and Covenants 44 which advises that until adequate provision is made for the poor and needy through response to "my law" (surplus and consecration to the storehouse) the church must "administer to their relief." In addition to the oblation funds received in Communion services, offerings may be made to the oblation fund at any time.

Social Ministries Commission. This commission is a part of the Field Support Services Division and functions in the area of helping the church to administer to those who are in need. The commission assists in identifying areas of ministry that enable persons to move from a condition of dependence to a life of productivity. The Social Ministries Commission stands ready to assist jurisdictions in the development of ministries to those who are poor and needy and who are without from time to time.

Meaningful Stewardship Response

One fact of the Christian life long recognized and taught by the church is the nature of our accountability to God for our lives and all the resources God places in our care. God's expectations are vividly seen as recorded in Doctrine and Covenants 72:1c: "It is required of the Lord, at the hand of every steward, to render an account of his stewardship, both in time and eternity." However, recognizing the importance of willing, participating, co-creating disciples, God has further counseled that persons "should be anxiously engaged in a good cause, and do many things of their own free will, and bring to pass much righteousness; for the power is in them, wherein they are agents unto themselves."[2] When Christians willingly choose to be accountable participants with God they are free to be productive and fulfilled in the kingdom-building process.

Financial stewardship accounting, although only a part of the total Christian stewardship response, is a significant and symbolic act in the life of a steward. It is a demonstration of a willingness to participate freely in a part of God's expectations for us. The implementation of the teachings of Christ dealing with stewardship accounting, increase, inheritance, tithing, offerings, surplus, consecrations, and the Storehouse all depend on a people who will freely choose the lifestyle of accountability.

The primary goal of the Christian family in its use of resources, money included, is to bear witness to its faith in God and the kingdom. Through its participation in the cause of the kingdom, in its concern for neighbor as for self, the stewardship-minded family is guided by this primary goal. Through the application of the law this goal may be achieved.

None Are Exempt from the Law. The temporal law should be observed as a part of the gospel of Christ. Compliance with the provisions of law will to a great degree indicate the sincerity of our repentance and desire to obey the whole law of Christ.

While observance of the temporal law is not made a test of membership in the sense that those who do not make stewardship accounting or pay tithing are denied membership; nevertheless, as in the case in every other phase of the gospel law, recognition of the stewardship of temporalities is part of the growth toward spiritual stature and effectiveness.

Guidelines for Response. In the interpretation given of the temporal law expressed in the General Conference Resolution 847, the Presiding Bishopric urges the Saints to respond to the stewardship of temporalities by doing these things:

1. Filing an inventory (first tithing statement)
2. Paying the tithe of the increase
3. Contributing surplus
4. Making offerings
5. Thereafter giving an account of one's temporal stewardship annually (annual tithing statement)

If those in the priesthood throughout the church will lead by example in responding to the temporal law, then their teaching among the Saints will be effectual and result in the advancement of the cause of Christ.

Money Management. Money is of particular importance for stewards. Its management carries a special responsibility. As with all resources, money is understood by the steward to belong to God, who is owner of both possessions and possessors. In the final analysis, the way in which our money is managed may be a more accurate reflection of what we believe about ourselves, the world, and God, than anything else that is said or done. The Master must have had this in mind when he said, "For where your treasure is, there will your heart be also."[3]

Some principles to remember in money management:
1. Live within your income.
2. Plan ahead.
3. Use credit properly and wisely.
4. Provide yourself with operating capital.
5. Set up reserves.
6. Develop good purchasing habits.
7. Determine your financial progress by periodic accounting.

Yearly Record Book. Many different types of record books have been prepared under the direction of the Presiding Bishopric and are available from Herald Publishing House to assist members in keeping financial records.

Teaching the Law

It is essential that prospective members be given an opportunity to understand the law of temporalities and to fulfill its requirements before, or immediately after, baptism. Those members of the church who have not rendered an accounting, paid tithing on their increase, or given their offering may lack understanding of the law. Patient efforts should be made to teach and win these members to complete obedience. Parents have the responsibility to teach their children the principles of life so that when they arrive at the age of accountability (eight years) they should then be making their steward-ship accounting and paying their tithing. Many children understand and wish to comply with this principle before they are eight years of age and actually begin their stewardship accounting earlier.

Children and young people may not have large in-comes, yet they should be given the opportunity to comply with the law to the full measure of their ability.

The church school should see that every child is grounded in the temporal law. Church school teachers should encourage the children to keep record books and make their stewardship accounting.

All priesthood members should feel responsible to the family in teaching children the temporal law and en-couraging parents to assist their children in making their stewardship accounting and paying their tithing. If we are to build soundly for the future of the church, we must see to it that the children of today are in-structed in the temporal law.

Program and Financial Resources

As a people called to participate in God's redemptive activity in the world, we come to understand that the "Stewardship of Temporalities" is that expression of Christian commitment in which life is lived out under the demands of faithfulness, wisdom, and temporal re-sponsibility.

Program and the Budgeting Process. This subject is more thoroughly covered in the *Leaders Handbook*, and priesthood members desiring greater detail regarding it should refer to that publication. However, it will be quite helpful for each priesthood member to understand the basics of the principles involved and the relationship between program and financial objectives, usually described as a budget. Priesthood members who have responsibilities as administrators or financial representatives will be particularly assisted by the following guidelines.

Planning ahead is a worthy objective for every jurisdiction as well as every individual involved in ministry. This involves time, talent, and treasure. A planning tool essential in every jurisdiction is the process of budgeting.

1. A budget is a financial expression of a program of ministry.
2. Program planning must always precede the development of the financial budget. These steps should be considered.
   a. Setting a budget based strictly on the prior years is not an adequate approach and does not reflect program evaluation.
   b. The program should be creative, imaginative, and challenging.
   c. Outline the program to be accomplished and establish priorities of the program.
   d. "Cost out" the various elements of the program.
   e. Relate program costs to anticipated financial capacity.
   f. The principle of increase and expansion should be evident in the budgeting process.

Communicating the Program and Needs for Human and Financial Resources

The total evangelistic thrust and the nurturing of moral and scriptural growth are dependent upon the diligent and skillful communication of the program and the commitment of the necessary human and financial resources to carry out the program.

The Commitment Enlistment Program is well established as an effective way of communicating the church program, both local and general, in enlisting the financial and human resources of persons in supporting the church program. In order to increase the level of commitment of church members to the total program of the church, this process needs to be supported by all priesthood members and promoted in all levels of church programming.

Resources prepared under the direction of the Presiding Bishopric are available through the Herald Publishing House.

NOTES

1. GCR No. 773.
2. Doctrine and Covenants 58:6d.
3. Matthew 6:21.

PART FIVE
HEADQUARTER'S
ORGANIZATIONAL
STRUCTURE,
INSTITUTIONS, AND
SPECIAL SERVICES

Chapter 1

HEADQUARTER'S ORGANIZATIONAL STRUCTURE

Ministerial Emphasis

Ministry is the heart of church administration. The church should be an extension of the revelation of God expressed in Jesus Christ. Its organizational forms and administrative procedures are designed to facilitate the witnessing, revealing, and redeeming ministry of the gospel.

The prophetic ministry of the church is centered in the First Presidency and the high priesthood. In a larger sense, the church as a whole is called to be prophetic.

Leadership in evangelism is centered in the Council of Twelve and Quorums of Seventy. However, all of the church is called to be a witnessing community.

Leadership in the management of temporal affairs is the function of the Presiding Bishopric and the Order of Bishops, but every church member is called upon to live the life of a good steward in all things.

Leadership in redemptive teaching and pastoral ministries requires presiding ministers. The church as a whole must live out redemptive teaching and shepherding ministry in the name of Christ.

Functional Emphasis

In response to a variety of human needs, the church

must adjust its ministerial function to minister at the place where people live. Since conditions in life change over the years, functions within the organization must be adjusted from time to time so as to focus on the persons needing such ministry.

Self-study must go on continually if the church is to use its resources in temporalities and persons effectively. Overlapping and ambiguous functions need to be eliminated while new opportunities to extend ministry must not only be met, but sought and anticipated.

Organizational Functions

Oversight of all of the programs of the church rests in the First Presidency. The First Presidency functions as a quorum. They identify policy issues and develop policy recommendations. This is done through broad consultation. The First Presidency refers certain matters to other quorums or to the Joint Council of the First Presidency, Council of Twelve, and Presiding Bishopric for counsel and advice. It should be remembered, however, that all major decisions of the First Presidency have either the explicit approval of the president or the implicit approval through the assignment of members of the First Presidency to their respective roles.

Counselors in the First Presidency are assigned responsibilities for administrative supervision of the presiding patriarch and the major areas of church management and operations. This frees the president to focus attention on overall coordination and other elements of the church-wide ministry.

Program Planning/Administrative Services Division

The Program Planning Section of this division identifies programs to be implemented throughout the church to interpret World Church objectives and goals. Various ministries are integrated into the total church program. The plans are submitted to the First Presidency for approval by the quorums and councils concerned and as required by the World Conference.

The Program Planning Section includes the following commissions:

The Research Commission: The Research Commission has been organized to plan, coordinate, and conduct all the research activities from the World Church headquarters. The commissioner, working within the Division of Program Planning/Administrative Services, assists all other headquarters divisions, commissions, and offices in designing and implementing various research projects. In addition to a variety of topics which come to the commission from time to time, there is an ongoing research program to help evaluate the progress of the program of the church at the congregation level. This includes the work on the Annual Data Reporting System. The commissioner also works with the First Presidency in the Faith to Grow award programs at the congregation level.

The Special Ministries Commission: This commission identifies the needs, interests, and abilities of specialized population groups. It recommends programs and resources to relate these needs and abilities to the work of the church. The commission studies special issues of concern to the church which otherwise would not be readily addressed in the established headquarters structure.

The Women's Ministries Commission: This commission is responsible for relating the needs and abilities of women to the total program of the church. Its work includes identifying the needs and concerns of women and ways by which women can effectively participate in the life of the church, consulting with field and headquarters officers regarding emphasis by and for women, recommending programs and resources to appropriate World Church divisions and participating in leadership training and development as requested by field and World Church officers.

The Zionic Community Commission: This commission studies the characteristics, concepts, and images of Zionic community life. On the basis of their study the commission recommends to the First Presidency development programs to increase Zionic relationships.

The Administrative Services Section of this division provides materials and procedures to support the administrative functions of World Church leadership and presiding officers in the field, with specific attention to providing assistance in the areas of health ministries, and ministerial recruitment, training, and placement. Basic statements of philosophy and procedure in these areas of concentration are prepared and presented to the First Presidency for review and approval by the Joint Council of the First Presidency, the Council of Twelve Apostles, and the Presiding Bishopric. When approved, they become the basis for consultation with field administrators and implementation through the normal line administration.

Specifically the Administrative Services Section includes the following commissions:

The Health Ministries Commission: The Health Ministries commissioner coordinates the church's health ministries in the field. The commission is made up of professional and lay volunteers in the various health disciplines. It is concerned with health education, training in hygiene, diet, and physical well-being, and specific programs related to clinics, ad hoc activities in areas of special need, and health evangelism. Its work includes the supervision, management, evaluation, and recommendation of appointee family health needs.

The Ministerial Personnel Commission: The Ministerial Personnel commissioner is responsible for developing policies and programs for ministerial personnel administration, including personnel planning, recruitment, job definition, performance appraisal, and recommendations to the Presiding Bishopric concerning compensation. He also serves as ombudsman/pastor to World Church Appointee Ministers and salaried staff executives and their families. The commissioner is also responsible for designing, installing, and operating systems and procedures for personnel administration.

A brokerage service is available to Level 3 and Level 2 jurisdictions to assist in selecting persons for staff functions and special ministries. The commissioner maintains a resource file from which selections may be made to meet the personnel needs at headquarters and in the field, either as volunteers or with church financial support in such categories as may be determined by policies developed by the Division of Program Planing/Administrative Services and approved by the Joint Council of First Presidency, Council of Twelve, and Presiding Bishopric.

The commissioner is responsible for recommendations for World Church Ministerial appointment. After recruitment, testing, and appraisal, recommendations concerning ministerial appointment are made to the division director who transmits these along with suggested assignments to the First Presidency with final approval given by the Joint Council of the First Presidency, Council of Twelve, and the Presiding Bishopric.

Temple School Division

The Temple School was established in 1974 at the initiative of the First Presidency and the approval of the World Conference to develop resources and supervise programs for the training of priesthood members and other leaders in the church. The document authorizing the organization of the Temple School emphasizes the partnership of study and faith in the learning process. Although such training and education may result in personal satisfaction and improvement, the basic purpose of Temple School programs is to enable ministry to others.

Basic Leadership Program: This program is designed to provide training for priesthood members and other leaders who serve in the local congregations. Specific series of courses are prepared for each priesthood office (elder, priest, teacher, and deacon) as well as for other leadership responsibilities. Each course is organized in a standard ten-hour form and may be taken through one of the numerous field schools conducted in the stakes, regions, districts, and congregations. Most courses are also available through home study. From time to time the Temple School also conducts leadership training schools at strategic centers such as Graceland or Park College.

Upon the successful completion of twelve courses in a planned program, students will receive the Temple School Certificate in Basic Leadership Studies.

Advanced Leadership Curriculum: In addition to the preceding program which focuses on the congregations, courses are also available for persons engaged in more general leadership roles. This program includes courses for high priests and seventies as well as for stake, region, and district leaders. New appointees assigned to advanced leadership and salaried staff executives working at headquarters or in the central stakes receive specialized training through this program.

For persons interested in pursuing studies at an advanced level in church administration, scripture, Restoration history, theology, church life and action, and worship, a certificate in Advanced Leadership Curriculum is offered upon the successful completion of ten units. These courses are offered in field schools where there is sufficient interest and through home study. For those who may be able to make suitable arrangements, advanced leadership curriculum courses are also offered in three-week sessions in Independence on a regular basis.

Leadership Training Field Services: With the assistance of field associates who have been appointed in each stake and region, Temple School assists local administrative officers in planning and conducting workshops or seminars to train local personnel in the skills and techniques of leadership.

Additional information or details regarding specific courses may be obtained by writing Temple School, the Auditorium, Box 1059, Independence, Missouri 64051. Announcements regarding new courses and special offerings in the field are also made through the *Saints Herald* and through the Temple School *Newsletter* sent periodically to local pastoral units.

The History Commission, World Church Library, Archives, and Museum are administratively a part of the

Temple School. The History Commission is responsible for the development of a records management program for World Church headquarters offices. An integral part of such a program, a records center, functions under the auspices of the History Commission.

As part of the commission's program, the church archivist's staff acquires, arranges, preserves, and catalogues documentary sources pertaining to church history. These sources (including letters, diaries, record books, photographs, and other institutional records) are then made accessible for research in the Library and Archives reading room at the Auditorium. Anybody wanting either to donate archival or manuscript materials, or to do research in such resources should call or write the church archivist, the Auditorium, Independence, Missouri.

The history of the church is more than the story of decisions made by the general officers or world conferences. It is in the various field jurisdictions that much of the vital history of the church transpires. Each administrative unit needs someone who intentionally preserves the corporate memory of that unit, compiling and sending in annual reports of the important trends and events of church life. A major function of the History Commission is to administer the church's program of writing and preserving the local history of the church in every place where the church is an organized, functioning body. Administrators at every level are encouraged to contact the History Commission if they wish to initiate the appointment of a jurisdictional historian to begin or resume the significant work of recording the history of a specific jurisdiction. On file in the commission office are guidelines for the various jurisdictional historians (mission, branch, congregation, metropole, stake, district, or region). These guidelines give specific instructions on what to report, how to go about it, and indicating the qualifications administrators should look for in recruiting persons for such a task.

Finally, the History Commission is a good place to write or call for help in addressing various kinds of questions arising in the study of church history. A knowledgeable, sensitive staff is ready and willing to respond to any sort of historical inquiry, and is glad to refer persons to further sources of information to strengthen the base of their inquiries.

Program Services Division

The Division of Program Services develops materials for the use of the congregations of the church. The personnel of this division are not involved in direct program implementation in field jurisdictions but provide resources and advisory service.

The Division of Program Services includes the following commissions and offices.

The Outreach Ministries Commission: This commission develops resources for ministry to those who are not members of the church. Included in the commission are the Missionary Office which provides resources for use in evangelism, and the Zionic Relations Office which provides resources for outreach in communities and other organizations.

The Christian Education Commission: This commission assists local workers in ministries to children, youth, and adults by providing resources for the church school, age-level groups, vacation church school, reunions, and other special educational settings.

The Worship Commission: This commission produces

resource materials for planning and conducting worship. The commission also produces music ministry such as *Messiah*, Auditorium Organ broadcasts, Auditorium Chorus, and music for the World Conferences.

The Pastoral Care Office produces resources that stress both preventive and redemptive ministries in the lives of persons and in families. Counseling programs, family and parenting workshop kits, crisis ministries, and numerous other "enabling" resources are produced by this office.

The Stewardship Office produces educational and motivational resources relating to good stewardship practices and principles. Emphasis is placed on developing a philosophy of stewardship over all the earth's resources including the development of talents and skills.

Division of Communication

The Communication Division provides for the efficient production of effective resources for use by the church. The dissemination of information and resources both internally and externally is also a concern of the division. The division generally does not provide direct program implementation but staff members are engaged in providing resources and advisory services.

The Communication Division consists of four areas— the Public Relations Commission, the Graphic Design Commission, the Electronic Media Commission, and the Resource Center.

The Public Relations Commission: This commission provides information about church leaders and staff, including photos and biographical data, as requested by local field jurisdictions. The commission also responds to requests for information about the church from the media and the general public. Media and promotional support for special events held at headquarters is also provided. Services to field jurisdictions include radio and television public service announcements and commercials, camera-ready newspaper ads, and workshops to develop communication skills both internally and externally for congregations and branches.

The Graphic Design Commission: This commission serves as a professional art studio providing a variety of visual services for the church including design, illustration, and photography for use with print materials and audiovisual projects, displays, and exhibits. Christian education graded resources, the *Leaders Handbook*, and *Commission* magazine are among the resources designed by the staff of this commission.

The Electronic Media Commission: This commission produces audiovisual resources for the World Church, its institutions, field jurisdictions, and other church-related organizations. The video periodical *Restoration: Today and Tomorrow* and radio broadcasts of the Auditorium Organ and Handel's *Messiah* are among the productions of this commission. Complete television studio and audio recording facilities are maintained in the Auditorium for use in headquarters productions.

The Resource Center: The Resource Center assists members in locating and obtaining a wide selection of resources for personal study as well as for use in congregational life. The center provides on a share-the-cost basis a vast number of electronic and film resources (videocassettes, 16mm films, audiotapes, records, filmstrips, slide sets, and kits). Resources are selected which will support and supplement World Church programs. A *Resource Directory* which lists all the collection and includes descriptions and ordering information is available on a subscription basis. The center can be reached at the Auditorium 816–833-1000, ext. 454, during working hours (Central Time). An after-hours answering service, 816–833-1014, is also provided to meet the needs of the membership.

In Summary

While the church has many functions which from time to time must be addressed in different ways, it tries to anticipate the needs of the people and provide the ministries appropriate to implementing the gospel in every situation. While the divisions set in the church to achieve these functions are very diverse, they are united and coordinated by the First Presidency who preside over the whole church.

Chapter 2

INSTITUTIONS AND SPECIAL SERVICES OF THE CHURCH

Introduction

The World Church is related to a number of institutions and special services that it promotes as a means of fulfilling its mission. Some of these are institutions which have their own corporate integrity and are administered by boards of trustees. Others are administered more directly by the church.

Those which relate most directly to the members of the local congregations are mentioned in this *Manual*. Priesthood members may receive personal assistance from some of these and may find other persons in their ministry who need the services of these institutions and special services.

Herald Publishing House

Herald House is the publishing division of the church. Management policy is vested in a Board of Publication selected at World Conference on recommendation of the Presiding Bishopric. The First Presidency are editors of all church publications and appoint their editorial assistants.

Purpose

For more than one hundred years the church's publishing endeavors have been aimed at instructing

315

leaders in the doctrine, programs, and goals of the church, and inspiring members to work toward fulfilling the purposes of the kingdom of God. This is accomplished through books, tracts, church school materials, manuals, magazines, and many miscellaneous publications and supplies.

Helps for You

Herald House is constantly engaged in a program to upgrade its publications—to meet the needs of our changing times. The following magazines will be of invaluable help to you in your ministry. The *Saints Herald*, published monthly, contains news, official anouncements, articles of an inspirational, informative, and educational nature, plus worship helps. *The Restoration Witness* is published bimonthly and contains missionary messages and testimonies for nonmembers.

The Herald House book steward program makes literature readily available in the local congregation while returning commissions to the church budget. The book steward's job is one of the most important in the congregation. It is an appointed position. Serious thought and consideration should be given to selecting a book steward. Please contact Herald House for more information.

How You Can Help

Each priesthood member should subscribe to the church magazines and encourage the congregation to participate in the Herald-in-Every-Home program which makes the *Herald* available to everyone in the congregation at a reduced price. It is particularly vital that all members, attending and nonattending, be kept informed of church news and other information. It has been found that nonattending members often are led to become active participants in the life of the congregation once more through the simple witness of the *Saints Herald* arriving in their homes.

Priesthood members should encourage others to keep up-to-date with new books, manuals, and other materials essential in church work. They should help spread the gospel by giving missionary materials to friends and helping promote the book steward program to the mutual benefit of both local and general church.

Book and supply catalogs listing church publications and church school curriculum and supplies (including descriptions and prices) are available on request. Write to Herald House, Box HH, Independence, MO 64055; Herald House Canada, 390 Speedvale Avenue East, Guelph, Ontario N1E 1N5.

Graceland College

Graceland College is a four-year liberal arts college sponsored by the church and accredited by the North Central Association of Colleges and Schools as a bachelor degree granting institution. Its teacher education program is accredited by the National Council of Accreditation for Teacher Education (NCATE). The nursing program is accredited by the National League for Nursing and Iowa Board of Nursing. It is governed by a board of trustees elected by the World Conference of the church. Cost of operation is financed through student tuition, World Conference appropriations, and special gifts and offerings.

Graceland offers over thirty major curricula and two special programs leading to a bachelor of arts or bachelor of science degree. During each summer, course work, seminars, and workshops are offered. Special programs frequently are provided. Every effort is made to assist students from junior colleges and other schools to transfer into Graceland's baccalaureate program in their junior or senior year.

The college attempts to develop a program aimed at helping young people receive an education in a wholesome social and academic environment. Graceland seeks to be a Christian-oriented community of learning. The college's religious heritage helps integrate the academic disciplines and campus life.

The college expects the student to possess requisite ability, preparation, and motivation. It is expected, too, that the faculty members will offer scholarly instruction reflecting a current understanding of their areas of competence and of its relation to other disciplines.

Graceland seeks to encourage commitment to a Christian purpose in life. At the same time it does not attempt to discourage the enrollment of students who do not share such convictions as long as such students respect the Christian commitments of their associates. The community seeks to broaden the vision as well as to refine the skills of all who attend. It attempts, then, to reaffirm the unity of the educational and the spiritual. It is hoped that this will help the students cope with the need to define their being in terms of usefulness to society while at the same time providing them with the ability to see their academic training as a prelude to, and not the end of, their contribution to society.

Park College

Park College was founded in 1875 as a Presbyterian-

318

related pioneer "work-college" in the liberal arts tradition and has been officially affiliated with the RLDS church since 1982. It is accredited by North Central Association of Colleges and Schools and offers course work leading to bachelor and master degrees with provisions for students to earn associate degrees and/or certificates in some programs.

The School of Arts and Sciences, located in Parkville, Missouri, enrolls primarily traditional, post-secondary-age resident and commuting students, but there is a mixture of differing cultures, races, ages, and religious backgrounds which enriches the students' educational and social experiences. There are special opportunities for outreach.

The School for Community Education is dedicated to serving learners wherever demonstrated need prevails with quality educational programs. The service is accomplished through its various off-campus components: (1) the Military Resident Center System which delivers degree completion programs on military installations throughout the United States, (2) the MetroPark program which serves part-time adult students in Metropolitan Kansas City, (3) the Portfolio Program, a nontraditional learning approach which focuses on serving people who are fully employed and who desire a degree completion program, and (4) special cooperative arrangements with businesses, agencies, etc.

The Center for Graduate Studies offers programs leading to masters' degrees in public affairs and religion. The MPA program is designed for upwardly mobile middle managers in government, business, and not-for-profit organizations. It is located at 934 Wyandotte in Kansas City with the MetroPark and Portfolio

319

portions of the School for Community Education.

The masters' of religion program has two concentrations: (1) religious leadership designed primarily for priesthood members and other church leaders, and (2) religious studies which provides advanced work in theology, Bible, and related social studies.

In addition, college credit may be earned for approved courses through the Temple School program, and persons of traditional college age to adults of all ages are encouraged to participate in this program.

Independence Sanitarium and Hospital

The Independence Sanitarium and Hospital is a church-sponsored institution governed by a board of trustees of twenty-three members, including representatives of the community served by the hospital. The following church officials make up the Corporate Body through whom the board membership is named.

1. The three members of the First Presidency
2. The three members of the Presiding Bishopric
3. The commissioner of Health Ministries

The first patients were admitted to the hospital in October 1909. Through the years, the hospital has grown to be a 337-bed institution with more than 1,000 employees. In addition to acute care and emergency care, the hospital provides clinical facilities in radiology, laboratory, electrocardiography, electroencephalography, respiratory therapy, occupational therapy, and rehabilitation therapy.

Specialized services available include Oncology Unit, Cardiac Cath Lab, Extended Care, Outpatient Surgery, Pain Management Center, Alternative Birthing Center, 24-hour Maternity Stay, Behavioral Development Center, and Drug/Alcohol Rehabilitation. Specialized services for the elderly are provided through the Community Assistance Services. Multiple health-related wellness sessions for businesses and community are available through HealthLine.

Graceland College is affiliated with the Independence Sanitarium and Hospital. The hospital provides clinical experience for students in Graceland's baccalaureate degree program in professional nursing.

Classes related to the following programs are also facilitated through the San:

1. Jennie Lund School of Practical Nursing—a one-year program in practical nursing
2. Surgical Technologist Program—a one-year program
3. Nursing Assistant in Acute and Long-Term Care—a six-week program
4. Unit Clerk—a five-week program
5. Medical Terminology—a 20-hour program
6. Medication Technician—a 48-hour program
7. IV Therapy for LPN—a 48-hour program
8. X-ray Technician School—a two-year program

Information about these educational programs may be secured by writing to the Health Occupations Department, Independence Sanitarium and Hospital.

Resthaven

Resthaven is sponsored and operated by the church as a service to elderly persons in harmony with the social ideals and principles accepted by the church. It is primarily a home which has been planned to offer comfort, protection, and care to its residents who have retired from active business or professional life, from domestic responsibilities, or who may be in need of special ministry.

It is administered by the Presiding Bishopric as a part of the function of the oblation fund.

The elderly persons who live here find comfort, security, and freedom from worry about their physical care. They find privacy and rest in their rooms, religious atmosphere, friendships, and companionship in the general living areas, and occupations in the hobby room. They have medical care as needed. They also have access to the services and conveniences of the city and at the same time a peaceful retreat from the rush and turmoil of the business world.

Charges for care are determined by the amount of care needed. It is anticipated that the rate will be paid by the person or the family, but the inability of a person to pay for his or her care does not bar entrance to Resthaven, as need is the determining factor for admittance among the members of the church.

For information concerning Resthaven, direct correspondence to Resthaven, Attention of the Administrator, 1500 West Truman Road, Independence, Missouri 64050.

Pacific Haven Convalescent Home

The Pacific Haven Convalescent Home is located in Garden Grove, California. It is sponsored and operated by the church as a service to elderly persons and maintains a social atmosphere in harmony with the principles accepted by the church. The facility is licensed for a capacity of ninety-nine persons as a Skilled Nursing Facility (SNF) in the state of California. The home is held and operated by a wholly owned church corporation known as the Casa Real Retirement Center, Inc. The Board of Directors for the corporation is appointed by the Presiding Bishopric and has responsibility for the operation of Pacific Haven Convalescent Home. For further information direct correspondence to Pacific Haven Convalescent Home, Attention of the Administrator, 12072 Trask Avenue, Garden Grove, California 92643.

Elbert A. Smith Retirement Center, Inc.

The Elbert A. Smith Retirement Center was established by the Presiding Bishopric for the purpose of providing additional services to those members of the church who have reached a certain age and desire to live independently in an apartment type living setting. The center is established under the continuing care concept which provides for life occupancy privileges and includes nursing home care when needed. The center is in close proximity to the Independence Sanitarium and Hospital and Resthaven Nursing Home. For information concerning the center, please write to Elbert A. Smith Retirement Center, Inc., 1500 West Truman Road, Independence, Missouri 64050.

How You Can Help

You can best serve the elderly persons by informing the members of your congregation of the program and objectives of the church and by encouraging them to comply faithfully with the law of stewardship, including the giving of their oblation offerings. The care of the elderly is an area of ministry which will require the continuing development of more facilities, so your financial help is always needed.

323

INDEX

A

Aaronic priesthood, 42; function of, 52-54; history of, 53, 54; bishopric preside over, 54.

Accountability of priesthood, 18, 29; to administrative officers, 37, 68, 69, 132-137.

Administration to the sick, 237-242; what is administration? 237; calling of elders, 238; preparation for, 238, 239; anointing the sick, 239; prayer of petition, 239; use of consecrated olive oil, 239, 240; use of hands in, 240; length of the call, 240, 241; prohibitions against prescribing treatment, 241; cleanliness of ministers, 241; contagious diseases, 241; administering to nonmembers, 241.

Appointment, 31, 75-79; family allowance, 77, 78; elders' expense, 77; procedure for appointment, 78-80.

Armed forces, 204-212; serving in the armed forces, 204, 205; church's stand on military service, 206; conscientious objection to military service, 206, 207; exemption from military service, 207, 208; serving in armed forces chaplaincy, 208-210; church's program of ministry to, 210, 211.

Attendance, church, 71, 72.

Authority of priesthood, 22-31; legal, 23-25; not limited to priesthood, 25; moral, 25, 26; spiritual, 26, 27; of competence, 27, 28; Joseph Smith statement on, 30, 31.

B

Baptismal service, 220-227; theology of baptism, 220-223; baptism in water, 223, 224; prerequisites for, 224; mode of, 224-226; order of service for, 226.

Bishop's agents, 91, 92, 105, 110.

Blessing of children, 243-245; significance of, 243; eligibility of, 243; conducting the service, 243, 244; arranging the service, 244, 245; follow-up ministry, 245.

Branches, 113-122; organization of, 113, 114; disorganization, 113, 114; names, 114; should not set by-laws, 114; president, 114, 115; business meetings, 115; election of officers, 116; secretary, 116; treasurer, 116, 117; church school director, 117; women's leader, 117; youth leader, 117; music director, 117, 118; solicitor, 118; recorder, 118, 119; historian, 119; deacon in charge, 119, 120; publicity agent, 120; priesthood education, 121.

C

Calls to priesthood, 124-131; ministerial dimension to all of life, 12, 13, 32-34, 38-43; sources of, 14, 124-127; consent of church members, 23, 30, 126, 127, 246; role of church in, 28, 29; those called to observe financial law, 46, 47; to high priesthood, 126; to First Presidency, Council of Twelve, and Presiding Bishopric, 126, 127; to Order of Bishops, 127; to Order of Evangelists, 127; to Seventy, 127; in unorganized areas, 127, 128; approaching calls originating in stakes, 128; approaching the candidate about a 130, 131.

Community relationships, 65, 66.

Confirmation service, 228-231; significance of, 228; conducting the, 228; prayer of confirmation, 229, 230; arranging the service, 230; follow-up ministry, 230, 231.

Conservatism, 67, 68.

Contractual assignees, 80-81; retired persons, 79; two-year, 80, 81; specific term, 81.

Council of Twelve, 44, 45; to regulate affairs of church, 44; chief missionary quorum, 44.

Courts, church, 85, 86; elders, 85; bishops, 86; stake high councils, 85; Standing High Council, 85, 86; actions, 86.

Covenant relationship of priesthood, 15, 16.

D

Deacon, duties of, 58-60.

District conferences, 106-109; order of proceedings, 106; special, 107; right to vote, 107, 108; representation at, 107; notice of, 108; nominations to elective offices, 108-111; appointive offices, 108, 109; secretary, 109; treasurer, 109, 112; director of Christian education, 109; women's leader, 109, 110; youth leader, 110; bishop's agent, 110; music director, 110; historian, 110; recorder, 110; departmental leaders, 111; boundary line changes, 112; budgets, 112.

Districts, 102-106; purpose of, 102, 103; presidency, 103, 104; president's files, 104, 105; bishops and bishop's agents, 105, 106; departmental officers, 106.

E

Education and growth, 17, 18, 37, 38, 41, 70, 71, 97, 121.

Ethics in church administration, 68, 69.

Ethics of priesthood, 62-73; basic, 62, 63; character of the ordained, 63, 64, 69, 70; in the home, 64, 65; in the community, 65, 66; in devotional life, 69; or preparation, 70, 71; financial responsibility, 72, 73.

F

Financial law, obedience to, 46, 47, 72, 73.

First Presidency, role of, 43, 44, 305, 306; presides over High Council, 44.

Funeral service, 191-203; significance of, 191; pastoral ministry at time of death, 192; the bier, 193, 194; preparing for, 194, 195; preparing obituary, 196, 197; funeral sermon, 197, 198; scripture for, 198; fraternal and military organizations, 198-200; graveside service and committal, 200, 201; follow-up ministry, 202; characteristics of the bereaved 202, 203.

G

Gathering, the, 292, 293.

General responsibilities of priesthood, 46, 47; characteristics and duties of all, 50-60; general administrative relationships, 68, 69.

Government of church through priesthood, 47-49; high priests as presiding officers, 47-49; priests, teachers, and deacons may preside over branch, 114; ethics in administrative procedure, 68, 69; Melchisedec priesthood hold right of presidency, 74.

Grace, priesthood witness of, 16, 17.

Groups, 120.

H

Headquarters, organizational structure, 305-316; ministerial emphasis, 305; functional organization, 305, 306; First Presidency, 306; Program Planning–Administrative Services Division, 306-310; Temple School Division, 310-313; Program Services Division, 313, 314; Division of Communication, 314-316.

Home Ministry, 172-183; role of, 172, 173; purpose of 174-176; family relationships, 176, 177; criteria for spiritual health and outreach, 177-179; who performs, 179, 180; preparation for, 180, 181; making priesthood calls, 181; reporting priesthood calls, 181, 182.

I

Institutions and special services, 317-325; Herald House, 317-319; Graceland College, 319, 320; Park College, 320-322; Independence Sanitarium and Hospital, 322, 323; Resthaven, 323, 324; Pacific Haven Convalescent Home, 324, 325; Elbert A. Smith Retirement Center, Inc., 325; Judicial procedure, 85, 86.

L

Legislative assemblies, 82-84; initiating legislation, 84.
Liberalism, 67, 68.

M

Marriage Counseling, 273-280; priesthood ministry to families, 273, 274; pastoral care, 274, 275; in times of crisis, 275-277; referral, 277-280.
Marriage, sacrament of, 249-271; basic belief about, 249-251; sacramental character of, 251-256; re-
marriage after divorce, 255, 256; premarital counseling, 257, 258; planning wedding service, 258-261; elements of wedding ceremony, 261-266; wedding rehearsal, 266, 267; sample wedding ceremonies, 267-271.
Melchisedec priesthood, 47-52; high priesthood is basic Melchisedec office, 47, 48; priesthood officers in high priesthood, 47, 48; duties of elder, 50-52; holds right of presidency, 74.
Mission organization, 120, 121.

O

Oblation, 295.
Ordinances and sacraments, 214-219; nature of, 214-217; preparation for, 217, 218; reporting, 218.
Ordination, 29, 30, 246-248; significance of, 246; preordination orientation, 246; conducting the, 247; prayer of, 247; arranging the service, 247, 248; of women, 32-40; follow-up ministry, 40, 248.
Organization of church, 43-46; 86-122; 305-316; terms of appointee assignment 75-78; stake, 86-98; region, 99-102; district, 102-113; branch, 113-122; mission, 120, 121; Program Planning–Administrative Services Division, 306-310; Temple School Division, 310-313; Program Services Division, 313, 314; Division of Communication, 314-316.

P

Pastoral Function, 20.
Patriarchal blessing, 281, 282.
Prayer service, 165-171; nature and purpose of, 165, 166; prayer service singing, 166, 167, 168, pastoral welcome, 167; scripture

reading, 168; theme talk for, 168; prayers in, 168, 169; testimonies in, 169; participation in 170, 171.

Preaching, 154-164; elements of, 154-159; preparation for, 159, 160; types of sermons, 160, 161; sermon preparation, 161-163; sermon delivery, 163, 164; funeral sermon, 197, 198.

Presiding bishopric, 46; functions of, 46.

Priest, duties of, 55, 56; qualities of, 56.

Puritanical extremism, 66, 67.

Purpose of priesthood, 14, 15; Joseph III statement on, 30, 31.

R

Regions, 99-102; definition of, 99; presidents and administrators, 99-101; bishops and treasurers, 101, 102.

Restoration of priesthood licenses, 136, 137.

S

Sacrament of the Lord's Supper, 232-236; significance of, 232, 233; preparation for, 233, 234; blessing of bread and wine, 234, 235; serving of bread and wine, 235; taking sacrament to sick and shut-ins, 236.

Seventy, 45; specialized function of, 45; seven quorums of, 45; presidents of, 45; in stakes, 88.

Silencing priesthood, 23, 24, 29 134-137; procedures in priesthood silences, 134-136; appeals from priesthood silences, 135, 136.

Solicitors, 91, 105, 110, 118.

Spiritual gifts, 26, 27.

Spiritual power of the priesthood, 18.

Stakes, 86-98; organization of, 86-88; presidency, 87; high councils,

87, 88; bishopric, 89-91; congregation, 92; bishop's agents, 91, 92; disorganization of congregation, 92, 93; conference, 93, 94; right to vote, 94, 95; nominations to elect officers, 95; appointment of officers, 95, 96; departmental officers, 96; congregational recorder, 96, 97; priesthood education, 97; reports to presiding officers, 98; terminology, 98.

Standing ministry, 74, 75.

Stewardship of temporalities, 284-303; basics of Restoration stewardship, 285, 286; God is owner, 286; doctrine of agency, 287; accountability, 287, 288; increase, 288-291; tithing, 291; inheritance, 292; the gathering, 292, 293; storehouse, 293-295; oblation, 295; response, 298-300; teaching financial law, 300, 301.

Storehouse, 293-295.

T

Teacher, duties of, 56-58.

Teaching, function, 20.

Tithing, 291.

V

Visiting the ill, 184-190.

W

Women, ordination of, 32-40

Worship, 139-153; characteristics of 139-141; elements of, 141-144; order of, 144; forms of, 144, 145; leadership in, 145, 146; planning services of, 146, 147; informal, 147; physical arrangements for, 147, 148; preparation for, 148, 149; ordinances and sacraments, 214-219.

Appendix A

Guidelines for Priesthood:

ORDINATION
PREPARATION
CONTINUING COMMITMENT

January 1985

Appendix A

Guidelines for Priesthood

ORDINATION
PREPARATION
ONGOING COMMITMENT

Table of Contents

Page

INTRODUCTION 5

I Perspectives on Priesthood Development........7

II Authority of the Priesthood.................18

III Organization of the Priesthood...............21

IV The Pastor and Calls to the Priesthood........24

Recommendation for Ordination Form........51

V Priesthood and Education...................54

Flow Chart for Processing Priesthood Calls....60

VI Giftedness and Calling.....................61

Definition of Terms........................61

VII Priesthood Review........................64

Flow Chart for Use of Priesthood Forms.......72

Priesthood Review Forms and
Sample Letters......................73–79

Plan for Service, for Deacon, Teacher,
Priest, or Elder.......................80–92

VIII Timeline for the Introduction of
Priesthood Policies......................93

Introduction

For some years the church leaders have felt a growing need for further clarification of the seriousness of priesthood and divine call. Many who have been ordained have indeed magnified their call, and they have been an inspiration to all of us. But there has also been a growing concern, both on the part of ministers and those who receive ministry, to enhance the effectiveness and commitment of our priesthood.

The revelation contained in Section 156 of the Doctrine and Covenants not only authorized the ordination of women — a most significant milestone in the history of the church — but it also called on the "proper administrative officers...to determine the continuing nature" of the commitment of priesthood members to their calling.

This booklet, *Guidelines for Priesthood: Ordination, Preparation, Continuing Commitment,* is the product of the labors of a committee appointed by the First Presidency, as reviewed by field administrators and by the Joint Council of the First Presidency, the Council of Twelve, and the Presiding Bishopric. It is intended to assist administrators and priesthood members in their responsible roles of ministry. A Temple School course of instruction based on this booklet is designed to educate leaders and priesthood in all aspects of the material included. Interested persons are urged to take advantage of this excellent training.

For the most part, these guidelines restate and support the concepts of priesthood which have long been with the church. However, in keeping with the divine instruction, the committee has suggested somewhat different approaches to the ministerial task in the following

5

areas: a priesthood review and commitment program, expectations of preordination and continuing education, a modified definition of "setting apart," and a modified Recommendation for Ordination form.

The committee selected by the First Presidency has labored diligently in preparing the contents of this study. We commend them for their service, and recommend the fruits of their labors for all priesthood members who are truly serious about their commitment to God and to ministry in Christ's name.

The First Presidency

I

Perspectives on Priesthood Development

Our religious heritage, continued in the church today, affirms the creative acts of God intervening in human history, calling persons and communities into being. From Abraham in Ur of the Chaldees to World Conference 1984, God has continued to work in the world to effect divine purposes. The form of the call of God to persons changes with the conditions of the world in which those persons live: from the burning bush to the still small voice of inspiration given a local pastor. The relatively simple organization of the first Christian community has developed, under divine direction, into the more comprehensive structures through which the ministries of the church have met human needs in each generation.

God issues the call in various ways and to a variety of persons. However, the call and the cause for which those called are sent does not change. In that which follows, some perspectives are offered concerning the call to priesthood. These perspectives offer the testimony of the constant, unchanging call of God to assist in the reconciling ministries for which priesthood are sent. They comment on the ways this constant call has been handled in the varied communities of disciples which have been the church throughout the ages.

At the center of Christianity stands the person of

Christ, the Word that became flesh. He was born in fulfillment of prophecy; he was the promised Messiah. His mission was redemptive and his message, the good news of the gospel, was the transformation of persons through love:

Thou shalt love the Lord thy God with all thy heart, and with all thy soul, and with all thy mind. This is the first and great commandment. And the second is like unto it; Thou shalt love thy neighbor as thyself. On these two commandments hang all the law and the prophets. — Matthew 22:36-38

It was the church's twofold mission to respond to the Divine and to the human that was central. The effective interrelationship of these two, through love, is at the heart of the Christian gospel.

How did Christ go about spreading the gospel of the kingdom? Beyond choosing twelve apostles, did Christ establish a church and institute a priesthood structure? These questions have been of particular importance to the Restoration movement.

The gospels, in delineating the work of Christ, deal not so much with how as with why. The account is testimonial. For that reason, as Arthur Oakman has said, "The New Testament is not a textbook in church organization." Certainly there are hints of developing structure but no definitive statement. What we do get is the spiritual conviction of the divinity of Christ. Christ tested that conviction in a question to his disciples, "Whom do men say that I, the Son of Man, am?" The question became more specific, "But whom say *ye* that I am?" Peter's answer, "Thou art the Christ, the Son of the living God," finds confirmation in the hearts of all those through the ages who have been similarly touched by the presence of the Divine. The conviction comes not through "flesh and blood" but through "my Father who is in heaven" (Matthew 16:14-18). Thus the physical presence of Christ takes secondary importance to his spiritual presence. It is that central experience that leads to the vision of the kingdom of God and of which the gospels most urgently wish to testify. Christ presented his followers with a choice: for or against the kingdom of God.

It is significant that as Jesus began his earthly ministry he called unto himself twelve "apostles" who lived and worked with him. It was to them he entrusted the continuance of his message.

And Jesus came and spake unto them, saying, All power is given unto me in heaven and in earth. Go ye therefore, and teach all nations, baptizing them in the name of the Father, and of the Son, and of the Holy Ghost. — Matthew 28:17, 18

To be apostolic was one of the gifts of the Spirit given to the church. The office of apostle was bestowed on those whose commitments and receptiveness to the Divine qualified them for this special calling. The apostles symbolized the pervasive power of witness inherent in the total fellowship of the church. It was in this sense that Paul wrote:

And God hath set some in the church, first apostles, secondarily prophets, thirdly teachers, after that miracles, then gifts of healings, helps, governments, diversities of tongues. — I Corinthians 12:28

The fact that apostleship stands first in this list is indicative of its importance. The church was true to its apostolic calling as its members bore witness of God's presence in their lives. That call through the movement of centuries has not changed. The call to membership, to go forth in power, is still the most significant call that any of us can receive. As F. Henry Edwards has written,

There is a sense in which all members of the church are ministers. The New Testament evidences nothing of any restriction of the truth to any inner circle of the specially elect. The glory of the apostolic church was that "from the least to the greatest" all might know "the unsearchable riches of Christ" (Ephesians 3:8)....We sometimes forget this basic "priesthood of all believers."...This principle of our common priesthood has been re-enunciated in this present dispensation in the instruction that "all are called according to the gifts of God unto them" (Doctrine and Covenants 119:8b). This call to sainthood is a call to ministry in a general but very important sense, so there is nothing strange in the references in modern revelation to "the office of member" (Doctrine and Covenants 104:5). — F. Henry Edwards, *Authority and Spiritual Power,* (Independence, Missouri: Herald House, 1956), 21.

The early Christian church, which included the apostle Paul, was more concerned with ministry offered than with particular ministerial office. Ministry is at the heart of the gospel. Jesus said, "I am come that they might have life, and that they might have it more abundantly" (John 10:10). And "whosoever will be great among you, let him be your minister....Even as the Son of Man came, not to be ministered unto, but to minister; and to give his life a ransom for many" (Matthew 20:26, 28). By example as well as by teaching, the Master established the "good news" of his mission among us to be a life of ministry for the sake of others. This mission was shared with his disciples in that early day, and has been the legacy of the disciples of all ages. The role of servant as portrayed so marvelously by Jesus himself stands forth indelibly written on the pages of human history. And each person whose life has ever been touched by the hand of the Master has at the same instant of healing felt the gentle encouragement to "go, and do likewise" (Luke 10:38).

The call to be witnesses of the gospel was a call to all, however lowly or exalted, to be transformed through love. It was a call to receive the gospel, to live the gospel, to be the gospel, for the sake of others. But most significantly it came not as a commission only, but with a divine assurance: "And lo, I am with you always, unto the end of the world" (Matthew 28:19). Ministry was to be done in the name of Christ and in the spirit of Christ. This promise guaranteed that the Lord would be with the servant as the ministerial task was being fulfilled. It was in response to the ministry of the Holy Spirit, Jesus' gift to the disciples as Comforter in his stead, that their call and commission came — and it was this self-same Spirit who would guide them in what they were to remember, say, and do.

One's life now found a meaning and purpose that had its origins in the love of God, extended most graciously without design of personal gain on the part of the Giver. That meaning was fulfilled in one's giving of oneself, in that same spirit, graciously and lovingly. Ministry came by the Holy Spirit, and it was to be given in response to that same Spirit. No one was beyond the reach of the grace of such a loving God. God was indeed no respecter of persons, and therefore all were loved, redeemed, and called to the task. It might have been the Samaritan of Jesus' parable, or the woman at the well, or even a persecutor of God's people, like Saul of Tarsus. Yet all could testify of God's love and gracious acceptance, of Jesus' healing ministry, and of the unmistakable call that came to them through that experience with the Lord. They, too, were called to serve.

Since the disciples of the Messiah were Jews, they for a time followed Jewish law and custom. In the beginning they had comparatively little institutional identity of their own. Worship in the temple was usual, though the followers of Christ often gathered for "love feasts," the breaking of bread together, and the sharing of the amazing new power that had touched their lives. Informality characterized the nature of their meetings, with no great necessity for detailed organization. Originally they were still Jews who practiced Judaism, but with the understanding that the hoped-for Messiah had indeed come.

Eventually, not all drawn to this new movement were Jews. Disputes arose over Jewish law between the Jews and the so-called Hellenists (non-Jewish Greeks). Congregations split on the issue of whether circumcision, for instance, was required of non-Jewish Christians. Jerusalem remained predominantly Jewish — Antioch predominantly Greek. Paul came into conflict with Peter and the "circumcision party" over what aspects of Jewish law were to be invoked. For a while Paul's whole credibility as a minister was at stake. Sometimes one group tried to undermine the other. Paul preached one way, but the Judaizers came after him (as in Galatia) and preached another way. Needless to say, that disturbed Paul. Great issues were at stake and change did not come easily. The process was both difficult and painful, particularly for those who had known Jesus in person. The feeling of "we know better than you" was hard to overcome. It required a humility in the face of changing circumstances. That is always difficult for those who are committed to a perceived truth that is limited. Eventually, congregations became Christian and lost their specific Jewish affiliation.

In all of this we see institutional forms changing to meet the needs of the people. Structure as such was not sacrosanct in the early Christian church. The admonition, "Rise up and experiment upon my word" finds practical expression as these early pioneers in the Christian way tried to find the means of most effectively incorporating and spreading the Christian message. Increasingly, the original, fairly loose structure of the Christian congregations was replaced by one more highly organized. While the early New Testament church was Spirit-directed, and led by gifted people who freely used their giftedness without restrictions of polity and hierarchy, the church soon had to deal with the problems of a growing institution.

First, there were distinctively different kinds of roles for the leadership in the early Christian church as compared with the practices of Judaism. The Old Testament reveals a priesthood which stood between God and humanity, but the New Testament describes leaders who were from among the people and who stood with them. It has been a problem historically for Christian churches to determine which of these two traditions they would prefer to institutionalize in their own experience. Some appear to be primarily oriented toward the Old Testament intermediary model for priesthood; the New Testament servant role is the preferred model for others. Such issues had to be faced by the first century church as well.

Second, priesthood was a division of labor and it emerged out of need. Each congregation developed the structure that best suited its particular situation. For example, the sixth chapter of Acts records the calling of seven "men of honest report, full of the Holy Ghost and wisdom," who were subsequently ordained by the apostles. They were called as a response to specific needs in the growing church: "In those days, when the number of the disciples was multiplied, there arose a murmuring of the Grecians against the Hebrews, because their widows were neglected in the daily ministration" to their temporal needs. The twelve said to the disciples,

It is not reason that we should leave the word of God, and serve tables. Wherefore, brethren, look ye out among you seven men of honest report, full of the Holy Ghost and wisdom, whom we may appoint over this business. But we will give ourselves continually to prayer, and to the ministry of the word. — Acts 6:1-4

A third illustration of forms developing in response to need is seen in the role of congregational leader. The "overseer" or presiding officer of a congregation was one of the first to be designated. Very soon problems arose over terminology, a debate that was to have repercussions for centuries to come. To acknowledge the truth of the situation, we need only to be aware that the very names used to identify the priesthood roles were themselves functionally descriptive. For example, the term *deacon* comes from the greek word *DIAKONOS* which means *servant*. The term *bishop* comes from the Greek word *EPISKOPOS*, which means *overseer*. The term *apostle* comes from the word *APOSTOLOS* which means *messenger*, or "those who are sent."

Because the term *elders* was applied in Judaism to those who were the traditional overseers of the Jewish communities, it was a simple matter for the Christian congregations which came from Jewish origins to accept a similar terminology for similar functions. However, other congregations began to use the term *bishop* for the ones who presided over their groups. This is reflected in the record of the twentieth chapter of Acts, when Paul called the elders of Ephesus together (verse 17). To these leaders he said, "Take heed therefore unto yourselves, and to all the flock, over the which the Holy Ghost hath made you overseers" (verse 28). The word *overseers* in this text represents the only time in the New Testament that the King James scholars translated *EPISKOPOS* to read *overseer* rather than *bishop*, as was done on the other four occasions where the same word appears.

In early times there was a natural confusion of roles and functions and titles of offices, due in part to communication difficulties, and in part to the practical necessities of congregations having to see to the effective carrying out of needed ministries. Organization and systematic consistency could and did come later.

By the time of the Puritan revolution in England in the seventeenth century these terms had taken on a life of their own. Among the many sects that developed, church government was a major issue. Should the church be governed by an episcopus or bishop like the Anglicans, by a presbyter (elder) like the Presbyterians, or should the determination be by individual congregations as the Congregationalist? The subject was not to be treated lightly, and it obviously gained momentum through time.

In the tradition of the Restoration movement, however, a form of priesthood emerged in response to divine guidance and initiation. This consisted of unfolding revelatory experiences expressed in offices and duties, which have continued to inform us in our theology of priesthood.

The rise of the church of Christ in these last days, . . . by the will and commandments of God . . . which commandments were given to Joseph Smith, Jr., who was called of God and ordained an apostle of Jesus Christ, to be the first elder of this church. — Doctrine and Covenants 17:1a

To say that structure was a gradual development in the early congregations and that priesthood office did not in practice emerge full-blown is not to underrate its importance. Divine involvement and commission are present everywhere. Whether it be Joseph Smith who is called to be a first elder and apostle, or Saul of Tarsus who wrote that he was "an apostle not of men, neither by men, but by Jesus Christ, and God the Father," no one may simply seek such an honor of responsibility, but must be "called of God as was Aaron." As F. Henry Edwards noted:

It is impossible to overemphasize the importance of the divine element in the sending forth of the priesthood. When God wanted John to preach and baptize he called him and sent him to do that work. . . . When he wanted a special group of forerunners to prepare the way before him, he called the seventy . . . (Luke 10:1–3). When he wanted Paul and Barnabas he called them by the Holy Spirit . . . (Acts 13:3, 4). When he wanted elders to guide the church at Ephesus, he called them by the Spirit and set them in their places (Acts 20:28). — Edwards, p. 23

The culmination of such a call comes in the rite of ordination. "The primary value of ordination is that it makes clear that the authority of the minister is not his own" (Edwards, p. 24). Once the ordained has accepted the call, the individual is truly the servant of the Divine engaged in a special mission. As a representative of the Divine each has access to divine empowerment as long as Christ is at the center of life. "But as many as received him, to them gave he power to become the sons of God" (John 1:12). The special empowerment that comes with ordination is for the purpose of ministry. It is an apostolic call to special function, not just within the church structure but to society at large.

The call that comes to the contemporary church is to effectively combine the ecclesia — the calling forth of each member — with priesthood structure. The particular joy and power that accompany the beginnings of a movement can easily be lost and bogged down in ritual and habit. We forget what it means to be firsthand Christians and become second- or thirdhand Christians. The Restoration was, among other things, a restorer of revelatory power, of renewed recognition of the importance of the Divine-human encounter. Such restoration, as we have seen, is always related to ministry. It is to be restorers in the sense President Smith enunciated in his keynote sermon to the 1984 World Conference:

Who will be the restorers? Are people willing to live close enough to the teachings of Jesus that their faith will become a compelling and powerful testimony of what true love, radical love, can really do? This is what restoration means to me—a willingness to build and heal and reconcile.—Wallace B. Smith, "Draw Near with a True Heart," *Saints Herald,* May 1, 1984, p. 19.

In effective group activity, however, some have to be leaders, to point direction, to channel energies, to make certain that all facets of the work receive attention. For these purposes priesthood is essential. In addition to the general call to all members comes a divine choice for specialized ministry. Such choice is in fulfillment of need, a Divine-human recognition of work to be done. It was such a divine initiative that sent Christ. As he was sent, so in turn he sent his disciples. "As my Father hath sent me, even so send I you" (John 20:21).

Priesthood ministry, though specialized, does not replace the call to membership, to be firsthand Christians in the most complete sense. The challenge to the contemporary church is to not let the original dynamic encounter of the movement fade and be lost in the prerogatives of office or in careless neglect of the individual right to the grace of God. To combine ecclesia with structure, to know doctrine not as lifeless dogma but as love and power, is true restoration. The attempt to slavishly follow perceived structure of an earlier time and to forget that structure follows function is to lose our opportunity of ministry. To be both in the world and not of it requires understandings of sociological and historical dynamics as well as the eternal purposes of the Divine. To be sensitive to this interrelationship and to meet its challenge has always been the call of the Christian church.

Surely this is the call to a prophetic church—one for which every member has a responsibility. Indeed the early Christian church has a major lesson to teach us which finds its expression here. Specific congregational or priesthood structures will, though important, be secondary to making the places we each occupy shine as Zion, the redeemed of the Lord.

Helpful Materials

Supplementary readings for the course, *Nature and Mission of the Church,* Temple School, Basic Orientation Program, August 1980.

Ernst Kasemann, *Essays on New Testament Themes,* Studies in Biblical Theology, First Series (London: SCM Press LTD, 1964).

II

Authority of the Priesthood

The concise statement in Hebrews may summarize best the several elements that combine in defining the authoritative priesthood relationship. Although explicitly applying to high priests, the principles apply to all priesthood. As the letter to the Hebrews states:

For every high priest taken from among men is ordained for men in things pertaining to God, that he may offer both gifts and sacrifices for sins; who can have compassion on the ignorant, and on them that are out of the way; for that he himself also is compassed with infirmity. And by reason thereof he ought, as for the people, so also for himself to offer for sins. And no man taketh this honor unto himself, but he that is called of God, as was Aaron. — Hebrews 5:1-4

The authority to act is from the call of God which was discussed in the previous section. This call is not simply self-understood and asserted, but expressed through others called to act in relation to God. The ones called are to act for others. These others must accept the call as valid if the ordinands are to act for them. The ordinands are not super persons, nor must they be perfect. Rather they are called to be gentle and compassionate, for those they serve will be fully aware of their weaknesses.

The key principles found here and applied in the Restoration movement's practices are as follows:

First, calls to priesthood are perceived by appropriate administrative officers, themselves priesthood called of God. Not just one such officer but at least another must bear testimony of the witness of the Holy Spirit in each call in order for there to be reasonable assurance of the genuineness of this foundational element in priesthood authority.

Second, while weakness will be found in the life of every person called, very private but reasonably comprehensive inquiry is made to assure that the life of each person called is in harmony with the teachings and practices of the church — the body that person shall serve.

Third, with appropriate assurance of the authenticity of the call and the acceptable quality of life, the person is advised of the call and given opportunity to express willingness to serve. Often the Holy Spirit blesses that person with an independent testimony of God's call to him or her, which is very reassuring. Others respond in faith to the general commitment they have made to serve the Lord to the best of their ability. Either response, from knowledge or faith, is an acceptable response of the individual disciple.

Fourth, after the call, examination, and affirmative response from the individual have occurred, the determination of the acceptance by the people is sought. This is best determined by vote of a conference of the congregation and/or jurisdiction of the church having knowledge of the individual. In cases where the church is not yet planted or sufficiently organized to have a conference, an apostle may act to express the acceptance of the candidate by the church.

Fifth, an additional dimension of the authority of the priesthood members is the competency with which ministry is offered to the body. Both before ordination and after, the quality with which the ministers act "for [persons] in things pertaining to God" commends their ministry to God and the church, and lends it an authority of competence. It is to reinforce this dimension of priesthood authority that standards of preordination and continuing education are being offered.

The sacrament of ordination symbolizes and confers through outward sign the authority of priesthood to act in the church on behalf of persons in relation to God. Although it is a simple act of laying on of hands with prayer, the many elements of authority and relationship come to focus in the sacrament of ordination. It will undoubtedly be noted that although the authority finally comes from God, it is through the agency of the church called into being by God that the call is expressed. Consequently, priesthood members may not consider themselves outside the claims of the church in the conduct of their ministry, but are accountable to the church and its policies, procedures, and authorities which are set in place to regulate the affairs of the body.

III

Organization of the Priesthood

The priesthood of the RLDS church consists of two major divisions. The first is known as the Melchisedec priesthood and is also referred to as the High Priesthood. The latter term is more applicable to functions or persons whose responsibilities are prescribed by law or other official acts of the church, to be administered by those holding the office of high priest. The president of the church is the president of the High Priesthood.

The second division is known as the Aaronic Order consisting of the offices of priest, teacher, and deacon. The presiding bishop is president of the Aaronic priesthood. This order is generally directed toward the temporal or social ministries of the church. The priest relates to families, and the teachers and deacons usually relate to individuals.

All the general officers of the church (including the First Presidency, Council of Twelve, Presiding Patriarch, the Presiding Bishopric and the Seventy) are members of the High Priesthood except the Seventy, who are elders. Specialized functions of the High Priesthood include evangelist-patriarchs and bishops.

The office of elder is described as an "appendage" of the High Priesthood. The law anticipates that every major or sizable organized unit should be under the leadership of a high priest or high priests. Such responsibilities would include the administration of stakes, regions, metropoles, districts, and large branches. The stake president, counselors to the stake president, and the Stake High Council are required to be high priests.

Elders may officiate in any office except those which by law or administrative policy require a high priest. All members of the Melchisedec priesthood may officiate in the sacraments and ordinances of the church, and the priest may lay on hands to ordain other members of the Aaronic Order. The latter may also officiate at weddings, serve the Communion, and perform water baptism.

The church's organizational forms and administrative procedures are designed to facilitate the witnessing, revealing, redeeming ministry of the gospel.

The church as a whole is called to a prophetic ministry, but leadership in that ministry is centered in the First Presidency and especially in the prophet.

The church as a whole is called to be a witnessing community, but its leadership in evangelism is centered in the Council of Twelve and the Quorums of Seventy.

Throughout the history of the church the members of the Council of Twelve have had primary responsibility for missionary work and for field administration; the latter upon specific assigment by the First Presidency.

Members of the Presiding Bishopric have responsibilities in temporalities, legal functions, and also serve as trustees for the holding of properties of the church where that is legally possible. The Presiding Bishopric are responsible to the First Presidency and to World Conference for their trusteeship.

Members of the Order of Bishops perform similar functions on election or approval by the respective jurisdiction with respect to the affairs of that jurisdiction.

The administrative line in the church runs from the First Presidency through members of the Council of Twelve, to presiding officers of field jurisdictions, to the congregational level. Administrative presidency is "of necessity" and is a means by which order is kept in the church and the appropriate decisions of the church are implemented.

In addition to the presiding and administrative roles, there are certain functional responsibilities that are to be carried out in the life of the church. These are generally those functions that are discharged by the members of the Order of Evangelist-Patriarchs, the Order of Bishops, and other high priests who may be assigned to special functions. All members of the High Priesthood not specifically assigned to the orders are formed into a quorum of high priests. The president of the Quorum of High Priests is appointed by the First Presidency and sustained by the action of the quorum.

Members of the Seventy are elders who are called by the action of the Council of Presidents of Seventy. There are seven presidents of Seventy and each one presides over one of the quorums of Seventy. The senior president of Seventy in addition presides over the Council of the Seven Presidents.

In general, all basic functions of the priesthood, including the approval and ordination of the several members, require the consent of the church at some appropriate level. This aspect of the doctrine of common consent is one of the undergirding principles of the Restoration movement. Without this supportive authority from the people, the divine calling exists in a vacuum: it is of little value in terms of ministry received, and institutional authority is withheld.

IV

The Pastor and Calls to the Priesthood

Perhaps one of the most significant and yet most demanding tasks of a pastor is the responsibility of calling persons to the priesthood. To be able to stand before the individual called and the congregation that ultimately must support that call and say, "I have evidence that this call is of God, is timely, and is in fulfillment of need" is indeed an awesome responsibility. However, the pastor is not alone in carrying this weighty burden, but may expect corroborating witness of the authenticity of the call by the stake or district president. The support and guidance of these administrative officers should be sought and welcomed. Experience is a great teacher, yet every call has elements of the new and unfathomed, of uncertainty and certitude.

A multitude of questions arise in the mind of the conscientious pastor: What is the purpose of priesthood? As calling officer, what is required of me as pastor? What are the needs of the congregation? What constitutes "evidence" in the discerning of a call? How does the Holy Spirit work in supportive confirmation or revelatory experience? How shall I be open to calls of women to priesthood? What is expected of the person called? What questions should I ask and what procedure should I follow in calling persons to the priesthood? What is the significance of the event of ordination? What is the role of the congregation? What is the pastor's role following ordination? Undoubtedly no final answers can be given to these questions but some guidelines can be established to assist presiding officers in decisions of ultimate significance.

1. What is the purpose of priesthood?

Simply stated, priesthood is designed to facilitate the witnessing, revealing, redeeming ministry of the gospel. According to the New Testament Jesus spent all night in prayer prior to choosing the apostles. Those who were chosen had gifts and potential in their lives to match the needs for ministry among the people to whom they were sent. As the early Christian church grew, so did the importance of priesthood. What we know of the congregational structure of those early days is limited. There seems to have been an emphasis on the ministry of each member. The call to all was to be apostolic: go forth in power and proclaim the gospel. All were called to be witnesses of God's presence in their lives. The gifts of the Spirit were bestowed on those whose commitment and receptiveness to the Divine qualified them to be representatives of the Christian message. The call of all believers to ministry was a firmly held conviction of these early Saints. Through the centuries, this recognition may have diminished in practice, but in importance the concept is more relevant than ever.

Because the mission was to all, early Christian congregations appear to have been rather unstructured. As congregations grew, however, leadership and specialized ministry became essential. The more complex a group becomes, the more its productivity depends on structural efficiency. As those early congregations struggled with the concept of priesthood, each met the need in its own way.

To say that the structural concept of priesthood was a gradual development in the Christian church is not to underrate its importance. Divine involvement and commission are present everywhere. We do not call ourselves as ministers. Though human agency is involved, the call is divine. So it has been from the beginning.

The church today proclaims that God is still calling disciples to specific ministerial responsibilities in light of their giftedness and in response to the needs of the church and of the larger community. As F. Henry Edwards suggests, "The church's function in relation to ministry is to recognize those to whom God has given the gifts of ministry and clear the way for the expression of their gifts."

Many revelations deal with priesthood and the specific responsibilities of various offices. Essentially, the priesthood of the RLDS church consists of two major divisions: The Melchisedec, also referred to as the High Priesthood, and the Aaronic. Each office within these major divisions has its own responsibilities which together facilitate the redeeming witness of the gospel. The call to priesthood comes through the administrative officers of the church — in the case of the congregation, the pastor. Calls to the offices of the Aaronic priesthood and to the office of elder may be initiated by the congregational pastor, while other ministers are called by the appropriate officers at other jurisdictional levels. Men and women are called to the priesthood and to specific offices within the priesthood by church officers responding to the spirit of inspiration, wisdom, and discernment. Through ordination the authority of the church is bestowed on the priesthood designate, though final authority and successful ministry reside in the life of each person called. As Apostle John Rushton once observed, "My authority is written into the biography of my life." If a member of the priesthood fails to carry that authority, opportunities for ministry are lost. If any of us as priesthood live contrary to the vows we have taken, inevitable deterioration among the membership will occur. The seriousness of this issue was addressed in Section 156 of the Doctrine and Covenants:

Hear, O my people, regarding my holy priesthood. The power of this priesthood was placed in your midst from the earliest days of the rise of this work for the blessing and salvation of humanity. There have been priesthood members over the years, however, who have...used it for personal aggrandizement. Others, through disinterest or lack of diligence, have failed to magnify their calling or have become inactive. When this has happened, the church has experienced a loss of spiritual power, and the entire priesthood structure has been diminished.

A genuine recognition of the purpose of priesthood and the dedicated function of all to whom the call of office has come is essential to the forward movement of the church, its mission to spread the good news of the gospel, and its call to witness in love and humility.

2. What is required of me as pastor?

A pastor, a shepherd, should not only preach the word but should live it. The demand placed on the pastor in this regard is no different from that placed on the membership; but anyone called to a position of leadership has increased influence. Furthermore, by embodying that which is spoken, the ministry of the pastor is immediately magnified. Perfection is not a requirement, but the continual striving for perfection is. The Christian gospel is rich in forgiveness to the truly repentant, and the strength to begin again is part of the endowment of the Spirit. The pastor participates in this great gift as does the membership.

If as pastors we truly wish to know the Divine in

greater measure we must strive to cleanse our lives. "Be ye clean, that bear the vessels of the Lord," admonished Isaiah (52:11). The principle is divinely instituted and finds memorable expression in the Doctrine and Covenants: "Therefore, sanctify yourselves that your minds become single to God" (Doctrine and Covenants 85:18).

The pastor-shepherd must know the flock. It is out of a knowledge of the needs of the congregation and the potential ministry of individual members that the pastor can effectively initiate calls to the priesthood. It is important in the internal struggles that so often take place in congregations that the pastor remain as objective as possible. Division over issues should never affect the love of persons or the recognition of their worth. A vindictive or jaundiced view growing out of struggle has no place in a pastor's life. Though the divine impulsion is essential in the calling of persons to the priesthood, human judgment always plays a part. This, as F. Henry Edwards points out, "arises out of the divine intention to share responsibility with us."

A pastor is called to minister and administer. Because of their nature, these two responsibilities do not necessarily relate well together. Administrative detail, the practical acumen necessary, the struggles over issues, organizational management, sheer busyness, and great activity, all can work counter to the stillness necessary for spiritual transparency and preparation for ministry. To so manage time and mental energy that the beauty of holiness and its consequent ministry can be an integral part of life is perhaps one of the greatest challenges facing us as pastors.

The responsibility of a pastor is indeed challenging, but the task is not one which is unaided. As we seek, so shall we find. A power will work through us that is not from us. Life and ministry become lifted to a plane that bespeaks the Divine.

3. What are the needs of the congregation? What is the relationship between need and call?

A crucial question in congregational life, as in professional life, is What kind of team with what qualifications will best accomplish our purposes? Two corollary questions follow: What kind of person, what kind of service are we in need of at the present time? Do we have anyone whose gifts and talents can fill that need? Such assessment related to priesthood may seem all too human and fallible. But such are the purposes of God as we learned in Oliver Cowdery's experience related in Section 9:3b-d of the Doctrine and Covenants:

Behold, I say unto you, that you must study it out in your mind; then you must ask me if it be right, and if it is right, I will cause that your bosom shall burn within you; therefore, you shall feel that it is right; but if it be not right, you shall have no such feelings, but you shall have a stupor of thought, that shall cause you to forget the thing which is wrong.

There is indeed a horizontal dimension to the revelatory experience. The call is to the partnership of the Divine and human. As persons we must be involved as well as God. "Without him," as Arthur Oakman once pointed out, "we cannot; without us, he will not."

As culture changes, so the needs of the church change. Though universal principles underlie the gospel, what is appropriate and efficacious in one time and place may not be so in another. No one illustrates this better than Paul.

On the one hand, Paul had a great spiritual vision: "There is neither Jew nor Greek, there is neither bond nor free, there is neither male nor female; for ye are all one in Christ Jesus" (Galatians 3:28). But Paul was also an administrator. He knew when to exercise control of a runaway congregation and when to push for principles that many were reluctant to accept. He exercised the latter option over the issue of circumcision of non-Jews. He took on the authority figures of the Christian church — people like Peter and the rest who had known Christ in the flesh, which Paul had not — and insisted that Jewish law, such as circumcision, should not apply to the Gentiles. Paul considered the issue important enough that he risked his ability to minister. He could have been cut off by the church and had no official recognition as a representative of Christianity. As it was, he endured the constant undermining of his position by "truth-tellers" who followed him in an attempt to undo his work. Paul, nevertheless, stayed with a principle in which he believed.

Decisions such as Paul made are pastoral in nature. Actions may have to be taken that, in the short run, appear to be inhibiting or even a serious break with tradition but which in the long run make possible a greater light and true Christian liberty.

Calls to the priesthood are an integral part of a pastor's understanding of the needs of a given congregation or area. No one method of calling can be specified, since no one has the right to dictate to another how wisdom must function or how inspiration is to be received. In some cases a pastor will consider a person's leadership potential and spiritual awareness in light of the perception of current needs. Insights about the person's candidacy for priesthood would then be tested and validated through prayer and possibly through discussion with the pastor's counselors. A growing conviction of the validity of the call may come through continuing observation of the candidate, prayer, and reflection on behalf of the candidate, and the needs of the church. In other cases a dramatic spiritual experience may be the event that triggers consideration of the call. This experience may draw attention in a powerful way to the candidate's capacity to minister to the needs of the people. In no case, however, should a call be consummated without the affirming Spirit of divine direction. The combination of the best of the human illuminated by the Holy Spirit makes the eventual invitation to ministry one of great meaning both to the person called and to the forward movement of the congregation.

4. What constitutes "evidence" in the discerning of a call? How does the Holy Spirit work in confirming or revealing power?

God through his Spirit may speak to us in many ways. The touch of the Divine may be as quiet and normal as breathing, ever-present, constantly sustaining life, assuring us that "the Eternal God is our home and underneath are the everlasting arms"; or it may come as the Hound of Heaven that follows us down the labyrinthine ways even when we are trying to escape. The experience may range from a sudden apprehension of wonder in the midst of the glory of creation to the certitude of divine self-disclosure; from a sensing of the mysterious to the affirmation of Saint Paul, "I know in whom I have believed"; from a vague longing to a commitment "costing not less than everything."

In matters that relate to church leadership, we sometimes expect God to "take over" and absolve us from the necessity of exercising our faith and taking the risks associated with actions of faith. God does indeed work in powerful and unusual ways, but at moments of God's own choosing and according to divine wisdom. Those moments of powerful direction are the exception and not the usual experience for reasons relating to our growth in faith and judgment. The personal experience of many pastors indicates that the clearest light or strongest spiritual assurance of a call may come when, for some reason, the call is resisted in the mind of the leader who has responsibility for the call. God works with us in a way that does not violate our agency or right of choice in all human-Divine interaction.

The most basic and substantial evidence of a person's call is in the nature of the person. What are his or her priorities, desires, and interests in life? The scripture reveals, "If ye have desires to serve God, ye are called to the work" (Doctrine and Covenants 4:1c). Many may evidence the fact that they are already called by their expression of "desires to serve" through active participation in the work. Some signal of the Holy Spirit which directs our attention to a given person through a strong impression, or at other times with a quiet, persistent thought of the possibility of the ordination, is helpful but does not represent the only evidence of a person's call. The Holy Spirit may find it necessary to direct our attention to a person when the call should already have been obvious to us and we were not responding.

The office to which a person should be called at a given time and place is related to the gifts, interests, and abilities of the person, and also to the need for particular kinds of ministry existing in that situation. There are some who could function in more than one office very adequately. With regard to the designation of an office of priesthood, the candidate's natural gifts, talents, potential for growth, and basic personality structure should be taken into account and used to match the person to an appropriate office. Of course, the needs of the congregation will also impact the designation of office. In the past there has been a tendency toward a vertical view rather than a horizontal view of the various offices, and consequently the Aaronic priesthood offices were sometimes seen as the training ground for the Melchisedec priesthood. By providing for a more realistic assessment of the person's gifts and the church's needs at the time of the first call, there will be inculcated into the system of priesthood service, more stability and greater longevity of service within the office of first call. This does not mean that calls from one office into another will not occur, but only that their incidence will be decreased with this more careful fitting to office at the time the first call is presented. If you do not receive clear spiritual evidence as to which office is indicated, "you must study it out in your mind" and move in faith to decide according to the nature of the person and the needs of the congregation.

As you carefully and prayerfully make these evaluations, the Holy Spirit may be depended on to be with you. You may feel assurance to proceed with a call, or in some instances, you may feel restraint for the present time. With others who are devoted and active, you will be expected to proceed if you feel no restraining influence; and the assurance you would like to receive before acting will come to you in the process of the calling and ordination procedure. These assurances may come through the testimony of the Spirit given to others, by the witness of the Holy Spirit in the presentation to the people, at the time of ordination, or during the ordinand's service in ministry. The Holy Spirit moves by divine initiative. We do not decide just when and how God will bear witness of divine callings.

For fallible human beings to speak for the Divine is indeed a humbling experience. To speak with certitude about divine or heavenly things has occasionally been a spiritual trap in Christian history. Where there is great potential for good, there is also great potential for harm. Yet within our history as a movement, there has always been the guiding influence of the Holy Spirit, to confirm, to control, to comfort, to guide to insightful truth.

When there are conflicting claims to authentic inspiration, especially regarding calls to priesthood, how may the pastor be helped? Imagination and feverish desire may lead some to believe an experience is divine which has only been created within themselves. Some may seek personal aggrandizement by declaring themselves special agents of the Divine. Certain forms of illness or even prescribed drugs may create hallucinatory images that have little foundation in fact. Emotion dissociated from clear thinking may cause some to revel in "great moments" that dissipate without consequence in thoughtful action. Some might be tempted to attribute divine origin to a certain position in order to vindicate a stance they have taken. Even persons of unquestioned integrity and sincere intent might bring differing interpretations to experience of the Divine. In all these and other similar situations, the calling administrative officer is solely responsible to the institutional church for the initiation of calls. Whether it be the pastor, district president, stake president, or other administrative officer, no other voice may claim comparable authority to initiate authentic calls for the institutional church.

However, we are not left with institutional support alone. The Lord has not left us comfortless. We need not be prey to distortions of divine self-disclosure. We have been promised as one of the spiritual gifts, the gift of discernment. If we seek guidance in humility of spirit, both for ourselves and for the claims of others, we can discern between that which is right and that which is wrong. Discrimination and growth in spiritual competence guide us in what can be the greatest of all human experiences.

In the universe in which we live, individuality is of great importance. In the divine-human encounter individuality is enhanced, not diminished. For some it is stillness and subtlety that matter. For others, only the dramatic carries weight. Though a pastor's recognition of the needs and talents of a given congregation may come from the slow accumulation of fact and the operation of the administrative mind, the dimension of knowledge so acquired can be expanded by the Spirit of God, not as a substitute for reason or sense data but as an illuminating power operating through them. Something which earlier had been intellectually apprehended takes fire and becomes an experience. The facts we confront and the knowledge we have may not be essentially different, but we refocus, we "attend" to that which we formerly missed. When the Holy Spirit so touches us it is not to destroy our human responsibility and understanding but to raise it to a more profound level of being.

To those who see, God communicates through action and contemplation. There are times to actively search and build. There are times in quiet contemplation to listen, "to be still and know that I am God." A mind too anxious or too busily occupied can often screen out the Spirit. For the searcher, belief in the possibility of "presence" is tremendously important. Without the belief that such a communion is possible between the human and the Divine, God's moment may pass unattended. Our own willingness to receive is as important as the willingness of the Divine to give.

God will evidence calls to priesthood through administrative officers of the church in a way that honors divine concern for the growing faith of the administrative officer as well as the response of the person being called. God will not cause an administrative channel for a divine call to become a "hollow pipe" for the purpose of running priesthood calls through without some involvement of the calling officer. Instead, it is the calling officer's responsibility to "study it out in your mind" (Doctrine and Covenants 9:3). There must be a willingness to exercise faith in the relationship to God and in the persons being called. The growth of all persons involved in the process of calling, ordaining, and responding to God's call is of concern to God.

In the revelatory experience of perceiving a priesthood call, such an illumination is a divine event interacting with the human. We recognize that it can easily be distorted by the human instrument and may be falsified in its expression. The event of revelation can never be totally equated with the human experience of it. We perceive but a fraction of the whole and are inadequate to totally describe the Eternal. But having with humility recognized our proper relation to the Divine and that at best in our human state "we see as through a glass darkly," we can still be representatives of the divine will and can affirm with assurance God's will for the people.

5. What should be the qualifications and expectations of the person called to the priesthood?

If the authority to minister centers at least partially in the personhood of the one called, quality of life is a major consideration. The person called must be someone of high ethical and moral standards, of significant personal stewardship, of a reasonable educational level, of devotion to individual development, of spiritual competence, of dedication to the mission of the church, and most of all, a participant in that abiding love that is first received and then lovingly given in ministry. The viability of the message is ultimately related to the person who utters it. Word and action cannot be separated.

Though no absolute educational standard should be set for the person called, the individual should have basic sensitivity, understanding, a willingness to learn. Dedication by itself is not enough. Every leader also wants to be competent. If formal education is lacking, the candidate for priesthood must evidence a strong interest in personal development. Motivation is the key which will lead to extraordinary effort from ordinary human beings. Maurice Draper writes:

Endowed ministry involves skill. It is not sufficient that one be designated and receive the laying on of hands. Well-intentioned error is error nonetheless. Devotion to a calling means that that calling be justified in effective performance.—"Endowment for Redemptive Ministries," *Saints Herald,* February, 1974, p. 14.

The invitation to priesthood will often be accompanied by confirmation to the one called. As the pastor receives evidence, so may the individual, although many may find their confirmation of the call through the rich experiences of ministry accompanied by divine empowerment. The call of God is intensely personal and gives the foundation from which ministry can proceed with assurance. To know, as stated in Isaiah, "I have called thee by thy name; thou art mine" (Isaiah 43:1), is to participate in the foundational love of the universe. To be known by name is to recognize individuality. In the body of Christ are many members with special gifts and functions. A calling makes us aware of these differences and, as in the parable of the talents, asks us to recognize our endowments, to make them grow and expand. As we do, the grace of God unfolds in our lives. The joy of ministry comes when we recognize our qualification is always from God and not from ourselves. "Not that we are sufficient of ourselves," wrote Paul, who knew what it meant to continually be on the frontier of ministry. "Our sufficiency is of God; who also hath made us able ministers of the new testament" (II Corinthians 3:5, 6).

Part of the humility of those called to ministry should be the recognition always that though a special need exists for their service, they are not thus superior to the rest of the congregation. "All are called according to the gifts of God unto them," and the responsibility of the member in fulfilling that call is just as important in the sight of God as is the call to priesthood. Though hierarchy appears to exist in priesthood structure—and operationally cannot be totally avoided—a sense of anyone being better than someone else merely through call to office has no place in the church of Christ. Any one of us may be an unprofitable servant, but whether the service we give is highly visible and publicly recognized or quiet and largely unnoticed, the important thing for us is the fulfillment of our vow to be the best that we can be. Having said that, we also know that when the word comes, "I have chosen you," we have been given additional responsibility that we cannot carry lightly. The joy of that responsibility comes when all are joined in the communion of Saints, and the congregation is lifted to a higher level of service and actively pursues the invitation to go into all the world.

Finally, all of us called to priesthood or to membership

in the church of Christ need a love we cannot know and a light we cannot reveal unless we have first received it in association with the Christ. It is God who calls us and gives us power to become his sons and daughters. Our Lord will not require of us more than we can give. All God asks is a reasonable service. But as in the experience of the loaves and fishes, Jesus takes our gifts, small though they may sometimes be, and enhances them to feed a multitude.

6. What are some factors surrounding my consideration of calls for women to the priesthood?

The issue raised in paragraph 9 of Section 156 was a long time in coming and was, as President Smith observed in the preamble, potentially divisive for the church. The position of the calling officer will also be difficult. It will be necessary to search honestly, in study, in thoughtful contemplation, in prayer and fasting. As the pastor in the past has experienced confirmation of call, so that same Spirit can work in enlightenment and understanding when the way is new and unknown.

From the beginning we have been called to be a prophetic church, to not be afraid, to rise up and experiment on the word of God. Of one thing we can be assured: the God who sends us out is also the God who goes with us and sustains us. That direction and sustaining power was truly present in the presentation of the document and, as many have testified, in the days and weeks that followed.

As we have all seen, times and needs change. The roles of men and women have been both imperceptively and dramatically changing over an extended period of time. The issue that confronts us in the ordination of women is related to a much larger issue of equal importance to society and the church: How shall we evaluate and reform our lives in terms of the full dignity, equality, and liberation of all, men and women? We tend to have fixed images of the roles of men and women, but as society changes, as our lifestyles change, roles cannot remain fixed. Service in the church of Christ is not dependent on one's gender, but on personal endowment, skill, and dedication.

When a pastor senses the possibility of a call for a woman, there are a number of factors which should also be included in the prayerful attitude of inquiry. Among the considerations are the following:

6.1 A period of transition is inevitable. General acceptance by the church membership in such significant matters is always gradual and largely depends on the resulting benefits derived from the change. Much will be required of the first women chosen. In the professional world women often have had to be better than men to receive equal recognition. Section 156, though it dealt with the ordination of women, was basically concerned with lifting the whole priesthood structure of the church to a higher level of performance. We should not, therefore, decry the inevitable demand for women of high quality, but should instead hope that all priesthood will be revitalized and will stand on a higher level of dedicated service.

6.2 In the next few years, in adjusting to this new mode of operation, the church will probably pioneer as it seldom has before. Part of that pioneering will relate to how men and women can work together in shared ministry. Can they be colleagues in service? Can true cooperation become a reality? To cooperate means to work together toward a common purpose. Cooperation is not subordination, to make subject or subservient to, nor is it integration, to blend together. It does not mean that everyone does the same thing. It means that men and women in responsible partnership make their specific contributions toward their God-given tasks, whatever those tasks may be; and that, further, they do so on the basis of equal worth before God and equal rights before church and society.

6.3 A risk in this new relationship between men and women is that women will be overly honored and protected or will be criticized and shunned. If we can recognize personhood before male and female, much of that problem will be solved. No doubt women as a group will have certain "feminine" characteristics to add to ministry as men as a group may have certain "masculine" characteristics. More important, however, is the recognition that our greatest religious leaders, including Christ, have had a blend of the masculine and feminine: strength and assertiveness on one hand, sensitivity and gentleness on the other; a harmonization of the rational and the intuitive; the power to stand and the humility of great vision; the ministry of both father and mother. Paul, one of the strongest of men, also wrote, "We were gentle among you, even as a nurse cherisheth her children" (I Thessalonians 2:7), and with parental concern he spoke of "my little children, of whom I travail in birth again until Christ be formed in you" (Galatians 4:19).

6.4 Many have expressed concern over a new relationship in ministry between men and women. It is one thing for a woman to be church secretary; it is another for her to join a male elder in calls for administration or as a pastor or counselor. In professional life most men and women have learned to work together as colleagues with appreciation for one another but without improper implications. Here truly is an opportunity to pioneer by learning what true friendship and support can be when warmed by the Holy Spirit. Such sharing is in the spirit of "Love ye one another as I have loved you," and can serve as a model for all men, women, and children of the congregation.

6.5 Special support, without patronizing, will be needed for the first women called. Loneliness compounded by internal and external pressures will likely be the lot of some: loneliness from being the first to forge a new way; internal pressure from self-doubt, from having been told for so long that she is not capable of fulfilling certain roles; external pressure from being on display, from the recognition that her performance will affect the attitude toward many others, and from both the expressed and unexpressed criticism she will certainly feel. Internal conviction of call with a vision of the work to be done will certainly sustain her in the difficult times, but acceptance by the male members of the priesthood and pastoral support from the rest of the congregation will make a difference.

In all these considerations, the ultimate and most essential question is, What is the will of God? If indeed the person is called of God, the church of faith will consequently respond in faithful ways.

7. What questions should I ask when considering calling persons to the priesthood?

Although it is not mandatory to have a favorable response to each question, every pastor should carefully consider them all before any call is completed.

    (1) Do you have a conviction that this person is being called to priesthood function in the Reor-

ganized Church of Jesus Christ of Latter Day Saints?

(2) What are the gifts and potential for ministry evident in this person's life for immediate and long-term ministry? How do they relate to a calling to a specific office?

(3) Is there need in the congregation or in other church settings for this person's ministry?

(4) How will this ordination affect the balance of ministry according to priesthood offices in the congregation?

(5) Is this person affirmative in testimony and positive in support of all levels of church life: congregation, district or stake, World Church?

(6) Is this person's life currently "in order" in regard to personal relationships, morality, response to the principles of personal stewardship, and family finances?

(7) If the person has been divorced, has inquiry been made regarding the circumstances?

(8) Does this candidate exhibit good stewardship of health and hold high standards of behavior, avoiding the abuse of chemical substances and refraining from the use of alcohol and tobacco?

(9) Does the candidate actively support the church to the best of his or her ability in terms of attendance, general and local contributions, and responsiveness to the principle of financial accounting?

(10) Does the candidate evidence a positive attitude toward study, personal improvement, and spiritual growth?

(11) If this person has been involved in any conduct which could reflect negatively on her or his abil-

ity to minister, have you counseled with your
supervising officers to determine if this should
be a factor in processing this recommendation?
(12) Is the candidate's appearance and manner of
dress acceptable to the congregation?
(13) Does the candidate enjoy adequate health to
fulfill the demands of the office?
(14) What is the reaction of your counselors to this
call?
(15) What will be the likely reaction of the people assembled in legislative conference to this call?
(16) What will be the likely reaction of the spouse and
other members of the candidate's family to this
call?

8. What are the needs of the congregation in relation to the functional offices of priesthood?

When considering the needs of the people, the pastor
must not ignore the fact that divine calling is expressed
finally in the specific ministries of particular kinds which
are offered to the Saints. As the apostle Paul pointed
out, the body is made up of various members with gifts
to serve the body in specific functions. If all the members of the body were eyes, the functions of hearing,
smelling, tasting, and touching would be lost. Similarly
there is need in the body of the church for all of the
priesthood offices because of their functions.

The pastor will do well therefore to give thought to
the numbers and qualifications of priesthood needed for
the sake of the body while remaining sensitive to the
divine will for guidance in selecting candidates for
ordination. There are some guidelines for assisting a
pastor in this process. These guidelines are based on
certain assumptions arising from experience in ministry

in the church. We assume the following:

(1) All the priesthood are active, and are performing their duties and respective tasks as described in Section VII.

(2) All individual priesthood members are competent to perform the ministry described for them.

(3) Members and friends will solicit and receive ministry from the priesthood in accordance with these descriptions.

(4) Priesthood efforts are complemented and supplemented by ministry appropriately provided by the unordained.

(5) Each priesthood member will spend 360 hours per year (approximately seven hours per week) in ministry beyond the usual church participation. Of these 360 hours, sixty will be spent in efforts directed toward ministerial growth, such as continuing education through Temple School. The remaining 300 hours will be spent directly in ministry.

Based on these assumptions, guidelines recommending possible numbers of priesthood by congregational size for the various offices are suggested to presiding officers as they consider the ministerial needs of the congregation. A range of numbers is offered, allowing greater freedom in responding to the needs of a specific congregation and to the inspiration received. Larger congregations may appropriately be organized into pastoral groups to most effectively utilize the ministry of the various offices.

These recommendations reflect the central focus of each office's ministry. For example, the suggested numbers for deacons and teachers are based on the number of enrolled members, while that for priests is based on the number of family units. Melchisedec recommendations consider not only the responsibility of the eldership to the corporate body, but the larger community as well.

The following table may be useful in observing how our current experience may compare with suggested numbers of a given priesthood office according to congregational size.

CURRENT EXPERIENCE VERSUS SUGGESTED NUMBERS OF PRIESTHOOD

Congregation Size	Deacon Curr.	Deacon Sugg.	Teacher Curr.	Teacher Sugg.	Priest Curr.	Priest Sugg.	Melchisedec Curr.	Melchisedec Sugg.
0–50	0.63	1	0.27	1	1.31	1–2	2.01	1–2
51–100	1.37	1–2	0.57	1–2	2.17	2–3	3.42	2–4
101–200	3.13	3–5	0.95	3–5	3.76	4–7	6.08	5–7
201–300	5.94	5–8	1.67	5–8	6.83	7–11	10.93	8–12
301–400	7.82	7–11	2.47	7–11	9.59	10–16	14.42	11–17
401–500	11.57	9–15	3.19	9–15	11.80	13–20	19.95	15–22

Notes: The average number of priesthood members currently serving in a given office includes all priesthood, active and inactive.

For the average ratio of members to the number of priesthood in a given office, the median number for each congregational size is used (e.g., for 101–200 the median of 150 is divided by the average number of deacons).

The average household size of 2.73 people per family as determined by the Bureau of Census for the United States of America was used to convert the recommended number of families to individuals (for the office of priest) in the recommended range.

9. What is the significance of the event of ordination?

Ordination, the confirmation of call and the invocation of the Divine, is a public occasion. It comprises a four-fold vow: the commitment of the candidate, the recognition of the Divine, the affirmation of receptiveness and supportive ministry by the congregation, and the formal authorization by the institutional church. There is reciprocal responsibility that comes from this authorizing sacrament: the individual minister is responsible to the church as an institution for his or her actions, and the church is responsible for the authoritative actions of the minister. The congregation can never simply be idle spectators at such an event. The doctrine of common consent is one of the undergirding principles of the Restoration movement.

We have the promise that the light of the Holy Spirit will work with us but not without the use of the best of human reason. Before the occasion of the laying on of hands, the congregation would have given its approval of the call. Not only should each voting member give that approval throughtfully and prayerfully, but the experience should remind them of their apostolic function to go forth in power to proclaim the gospel. The culmination of that recognition comes in the ordination ceremony itself. As the vow of the ordinand is received and blessed, so the vow of each member, in once more affirming personal responsibility and ministry, is received and blessed. We renew our vows at the Communion service but the vows we make as we participate in the other sacraments of the church are equally important. Throughout the New Testament virtually every reference to the work of the Holy Spirit is related to the group: "Where two or three are gathered together in my name, there am I in the midst of them" (Matthew 18:20). As we lend our minds, our talents, our skills to one another, the Holy Spirit recognizes our efforts and enhances our gifts. Ordination is divine recognition, not just of the one called but of the group who has given supportive assistance, and to whom the word comes, saying in essence, "I have not forgotten you. I have chosen servants to minister in your midst." Not only does the ordinand recognize that he/she has a specific vocation to minister, but the congregation affirms its support. "As Thou hast given, so we will give." In such sharing with one another and with the Spirit, we each leave stronger than we were before and with the assurance that we do not walk alone. We are engaged in mutual support for a common purpose.

In the ordination itself, where receptiveness and preparation are present in the candidate, there comes the enabling power of the Divine. What happens is the affirmation of a covenant relationship. The vow given at that moment is mutual — the individual to the Divine and the Divine to the individual; the individual to the institution and the institution to the individual. Such an experience and such a vow are possible for all, but call to office and ordination is a selective process for selective work, one covenanted to and supported by both the individual and the Divine. As the endowment of the Holy Spirit is bestowed on the candidate in the ordination ceremony, so the outstretched hand of the Divine will be ever there.

10. What is the pastor's role following ordination?

The pastor is to a large extent responsible for directing the priesthood members and helping them to function in their office and calling. Particularly for those newly ordained, instruction, guidance, and positive reinforcement are very important. The communication of appreciation for work well done may often give enough confidence to the newly ordained to inspire increased effort and stronger ministry. An important aspect of that appreciation is instilling confidence in the ordained regarding the worthwhileness of the task. Such worthwhileness can be communicated only when the pastor is a genuine leader. If the congregation is on the move, then all desire to be part of an important endeavor. The tragedy of many congregations is internal quarreling over issues that divide member from member and friend from friend. Though the issues are nearly always centered around interpretation of the gospel, its true significance is forgotten. Loving concern for one another and our Christian purpose for being become lost. We are certainly not all required to think or believe alike, but we are called to have our lives centered in the Christ and to be his witnesses in the world. Though all share in the responsibility for the spiritual welfare of the group, the pastor is in the best position to radiate a spirit of reconciliation and love. If the priesthood become quarrelsome or the membership begin to stray, the pastor must speak the redeeming word. This is indeed an awesome responsibility but perhaps more necessary in this particular time in our history than ever before.

To assist priesthood in performing at their maximum level, evaluations of their work are in order. Such evaluation should always begin with self-assessment on the part of the priesthood member. Along with that assessment should also be a growth plan in which annually the individual would consider and write down plans for personal development and ministry. Such creative exploration of ministerial possibility may be viewed in the light of a position description. Seeking to "magnify our calling" requires a constant concern for the possibilities within the call, and a willingness to involve ourselves in the discipline that will release our true potential. Self-discipline, especially in the light of our calling to be disciples of the Christ, is the very essence of our calling to priesthood.

Personal assessment and growth plans tend to have more effect if someone else is evaluating progress. That is the role of the pastoral leadership. Pastoral evaluation of progress is formalized so that no one feels himself or herself a victim of bias or discrimination. Though suggestions for procedure may come from the World Church, each congregation will need to adapt method to its own needs. Whatever this method, everyone should be quite clear about what is involved and inspired to participate actively and willingly in the process.

The days before us are indeed filled with opportunity. The call is to go forth for the blessing and salvation of humanity. The closing words of Section 156 give us our admonition and promise:

Dear Saints, have courage for the task which is yours in bringing to pass the cause of Zion. Prepare yourselves through much study and earnest prayer. Then, as you go forth to witness of my love and my concern for all persons, you will know the joy which comes from devoting yourselves completely to the work of the kingdom. To this end will my Spirit be with you. Amen.

RECOMMENDATION FOR ORDINATION FORM

I recommend _____ Register Number _____
For ordination to the office of _____
Candidate's residence (address) _____
Currently enrolled in (congregation) _____
District/Stake _____ Region_____
Date of birth: _____ Sex _____ Vocation _____
Approximate number of years as: Church Member _____ Priesthood _____
Any previous priesthood offices held _____
Current marital status, approximate number of years: Married _____ Single _____
Check if candidate has to your knowledge ever been: Widowed _____ Divorced _____
Spouse is member of: RLDS church _____ Other church or faith _____ None _____
Spouse will be comfortable with this call: Highly _____ Fairly _____ Little _____
Education (show graduation or degree, or number of years attended):
    Elementary _____ High School _____ Four-Year College _____
    Postgraduate Work _____ Other Training _____
Further training needed for this office: Extensive _____ Moderate _____ Little _____
As pastor (or other appropriate administrative officer), I present this recommendation as my own serious conviction of this call.

                    Signature _____
                    Official Capacity _____
                    Congregation _____ Date _____

Approved by:
    Stake or District President _____ Date _____
    Regional Administrator/President _____ Date _____
    Apostle in Charge (if required) _____ Date _____

[Note: This call should be discussed only with proper administrative officers or others who will not share confidential information.]

Conviction concerning the candidate's call came to me as pastor/administrator in this manner (general conviction, any special feelings or experiences):

Any other remarks by the officer making recommendation:

Remarks by the stake/district president:

Remarks by the regional administrator/president:

Remarks by the apostle in charge:

Priesthood Standards and Qualifications

The following qualities and factors should be considered when reviewing the history and call of the candidate. Be sensitive to anything which might be a problem in acceptance or ministry of the candidate. Make a brief notation, or if necessary explain on a separate sheet of paper.

1. Do you have a conviction that this person is being called to priesthood function in the Reorganized Church of Jesus Christ of Latter Day Saints?
2. What are the gifts and potential for ministry evident in this person's life for immediate and long-term ministry? How do they relate to a calling of a specific office?
3. Is there need in the congregation or in other church settings for this person's ministry?
4. How will this ordination affect the balance of ministry according to priesthood offices in the congregation?
5. Is this person affirmative in testimony and positive in support of all levels of church life: congregation, district or stake, region, and World Church?
6. Is this person's life currently "in order" in regard to personal relationships, morality, response to the principles of personal stewardship, finances?
7. If the person has been divorced, has inquiry been made regarding the circumstances?
8. Does this candidate exhibit good stewardship of health and hold high standards of behavior, avoiding the abuse of chemical substances and refraining from the use of alcohol and tobacco?
9. Does the candidate actively support the church to the best of his or her ability in terms of attendance, general and local contributions, and responsiveness to the principle of financial accounting?
10. Does the candidate evidence a positive attitude towards study, personal improvement, and spiritual growth?
11. If this person has been involved in any conduct which could reflect negatively on her or his ability to minister, have you counseled with your supervising officers to determine if this should be a factor in processing this recommendation?
12. Is the candidate's appearance and manner of dress acceptable to the congregation?
13. Does the candidate enjoy adequate health to fulfill the demands of the office?
14. What is the reaction of your counselors to this call?
15. What will be the likely reaction of the people assembled in legislative session of conference to this call?
16. What will be the likely reaction of the spouse and other members of the candidate's family to this call?

Information for the calling officer

1. This form is to be completed by the administrative officer initiating the call of a person to priesthood. On completion, it should be forwarded to the stake/district president for further consideration and approvals. You are not to approach the candidate about the call until administrative approvals have been obtained, and you have been notified to discuss the call with the candidate.

2. An indication of divine call is *required*. Having said this, it should be understood that your experience as initiating officer need not be dramatic or completely without question on your part. You are to use your best judgment — not only concerning the spiritual experience regarding the call, but on every aspect which might affect ordination. That is, you are to take a "wholistic" approach to the leadings of the Holy Spirit. You will *not* be asked to "defend" your discernment of the call, simply to share it.

3. Confirmation of the call (from a second person in the congregation sensing the divine intent) is appropriate but not mandatory.

4. If you sense the call, but are unclear as to the office, contact your supervising administrator for further counsel.

5. As the initiating officer regarding this call, you are part of a team which will determine the appropriateness of ordination. You should see yourself as a member of that team, rather than strictly the proponent of this particular call. Our system relies on the Holy Spirit working through the administrative officers of the church, not only to discern the divinity of the call, but to identify the candidate's strengths and weaknesses, the needs for ministry, etc. The strength of this system is in gaining a number of perspectives. It is possible that on occasion other administrative officers will evaluate the situation differently, in which case this form will be returned to you for further consultation to occur. Your integrity in response to the light you have received is fulfilled by initiating the recommendation for ordination.

6. There are a number of considerations for ordination: acceptance of his/her ministry by the people, personal standards to be met, the need for the candidate's ministry in a priesthood capacity, and ultimately the readiness of the candidate.

7. Personal standards should be met before ordination, as well as to retain a priesthood license. These include stewardship compliance, continued training, and standards of personal conduct (see the statement of Priesthood Standards and Qualifications printed on this form).

8. If you have felt moved to process a call, but you know the candidate does not meet some of the priesthood standards, first give ministry to the person in the area of inadequacy, obtaining some response without revealing a specific call. If your conviction of the call persists, you should process the call with a notation explaining the deficiency, ministry given, and the candidate's response. But a specific call should at no time be shared with the candidate prior to the usual approvals by the administrative officers. After all other considerations have indicated the appropriateness of ordination, the candidate may be approached about the call, and encouraged to meet the standards. If the candidate subsequently meets all the standards, ordination can proceed.

9. *After* approval for candidacy is given by the church and you are notified to proceed, you as the initiating officer may approach the candidate. The candidate should be informed of your role in the process, and that other approvals have been obtained. You should review the Priesthood Standards and Qualifications with the candidate and administer the Priesthood Interview. (It may be at this time that you become aware of personal standards which are not being met.)

10. The candidate should give prayerful consideration before accepting the call, realizing the commitment to training and the service which the call requires. While the candidate may want personal validation of the call, this is not strictly necessary. You might encourage the candidate to weigh *all* considerations — the needs of the church for ministry which he/she can give, the time demands for preparation, and the skills, talents, and gifts which the candidate possesses, together with his/her sense of being called.

11. If the candidate has questions regarding the office, the standards, or the timing of ordination, you should feel free to contact the next level administrator to help answer such questions. You can also expect help from administrators in your stake/district to establish the Plan for Ministry.

Send this form to the stake/district president. *Do not* approach the candidate about the call until you have received clearance to do so.

V

Priesthood and Education

1.0 *Preordination Training and Education.* A significant distinction exists between calling and ordination. An important difference exists between the divine power of the *calling* and the *ordination* which empowers one in the work of the church. While the first reflects the personal relationship between God and the person, the second makes us aware that the Spirit of God moves in the church concerning the church. Thus the church is *led* in its organizational requirements, not unlike the way the individual may feel led in terms of the call. Ordination to office implies the permission to function within an office within the church, and thus it is a legitimate function of the church to control the evaluation and licensing of persons.

Education has always been held in high esteem in the Restoration movement, especially due to instruction which the church has received periodically through the prophet on the importance of preparation for ministry, and study which is accompanied by faith. At various times and places in our history, formal education for priesthood has been eagerly offered and received. The first of these was very early in our history, at Kirtland, under the general direction of Joseph Smith, Jr. In our present era, virtually every facet of human endeavor has established criteria of professional qualifications to authorize acceptable service. The widespread expectations of the people of today are for expertise from those who serve them. Thus the following educational expectations are set in the context of Restoration history and scripture, and are fully in keeping with the earnest hope and expressed desire of the people for priesthood of excellence.

1.1 In preparation for service and responsibility, and prior to ordination to office, the candidate is expected to complete the Temple School course "Introduction to Ministry."

1.2 In addition, the candidate will be expected to complete the Temple School course designed for the anticipated office (deacon, priest, or other)

1.3 The candidate also will be expected to complete the Temple School course, "Introduction to Scripture," or a course of equal content and study provided in a form acceptable to the ordaining authority.

1.4 The candidate may begin the recommended courses of study immediately on notification of the call and acceptance by the candidate.

1.5 Under unusual circumstances where existing conditions may impose a hardship on the ordinand, a mutual agreement may be reached with the presiding officer as to the nature of the preordination training to be provided. This should be done in consultation with the district or stake president. Without such agreement, the expectations will remain.

1.6 The provisions of paragraphs 1.1 through 1.5 apply to all ordinands, whether the present call is a first call or a successive call. If a course (such as "Introduction to Ministry") has already been taken, it need not be repeated. However, a course in the scriptures should be included in preordination studies for each calling.

2.0 *A period of preparation exists* between the time of administrative approval authorizing a call and when ordination takes place. The status of persons in this category of designation and candidacy for priesthood usually lasts no more than one year, and therefore terminates no later than one year after the conference action which authorized it. During this time the designated candidate is seen as having been called to service but is not yet authorized by the institutional church. It is a time of consideration, preparation, and training.

2.1 During this period there is opportunity for practicum in the office under consideration. Within this structure, the person may perform the functions of the office (other than ordinances) while under the direct supervision of a member of the congregation (or other appropriate jurisdiction) who occupies, or has occupied, the office.

2.2 The individual will have the opportunity to prepare and to meet the standards and expectations of the office.

2.3 The candidate will have completed all educational requirements established for the office during this period of time.

2.4 The candidate also considers the responsibilities and opportunities of the priesthood office. The priesthood designates take a serious look at whether they wish to be deeply involved, if they are willing to abide by the expectations of the church, and if they see this call and ordination as significant to their own life's direction.

2.5 The candidates test where they fit into the church,

both in terms of activity, responsibility, and authority, but also in terms of theological understanding, behavioral modes, and relationships to the church.

3.0 *Preordination Expectations.* Prior to the actual ordination of an individual, it is recommended that the following standards for all ordinands be met:

3.1 A conviction that this person is being called to priesthood function in the Reorganized Church of Jesus Christ of Latter Day Saints.

3.2 An awareness of the gifts and potential for ministry which are evident in this person's life for immediate and long-term ministry, and how they relate to a calling to a specific office.

3.3 An awareness of need in the congregation or in other church settings for this person's ministry.

3.4 A concern for how this ordination will affect the balance of ministry according to priesthood offices in the congregation.

3.5 The knowledge that this person is affirmative in testimony and positive in support of all levels of church life: congregation, district or stake, and World Church.

3.6 An assurance that this person's life currently is in order in regard to personal relationships, morality, response to the principles of Christian stewardship and family finances.

3.7 An awareness that this candidate exhibits good stewardship of health and holds high standards of behavior, avoiding the abuse of chemical substances and refraining from the use of alcohol and tobacco.

3.8 A knowledge that the candidate actively supports the church to the best of his or her ability in terms of attendance, general and local contributions, and responsiveness to the principle of financial accounting.

3.9 Evidence that the candidate has a positive attitude toward study, personal improvement, and spiritual growth.

3.10 A determination has been made, via counsel with the supervising officers, that any history of conduct or divorce which could reflect negatively on her or his ability to minister has been properly considered.

3.11 An assurance that the candidate's appearance and manner of dress are acceptable to the congregation.

3.12 Some assurance that the candidate enjoys adequate health to fulfill the demands of the office.

3.13 A supportive testimony of the pastor's counselors to this call.

3.14 An assessment of the likely reaction of the people when assembled in legislative conference to this call.

3.15 An awareness of the likely reaction of the various members of the candidate's family to this call.

4.0 *Continuing Education.* Following ordination, persons holding priesthood office are expected to be involved in the process of continuing education.

4.1 Each priesthood member is expected to take at least two units (CEU) per year (six in a review period). This is an equivalent of two ten-hour Temple School courses, or would be the equivalent of two long weekend workshops, or a single four-day seminar or workshop. All of these are available through Temple School programs including the Home Study program. Equivalent programs of continuing education may be found in other institutions of higher education, and may be accepted by the Priesthood Training and Education officer (see 5.0 below) in lieu of Temple School course work. In addition, retreats, workshops, seminars, and other similar offerings by the region, stake or district may carry CEU credits which the Priesthood Training and Education officer accepts.

4.2 This education is directed both toward further understanding and training in the office held and, as much as possible, in wider scriptural, historical, theological, pastoral, and organizational areas.

4.3 Those seeking active priesthood status are expected to show evidence of having completed their planned continuing education courses.

5.0 *Priesthood Training and Education Officer.* It is recommended that each congregation have an officer who assists in the implementation of the program outlined above.

5.1 The pastor appoints the officer, who becomes an assistant to the pastor. In small congregations, the pastor may choose to serve in that role. The congregation sustains the P.T.E. officer.

5.2 It is the task of the P.T.E. officer to coordinate the training and education functions for the priesthood. This includes the following:
   — arranging for preordination education opportunities as described in paragraph 1.1 through paragraph 1.3 above;
   — recommending practicum possibilities as described in paragraph 2.1 above;
   — arranging for continuing education opportunities as described in paragraphs 4.0 through 4.3 above;
   — identifying ways in which the priesthood of

the congregation may take advantage of additional training through retreats, workshops, and seminars as described in paragraph 4.1 above.

5.3 In this coordinating task, the P.T.E. officer serves as liaison with
- Temple School;
- district, stake, and regional training and educational officers;
- other institutions and organizations offering suitable courses of study;
- the pastor;
- the individual priesthood member.

5.4 In all these functions, the P.T.E. officer assures that educational and training opportunities are available for all who should have access to means of preparation for service in the priesthood.

FLOW CHART FOR PROCESSING PRIESTHOOD CALLS

Seek and receive inspiration regarding priesthood call.

Initiate priesthood call. (Complete ordination form.)

Obtain administrative approvals and clearances.

Interview priesthood candidate*

Present recommendation to appropriate conference for approval

Candidate begins practicum and completes preordination training*

Service of ordination

First year review

Triennial review

*Training may begin after the candidate has accepted the call, or following approval by the appropriate conference. Conference action may stipulate that approval is given, "subject to satisfactory fulfillment of the preordination expectations."

VI

Giftedness and Calling

1. *Giftedness*

Gifts of ministry differ from person to person through differing genetic qualities, impact of milieu, or through whatever means God chooses to endow persons with those qualities labeled as "gifts of God unto them." Gifts inherent in the personality of certain church members are perceived within the church as those qualities of ministry which are appropriate for expression through priesthood ministry. Thus the church, through its authorized representatives and formal procedures, calls those persons to priesthood with specific categories of ministry implied by office designation which relate to the giftedness of the person who is called and ordained. Gifts and their expression are developed according to life's circumstance, personal interest and needs, and capability of the church to receive the varieties of ministry offered by each member.

2. *Calling*

Persons need to experience the call of God personally if they are to be affirmed as chosen of God, and able to accept the givenness of their life's present situation within which ministry is to be offered.

The call of God is received as something intensely personal rather than a call to something in general. "I have loved thee" (Jeremiah 31:3), "I have called thee by thy name, thou art mine" (Isaiah 43:1). It is this sense of personal calling which makes faith real. One may well say, "Faith is the assurance that *I* am called of God and that *I* have been ***chosen***. God's purpose in my life is recognized in the call of God extended to me. Being called is to recognize that I belong to God and thus I live in dependence on God."

We recognize the importance of each person sensing very deeply that "***I am called*** according to the gifts of God unto me" as well as being able to recite that "***all are called*** according to the gifts of God unto them." Members should be encouraged to see their baptism and confirmation as the church's official recognition of their calling to "the office of member."

The ***office of member*** designation is applied to any person who has a sense of personal calling to the work of a Christian, as expressed through water baptism and confirmation in the church. The office of member is synonymous with full membership in the church. One who thereby holds the office of member may perform any function of the church, other than the presiding and sacramental roles which would continue to be the responsibility of specific priesthood offices. This safeguards the long-standing tradition and polity of the church, reflecting the right and authority of a believer to represent Christ in the life of the body of Christ. As with priesthood, so also will members who take their responsibility seriously want to magnify their calling of member through Temple School courses of study and preparation. All courses offered by Temple School are available to any member.

The church should be looking for innovative ways to impress on its members that they continue to play vital roles in the church. This may be a time in our history when those not desiring or not called to priesthood might feel severely left out. Church leaders are encouraged to create and share innovative suggestions applicable to field situations.

3. *Definitions of Terms*

Some semantic confusion exists concerning the difference between *ordination* and *setting apart* by the laying on of hands. Therefore we define these terms as follows:

3.1 *Ordination* is to membership in the various offices, quorums, and orders of priesthood (i.e., deacon, teacher, priest, elder, seventy, presidents of seventy, high priest, bishop, presiding bishopric, evangelist-patriarch, presiding patriarch, apostle, First Presidency, prophet-seer-revelator).

3.2 *Setting apart* by laying on of hands is to presiding roles within quorums, councils, orders, and field jurisdictions of the church, including districts and congregations. For example, the person may be said to be ordained an elder and set apart as the pastor of a congregation, or as the president of a district. In congregations, the setting apart is performed by elders under the direction of the stake or district president whenever there is a change in pastor.

This modified definition constitutes a new application of setting apart as interpreted by the First Presidency.

Counselors to these presiding officers in congregations and districts do not need to be set apart, as their authority is delegated by and derived from the presiding officers. In regions and stakes, counselors to the president and bishop and members of high councils are also set apart.

VII

Priesthood Review

Introduction

The evaluation of the performance of priesthood in the church takes on many forms. At the World Church level the use of position support statements, combined with goals which are reviewed annually, has proven to be relatively effective. This also permits supervisors to spend some time with each person for purposes of consultation, morale, and direction.

Our research indicates that insofar as possible priesthood evaluation in the field should be decentralized. It should also be operated wherever possible at the level of congregational or stake and district administration, with the priesthood interview by an immediate supervising administrator. The World Church will assist in this process by providing guide sheets and motivational resources. This procedure will apply to both men and women.

1. *Priesthood Accountability*

1.1 A person's priesthood is initiated by divine call, and approved by common consent. Authority is symbolized and confirmed through the sacrament of ordination.

1.2 Priesthood is of a continuing nature. Priesthood authority is granted by the church as a privilege, with continuing expectations. One is called to enlarge and expand personal gifts in the process of ministry—in brief, to magnify one's calling. In recognition of these factors, continuing education and accountability for one's ministry are accepted by each ordinand as essential to fulfilling the call of God.

2. The Priesthood Interview Process

2.1 Each person ordained to priesthood office receives a formal review every three years. In addition, the pastor is encouraged to offer an informal review at the end of the first year to new ordinands.

2.1.1 Priesthood members receive a formal review of their performance in ministry on at least a triennial basis by the pastor or other designated officer of the congregation. This formal review consists primarily of the priesthood member's self-evaluation, feedback to the pastor, and a plan for future service. It is a time for seeking and sharing a testimony of one's awareness of God's intention in the call to ministry, and an assessment of one's God-given gifts for ministry.

2.1.2 Persons assigned to inactive priesthood status will also be reviewed every three years. In addition, the pastor is encouraged to offer an informal review each year. This is to assure that regular attempts are made to assist someone who is inactive to return to full active priesthood status.

2.1.3 One-sixth of the priesthood of a congregation will be interviewed and status determined every six months. The cycle of interviews will thus be completed in a normal three-year period.

2.1.4 Priesthood officers whose assignment or election makes them responsible to a jurisdiction higher than the local congregation (i.e., pastor, district president, stake president, etc.) are interviewed by the jurisdictional presiding officer or representative at the next higher level. This principle also applies to any priesthood officers (e.g., seventy or evangelists, etc.) who report to other jurisdictional authorities at levels II or III. All other Melchisedec and Aaronic priesthood members are interviewed by the pastor (or the pastor's representative) as described in the paragraphs above. In some ambiguous instances, the field administrators concerned may determine at which level a given priesthood member's interview will occur.

2.2 Categories of priesthood activity

2.2.1 Active

This category describes the large body of priesthood members who provide ministry appropriate to their abilities, life's circumstances, and the congregation or other jurisdiction to which they are responsible.

2.2.2 Superannuation

Superannuation is an honor in recognition of long and faithful service. Therefore, "the honor of superannuation" releases a priesthood member from the responsibility of office, and subsequently the necessity, obligation, or expectancy to function in all the duties of that office. Superannuation continues to recognize the authority to administer the ordinances and/or sacraments pertaining to the office; however, such participation becomes permissive and voluntary. This honor is appropriate when permanent or long-term limitations prohibit one's full functioning in priesthood office. Such limitations may be related to age, increasing degrees of infirmity, or disabling conditions.

a. At the time of the priesthood interview, either the priesthood member or the interviewing officer may suggest superannuation. The priesthood member may request an interview at any time without awaiting the normal three-year cycle.

b. Procedurally, the request would follow the same administrative and legislative processes that would be involved in a call to priesthood.

c. Recognition of the honor of superannuation may then occur at a stake or district conference, at which time the meaning of superannuation would be clearly communicated and celebrated.

d. The superannuated minister is issued a new priesthood license as a minister of the church, indicating the office of last ordination with the additional term "superannuated," and official membership records will show that the priesthood status is that of superannuation.

2.2.3 Inactive

The inactive priesthood status recognizes that personal and/or situational conditions may determine that the priesthood member is not actively functioning in the office and calling for a period of time. Inactive status recognizes that there is no ethical/moral breach of the church's normative expectations for the personal conduct of priesthood members. This category carries no pejorative connotation on the person's church record. If there is cause for silence, the person will not be placed on inactive status.

a. The inactive priesthood status will usually be agreed on in the priesthood interview. At the time a member is placed in the "inactive" category, he/she is notified that should there be inactivity through two triennial reviews, it will be the duty of the pastor to initiate proceedings for release from priesthood. (See 2.2.5)

b. In cases of difficulty in status assignment, the member has the right of administrative appeal to the same administrative level required for approval of ordination to the office presently held.

c. Reinstatement to active status is recommended by the pastor and approved by the district or stake president.

d. Inactive priesthood participate in the interview process on an annual basis, looking toward their being restored to active ministerial roles.

2.2.4 **Silence**

Church policy regarding priesthood silence is clearly defined in existing policy statements. All rights of administrative appeal in the law are available to persons placed under ministerial silence. The formal priesthood interview should not be normally perceived as the arena for invoking the priesthood silence.

a. Silence is for cause and usually involves need for frequent and specialized ministry.

b. Silenced members are required to relinquish their priesthood license and their membership records will indicate the priesthood category of "silenced."

c. Silenced members of the priesthood have the same status as the unordained.

2.2.5 **Release**

A member may choose to be released from the responsibility of priesthood for reasons of conscience or life's circumstances. If there is no cause for *silence*, the person's request is handled administratively in the same manner as that required for approval to the office to which the person was ordained. It is not a matter for legislative action.

a. Members of the priesthood who have been classified as *inactive* through two triennial reviews are released. (This will usually average approximately five years.)

b. A released priesthood member relinquishes the priesthood license, and the membership records will indicate the priesthood category of "released." Reinstatement to priesthood office for released persons follows the same procedures as for silenced persons.

c. A member may request release for the purpose of serving in an office with a more narrow scope of responsibility than the one currently held. (For example, an elder may request release to accept the role of ministry in the office of priest, teacher, or deacon.) Such a request should originate with the member rather than the administrative officers. On rare occasion, and with the dignity of full respect and spiritual concern, an administrative officer may initiate the subject of release or acceptance of another priesthood role in tactful conversation with the minister. To accept release, however, does not assume that another call and ordination will necessarily follow.

d. Any additional or future ordination (such as in c. above) for a member granted release would be through divine initiative, and administrative and legislative actions. These would be conducted in the normal manner, and a new license for the new office would be provided.

2.2.6 Suspension

A member of the priesthood who is encountering the difficulties of a divorce from his/her spouse should voluntarily accept suspension of priesthood duties. This means only that the member refrains from priesthood functions, retaining the certificate of ordination. After the problems surrounding the divorce are resolved, and the minister and the pastor are agreed that he/she is ready to resume ministerial duties, the suspension is lifted. No report is made to the Office of the First Presidency of suspension or resumption of duties.

2.3 The Review Procedure

2.3.1 In March and September of each year, mailings will be sent from the Auditorium to the presiding officers of all reviewing jurisdictions. (See forms A-1 and A-2.)

a. Form A-1: A letter described as a periodic priesthood review list, is sent from the First Presidency to each pastor. It contains a listing of one/sixth of the priesthood of the jurisdiction, which are to be reviewed within the following six months.

b. Form A-2: Supplemental information is provided the pastor for assistance in the Periodic Priesthood Review.

c. Additional helps are found in the *Church Ad-*

ministrators Handbook, and include the following:

(1) Priesthood Self-Evaluation and Feedback forms (Form C)

(2) Guidelines for Priesthood Evaluation (Form D)

(3) Plans for Service: Position descriptions for each priesthood office (Forms E-1 through E-4)

2.3.2 Scheduled mailings to individual priesthood members (Forms B-1 and B-2) will be sent from the Auditorium at a time to coincide with the mailings sent to the presiding officers, described above.

a. Form B-1: The *Periodic Priesthood Review* form is the means for officially reporting completion of the Priesthood Interview process, and any recommendations for changes in status which may result from it.

b. Form B-2: A sample letter from the First Presidency to each individual priesthood member.

c. Additional helps are found in the *Church Administrators Handbook,* and include the following:

1) The Priesthood Self-Evaluation and Feedback forms (Form C)

2) Guidelines for Priesthood Evaluation (Form D)

3) Plans for service: position descriptions for each priesthood office (Forms E-1 through E-4)

2.4   Forms and Sample Letters

FLOW CHART FOR USE OF PRIESTHOOD FORMS

Form	Usage
Recommendation for Ordination.	May be used at any time by administrators.
Certificate of Ordination.	The First Presidency provides to each Ordinand after ordination or change of status.
Form C and Forms E-1 through E-4.	The pastor provides to each new ordinand prior to first interview following ordination.
Form D.	The pastor uses for interview in conjunction with Forms E-1 through E-4 and Form C.
Time Lapse:	Informal reviews occur for *newly ordained*—after one year; inactive priesthood members—annually. Formal reviews occur for all priesthood members triennially.
Form A-1, Form A-2, and Form B-2.	Mailed from Headquarters to pastors in March and September of each year.
Form B-1 and Form B-2.	Mailed from Headquarters to one-sixth of priesthood members each March and September in a three-year rotation.
Form C and Forms E-1 through E-4.	The pastor provides each priesthood member in preparation for the interview.
Form D.	The pastor uses for inteview in conjunction with Forms E-1 through E-4 and Form C.

Form A-1

PERIODIC PRIESTHOOD REVIEW LIST

To: Pastor John Doe
Anywhere Congregation
1234 Fifth Street
Nowhere, Missouri 65432

Date: (March 1, 19____ or September 1, 19____)

Dear Brother Doe:

The priesthood status of the following individuals is to be reviewed within the next six months. As the congregational presiding officer, it is your responsibility to meet with and discuss the status for each person for the next three years. Please refer to the attached supplemental information for help in conducting this process, and to the *Church Administrators Handbook* and your jurisdictional policies for guidelines. If a change involves granting superannuation, imposing silence, changing office, or permitting release, then additional procedures must be followed. (See the *Church Administrators Handbook,* or check with your administrative officer.)

Name	Office	Date of Last Review	Current Status	Interview Date	Recommendation
John Jones	Priest	_____	Active	_____	_____
Peter Smith	Elder	_____	Inactive	_____	_____
Susan Brown	Teacher	_____	Active	_____	_____

Please notify Membership Records, the Auditorium, Post Office Box 1059, Independence, Missouri 64051 if any of the above information is incorrect, or if an individual is no longer in your congregation. You may keep this list for your records. Thank you for your help in conducting this important process.

Very sincerely yours,

THE FIRST PRESIDENCY

SUPPLEMENTAL INFORMATION REGARDING PERIODIC PRIESTHOOD REVIEW

Sample Letters

Enclosed you will find samples of the letters sent directly to each active and inactive priesthood member. These letters describe the steps that the individual must take in order to complete the review process.

Extra Forms

You are at liberty to photocopy extra forms in case you need them for priesthood who have been recently transferred into your congregation, to replace lost forms, or for other needs.

Interview

Individuals should each take the initiative to contact you, or your designate, to arrange a meeting. However, if they fail to contact you within a reasonable period of time, then you should contact them. The purpose of this meeting is to accomplish the following:
1. Assist the individual in ministerial growth and development.
2. Assess the individual's interest and giftedness in order to match them with ministerial assignments.
3. Receive feedback that will enhance your presiding ministry, suggest needed efforts, indicate priorities, or share other information that will be helpful to you and/or other church leaders.
4. Provide you with the basic information you need in recommending the individual's priesthood status.
5. Establish lines of communication that will enrich a sense of teamwork and result in more effective ministry by all involved.

Checklist

The following items outline your responsibility in this process:
1. Make sure that a meeting is scheduled with each individual at least sixty days prior to the review date.
2. During this meeting listen carefully to the feelings expressed by the individual as the Self-Evaluation and Feedback form is reviewed and related items discussed. Feel free to take notes to remind you of follow-up actions or issues you may want to pursue or pass along. The individual should keep the Self-Evaluation and Feedback form.
3. Have the individual complete his/her portion of the Periodic Priesthood Review form, then complete your portion.
4. Be certain that photocopies of the completed Periodic Priesthood Review form are forwarded directly to the priesthood records office, to your administrative officer, and to the priesthood member concerned. You are also to retain a copy for the pastor's files.
5. If necessary, follow up with your administrative officer the additional procedures for superannuation, silence,* release,* or change in office.* (*These items are not listed as options on the Periodic Priesthood Review form, but may be recommended under "Comments.")
6. Reflect on the feedback received in the interviews and take any appropriate action that might be suggested.

Form A-3

CERTIFICATE OF ORDINATION

_____
(name)

was ordained _____ to the office of
(date)

_____
(office printed here)

in the Reorganized Church of Jesus Christ of Latter Day Saints
and is hereby authorized to minister in such office
according to the rules of said church.

THE FIRST PRESIDENCY

(*signature printed*)   by (*signature printed*)
Secretary

(The reverse side is to be left blank for governmental validation where applicable. The following text will appear on the folder in which the certificate is presented to the ordinand.)

Priesthood is of a continuing nature. Priesthood authority is granted by the church as a privilege, with continuing expectations. One is called to enlarge and expand personal gifts in the process of ministry—in brief, to magnify one's calling. In recognition of these factors, continuing education and review of one's priesthood stewardship are accepted by each ordinand as essential to fulfilling the call of God.

Form B-1

PERIODIC PRIESTHOOD REVIEW FORM

NAME _____ BAPTISMAL REGISTRATION NO. _____
ADDRESS _____
CONGREGATION _____ STAKE/DISTRICT _____
PRIESTHOOD OFFICE _____ REVIEW PERIOD _____
PRIESTHOOD STATUS _____

***********************TO BE COMPLETED BY PRIESTHOOD MEMBER*********************

PLEASE CHECK ONE:

____ It is my desire and sincere intention to serve diligently in my office and calling.
____ After prayerful consideration I request that I be placed on inactive status at this time.
____ I would like to be considered for superannuation.

COMMENTS

***********************TO BE FILLED OUT BY PRESIDING OFFICER***********************

PLEASE CHECK ONE:

____ I concur with the status requested above.
____ I do not concur with the status requested above. My recommendation is described below.

COMMENTS

_____   _____   _____
Signature   Title   Date

Copy 1—Please send to the First Presidency, Priesthood Records, Post Office Box 1059, the
        Auditorium, Independence, MO 64051
Copy 2—Next higher administrative officer
Copy 3—Priesthood member
Copy 4—Pastor's file

76

LETTER TO PRIESTHOOD MEMBER

To: Mr. John Jones
5678 Middletown Street
Nowhere, Missouri 65432

Date: (March 1, 19____ or September 1, 19____)

Dear Brother Jones:

According to our records your priesthood status is to be reviewed within the next six months. It will be necessary for you to complete the following prior to your review date.
1. Take time to reflect back over your ministry and record your feelings on a copy of the Self-Evaluation and Feedback form which you may obtain from your pastor. An office-centered position description entitled "Plan for Service—Deacon" is designed to aid you in your consideration. It is published in the *Church Administrators Handbook*, and you may obtain a copy from your pastor.
2. Please contact your presiding officer (or designate) to arrange for a meeting.
3. Meet with your presiding officer (or designate) to discuss your Self-Evaluation and Feedback, as well as the enclosed Periodic Priesthood Review form.
4. Be certain that a copy of the completed Periodic Priesthood Review form is sent directly to
Priesthood Records
The Auditorium, Box 1059
Independence, Missouri 64051

Thank you very much for your cooperation in this important process. We pray that God will continue to bless you in your ministry for the Christ.

Very sincerely yours,
THE FIRST PRESIDENCY

Wallace B. Smith

WBS:

encls: Periodic Priesthood Review Form

PRIESTHOOD SELF-EVALUATION AND FEEDBACK

Name _____ Present priesthood office _____

Branch/Congregation _____ Years in present office _____

Period covered by this self-evaluation: from _____ to _____

The periodic priesthood self-assessment is an opportunity for persons to engage in reflection on past achievements and future goals. It is a time for persons to assess their gifts and talents, and plan for personal growth and development.

Following completion of the self-assessment, schedule a time to meet with your presiding officer in order that you can plan together for the coming period.

----

1. When you consider the particular roles of your priesthood office, for which types of ministry do you feel you have particular skill or aptitude?
2. In what types of responsibility have you functioned as a priesthood member during the recent calendar year? Rank order your list according to the amount of time you spent in each activity.
3. In what types of ministry would you have liked to participate had you been asked?
4. Do you feel you have been given sufficient opportunity to serve in areas of your interest?
5. In what areas do you feel you need more knowledge, skill, or training in order to function more effectively? List them in order of need (i.e., No. 1 = area of greatest need, No. 2 = area of second greatest need, etc.) You may find it helpful to refer to the list of current Temple School offerings as you contemplate this area of the self-evaluation.
6. In what areas would you like to participate in classwork or additional training during the coming year?
7. What courses, continuing education, or other training, have you completed during the time period covered by this evaluation?
8. Do members of your family recognize the importance of their support to the success of your priesthood ministry?
    Do you consider your family as you schedule your priesthood activities?
    Is your family aware of how you feel about your priesthood responsibilities?
9. Do you have any personal conflicts or concerns that are affecting your ability to give ministry?
10. Do you feel a need for assistance in the area of your own personal financial stewardship?
    Do you contribute regularly to local and general offerings?
    When was the last time you filed an Annual Financial Accounting? _____
    If you have not filed within the last twelve months, why not?
11. Frequently, you may note a marked difference between the standards of Christ and the usual standards of behavior and ethics in the various professions, the political arena, practices of labor, and personal conduct. As someone who must work and minister in the real world as well as everyday life within the church, how is your personal stewardship affected in light of this difference?
12. How do you view your ministry for the coming year? What would you like to work toward? Accomplish?
13. In what direction should the congregation/branch be focusing its energies collectively during the next year? How does this relate to the total mission of the church?
14. In what ways do you see the Spirit moving in the congregation and/or surrounding community?
15. How do you feel about your efforts toward personal spiritual development? (i.e., prayer, fasting, study, or other)
16. Identify your specific accomplishments since your last periodic self-evaluation. Relate these to your goals and priesthood responsibilities. You may find it helpful to refer back to your copy of your last evaluation and your goal statements. Use additional pages as necessary.

GUIDELINES FOR PERIODIC PRIESTHOOD EVALUATION
WITH THE PRESIDING ELDER

Name _____ Priesthood office _____
Branch/Congregation _____ Date _____
Presiding Elder _____

I. Items related to Self-Evaluation
   A. *Questions designed to promote reflection on key issues of ministry.*
     How would you describe this period, time, or phase of your life?
     Describe a meaningful experience in your ministry during the past year?
     What gifts or talent do you feel you have that can or have helped in your ministry?
     Is there a significant personal goal you are working toward right now?
     Do you have any personal conflicts or concerns that are affecting your ability to give ministry?
     At this particular time in your life, what do you feel God is calling you to do?
     What responsibilities of your office do you most enjoy?
     In what responsibilities of your priesthood office do you feel least prepared to function, or enjoy the least?
   B. *Questions designed to focus on goal setting and future planning.*
     What do you need to help you accomplish your goals (personal and ministerial)?
     How do you feel about the present program of the congregation?
     In what ways do you see the Spirit moving in the congregation and/or surrounding community?
     What are your thoughts about the future mission of the congregation and the church?
II. Mutually established goals in relation to priesthood office/responsibility.
   A. Participation in congregation/community
     Action:
   B. Personal
     Action:
   C. Continuing development/education/preparation
     Action:
   D. Related to family
     Action:
   E. Other
     Action:

Date of last annual financial accounting: _____
Recommendations: Status_____ Office_____
_____
_____

Signature of priesthood member _____ Date _____

Signature of presiding elder _____ Date _____

PLAN FOR SERVICE—Deacon

Name_____ Date_____

Instructions: This form is to be used in conjunction with the Periodic Priesthood Interview process. A separate form (Form C) titled Priesthood Self-Evaluation and Feedback is to be completed by the minister. The minister and administrative officer utilize the form (Form D) titled Guidelines for Periodic Priesthood Evaluation as they jointly discuss the person's ministry.

This form is intended to assist the minister and the presiding officer to discuss the service of the minister, and to plan for the next three-year period (or portion thereof). Two copies of this form are needed—one for the minister and one for the confidential file in the interviewing minister's office.

The plan for service may be amended before the three-year period is completed if a change is needed. This form may also be used for such amendment. The amendment is made in discussion with the appropriate presiding officer.

POSITION DESCRIPTION FOR THE DEACON

Qualifications: Deacons are committed to Jesus Christ and the cause of God's kingdom. Priesthood members are to lead clean lives, free from all chemical dependence; they are to be honest, humble, clean, and neat in appearance and walk uprightly before the Lord. They avoid all immoral activity and appearance of evil. Deacons respond affirmatively in their temporal stewardships. They are faithful in church attendance and in their priesthood duties; they should continually seek to magnify their calling.

Supervision: The deacon is a congregational minister and serves under the general guidance of the pastor of the congregation or anyone the pastor may delegate for a specific purpose. The deacon may assist teachers, priests, and elders in their duties as requested.

Specific Duties of Office

1. The deacon is concerned with the physical welfare of church members and their families.
1.1 The deacon identifies closely with the poor, the sick, the helpless and needy, and assists them in every way possible to meet their needs. The deacon is their advocate and presents their needs to financial officers if financial assistance is required, the pastor and elders for spiritual ministries, the priests and teachers and others for home ministry and friendly visits.
1.2 The deacon identifies community and governmental assistance programs relevant to the physical needs of the poor among the Saints and assists in assuring that their needs are met by the proper agencies.
2. The deacon is concerned with the care, maintenance, and appearance of the properties of the church.
2.1 The deacon is the advocate for the physical properties of the church. The deacon identifies and works to develop adequate programs of cleanliness and maintenance of church property.
2.2 The deacon is concerned with the appearance and contribution of the church property to the neighborhood of which it is a part. Physical appearance, order, and neatness of lawn, signs, and building are of special importance to the deacon.
3. The deacon is concerned with the physical comfort of the Saints whenever the congregation assembles.

3.1 The deacon assures cleanliness, order, and proper temperature in the building.
3.2 The deacon assures friendly and orderly ushering and decorum in congregational meetings.
3.3 The deacon receives the offerings in public worship and assures their transmittal to the congregation's financial officers.
3.4 The deacon opens the church for congregational meetings and assures the building's security at the close of meetings.

Ministries the Deacon May Be Requested or Elected to Perform

1. Serve as solicitor.
2. Serve as congregational treasurer.
3. Serve as member or chair of the church building committee.
4. Serve as member or chair the stewardship commission.
5. Serve as head deacon or usher.
6. Serve as member or president of a deacon's quorum.
7. Assist priests and teachers in home ministry.
8. Teach classes as requested in church school, or other settings.
9. Provide financial management teaching to families and congregation.
10. Visit the homes of Saints with special concern for those in physical need.

General Duties

As a member of the Aaronic priesthood, the deacon is to minister primarily in the congregation, teaching the value of temporalities in personal spiritual development, and serving the temporal needs of the Saints. The deacon and all priesthood are to invite people to come to Christ. They are to teach and encourage people to respond to the gospel of Jesus Christ, and be reconciled to Christ through faith, repentance, baptism, and other gospel principles.

CHECKLIST: Check ( ) below the ministries you have offered during the past review period, and those you wish to focus on during the next period. You need not check a specific number of areas.

General Ministries	*Past Period*	*Next Period*
Home Ministry	_____	_____
Personal Counseling	_____	_____
Cottage Meetings	_____	_____
Public Worship		
Specify _____	_____	_____
Teaching Classes		
Specify _____	_____	_____
Commission Work		
Specify _____	_____	_____
Specific Areas of Calling		
Assist the Saints in personal		
financial planning.	_____	_____
Assist the Saints in financial		
accounting (tithing statements).	_____	_____
Oblation processing and counseling	_____	_____
Organize custodial service for		
the church building.	_____	_____

Supervise or help with church
building maintenance.   _____ _____

Serve on the building committee.   _____ _____

Teach about health, personal money
   management, and other stewardships.   _____ _____

Encourage members to file tithing
   statements.   _____ _____

Serve on the stewardship commission
   for your congregation.   _____ _____

Serve as head deacon for the
   congregation.   _____ _____

Serve as usher in church services.   _____ _____

Participate in a deacon's quorum.   _____ _____

Serve as solicitor or treasurer.   _____ _____

Other _____   _____ _____

Plan for training (list possible courses).

_____

Briefly describe your plan for service for the next three years.

_____

Minister_____   Signature _____

82

Form E-2

PLAN FOR SERVICE—Teacher

Name_____ Date_____

Instructions: This form is to be used in conjunction with the Periodic Priesthood Interview process. A separate form (Form C) titled Priesthood Self-Evaluation and Feedback is to be completed by the minister. The minister and administrative officer utilize the form (Form D) titled Guidelines for Periodic Priesthood Evaluation as they jointly discuss the person's ministry.

This form is intended to assist the minister and the presiding officer to discuss the service of the minister, and to plan for the next three-year period (or portion thereof). Two copies of this form are needed—one for the minister and one for the confidential file in the interviewing minister's office.

The plan for service may be amended before the three-year period is completed if a change is needed. This form may also be used for such amendment. The amendment is made in discussion with the appropriate presiding officer.

POSITION DESCRIPTION FOR THE TEACHER

Qualifications: Teachers are committed to Jesus Christ and the cause of God's kingdom. Priesthood members lead clean lives, free from all chemical dependence; they are honest, humble, clean, and neat in appearance and walk uprightly before the Lord. Teachers are motivated by Christian values rather than worldly pursuits. They avoid immoral activity or entanglements. They respond affirmatively in their temporal stewardships. They are faithful in church attendance and in their priesthood duties; they should continually seek to magnify their calling.

Supervision: The teacher is a congregational minister and is responsible in priesthood duties to the pastor, or to anyone the pastor might delegate for a specific purpose. The teacher assists the priest and elder in their duties and may be assisted by a deacon.

Specific Duties of Office

1. The teacher is the advocate of full participation, healthy relationships, and development of a healing, redeeming attitude among the Saints. This is what it means for the teacher to "watch over the church."
1.1 The teacher is the attendance officer of the congregation. If members are not in attendance, the teacher contacts them promptly through visit, call, or on occasion, personal note. Participation is the key to right relationships in the congregation.
1.2 If relationships are broken between families or members, the teacher will persist in either offering the ministry or making the ministry of the pastor or elders available to heal the relationships. (If especially qualified in this field, the teacher may serve as the minister of reconciliation.)
1.3 The teacher is responsible for the membership records of the congregation. In this role every person is known and encouraged to participate.
1.4 The teacher, in concern for healthy relationships, provides home ministry to the lonely, shut-ins, single person households, as well as others who may be overlooked.
1.5 The teacher promptly visits any newly transferred members and assists them to be introduced to congregational fellowship.

1.6 The teacher serves as advocate for home ministry programs as a means of prompting understanding and participation in the congregation.
2. The teacher is aware of community programs relevant to the needs of the Saints, such as counseling services for families, individuals, alcoholics anonymous, or other.
2.1 The teacher assists the Saints in obtaining the needed community services.

Ministries the Teacher May Be Requested or Elected to Perform
1. Serve as recorder of the congregation.
2. Assist priests and elders as requested.
3. Teach classes on personal relationships, etc.
4. Teach clases on unity and peace.
5. Serve as member or leader of a teacher's quorum.
6. Assist in cottage meetings if requested.
7. If properly trained and gifted, serve as "lay counselor."
8. Work in community agencies providing help to the lonely and those needing help in interpersonal relationships.
9. Provide "friendly greeting" at congregational meetings.
10. Participate in congregational meetings as requested.

General Duties
The teacher is to "watch over the church" and promote unity and harmony among the Saints. As a member of the Aaronic priesthood, the teacher is to minister primarily in the congregation, teaching and promoting the benefits of acceptance, understanding, and unity among the Saints. The teacher and all priesthood are to invite people to come to Christ. They are to teach and encourage people to respond to the gospel of Jesus Christ, and be reconciled to Christ through faith, repentance, baptism, and other gospel principles.

CHECKLIST: Check ( ) below the ministries you have offered during the past review period, and those you wish to focus on during the next period.

General Ministries	*Past Period*	*Next Period*
Home Ministry	_____	_____
Personal Counseling	_____	_____
Cottage Meetings	_____	_____
Teaching Classes		
Specify _____	_____	_____
Public Worship		
Specify _____	_____	_____
Commission Work		
Specify _____	_____	_____

Specific Areas of Calling		
Assist as lay counselor.	_____	_____
Work on congregational newsletter.	_____	_____
Serve as congregational minister for conflict resolution.	_____	_____

Serve as recorder for the
congregation. ———————   ———————
Serve as greeter at church
functions. ———————   ———————
Visit the inactive—especially
the single and those without a
family unit. ———————   ———————
Teach classes on interpersonal
relationships. ———————   ———————
Teach classes on unity and peace. ———————   ———————
Do periodic reviews for members
and families "to see that they
do their duty." ———————   ———————
Keep attendance records for the
congregation. ———————   ———————
Visit new members of the
congregation. ———————   ———————
Lead a youth group or other
special interest group. ———————   ———————
Participate in a teacher's quorum. ———————   ———————
Other _____ ———————   ———————

Plan for training (list possible courses).

——————————————— ——————————————— ——————————————————————————

Briefly describe your plan for service for the next three years.

Minister_____   Signature _____

PLAN FOR SERVICE—Priest

Name_____ Date_____

Instructions: This form is to be used in conjunction with the Periodic Priesthood Interview process. A separate form (Form C) titled Priesthood Self-Evaluation and Feedback is to be completed by the minister. The minister and administrative officer utilize the form (Form D) titled Guidelines for Periodic Priesthood Evaluation as they jointly discuss the person's ministry.

This form is intended to assist the minister and the presiding officer to discuss the service of the minister, and to plan for the next three-year period (or portion thereof). Two copies of this form are needed—one for the minister and one for the confidential file in the interviewing minister's office.

The plan for service may be amended before the three-year period is completed if a change is needed. This form may also be used for such amendment. The amendment is made in discussion with the appropriate presiding officer.

POSITION DESCRIPTION FOR THE PRIEST

Qualifications: The priest is committed to Jesus Christ and the cause of God's kingdom. Priesthood members lead clean lives, free from all chemical dependence; they are honest, humble, clean, and neat in appearance and walk uprightly before the Lord. They are motivated by Christian values rather than worldly pursuits. They avoid immoral activity and appearance of evil. Priests respond affirmatively in their temporal stewardships. They are faithful in church attendance and in their priesthood duties; they continually seek to magnify their calling.

Supervision: The priest is a congregational minister and is responsible in priesthood duties to the pastor, or to anyone the pastor may delegate for a specific purpose. The priest is to assist the elders in their duties, and may be assisted by deacons and teachers.

Specific Duties of Office

1. Develops a close "good friend" relationship with the families of the church.
1.1 Visits the homes of church members to help the family's communication process on the subjects of prayer and scripture reading.
1.2 Provides friendly support to families in studying the scripture and in praying together.
1.3 Serves as advocate for family-type ministries in the congregation.
1.4 Observes the dynamics of family relationships and contacts the pastor and specialized ministers whenever difficulty arises in a family.
1.5 Promotes family participation in reunions, retreats, or other church activities.
1.6 Promotes family projects of contributions to special projects which may help in missionary outreach, care of the poor, or other.
1.7 Promotes family participation in the church's stewardship program.
2. The priest is familiar with personal and family counseling and other assistance programs in the community.
2.1 Assists members to acquire any needed counseling through community mental health programs or other sources.

2.2 Promotes family participation in community recreation programs, hobby development activities, or other.

Ministries to Which the Priest May Be Assigned or Elected
1. Supervise home ministry program.
2. Conduct cottage meetings with persons not yet baptized.
3. Participate in or be leader of a priest quorum.
4. Participate in community agencies dealing with counseling families, mental health, alcohol and other chemical substance abuse problems, recreation programs, teaching hobbies, and other continuing education programs.
5. If qualified, teach and conduct seminars related to family life.
6. Administer the sacraments of baptism, the Lord's Supper, marriage, and ordain other priests, teachers, or deacons.
7. Preach and participate in public worship as requested by the pastor.
8. Preside over a congregation if circumstance requires.
9. Serve as financial officer of a congregation.
10. Serve as a member or chair the stewardship commission.
11. Serve as a member or chair the building committee.

General Duties

The priest is to offer ministry to the family and to administer the "outward ordinances" of the church: baptism, the Lord's Super, and marriage. As a member of the Aaronic priesthood, the priest is to minister primarily in the congregation, teaching and preaching the importance of the gospel, especially in family life. The priest and all priesthood are to invite people to come to Christ. They are to preach, teach, and encourage people to respond to the gospel of Jesus Christ, and be reconciled to Christ through faith, repentance, baptism, and other gospel principles.

CHECKLIST: Check ( ) below the ministries you have offered during the past review period, and those you wish to focus on during the next period.

General Ministries	*Past Period*	*Next Period*
Home Ministry	_____	_____
Personal Counseling	_____	_____
Cottage Meetings	_____	_____
Public Worship		
Specify _____	_____	_____
Teach classes		
Specify _____	_____	_____
Commission work		
Specify _____	_____	_____

Specific Areas of Calling		
Visit inactive families.	_____	_____
Serve on pastoral care commission.	_____	_____
Supervise a visiting program.	_____	_____
Teach a class on parenting.	_____	_____
Organize a visiting program for the congregation.	_____	_____

Teach a class on family
   relationships.   _____   _____
Preach   _____   _____
Serve on worship commission.   _____   _____
Serve on Christian education
   commission.   _____   _____
Administer the ordinances of
   marriage, the Lord's Supper,
   and baptism.   _____   _____
Lead a youth group, or other
   special interest group.   _____   _____
Serve as congregational missionary
   coordinator.   _____   _____
Other _____   _____   _____

Plan for training (list possible courses).
_____
_____

Briefly describe your plan for service for the next three years.

Minister_____   Signature _____

PLAN FOR SERVICE—Elder

Name_____ Date_____

Instructions: This form is to be used in conjunction with the Periodic Priesthood Interview process. A separate form (Form C) titled Priesthood Self-Evaluation and Feedback is to be completed by the minister. The minister and administrative officer utilize the form (Form D) titled Guidelines for Periodic Priesthood Evaluation as they jointly discuss the person's ministry.

This form is intended to assist the minister and the presiding officer to discuss the service of the minister, and to plan for the next three-year period (or portion thereof). Two copies of this form are needed—one for the minister and one for the confidential file in the interviewing minister's office.

The plan for service may be amended before the three-year period is completed if a change is needed. This form may also be used for such amendment. The amendment is made in discussion with the appropriate presiding officer.

POSITION DESCRIPTION FOR THE ELDER

Qualifications: Elders are deeply committed to Jesus Christ and the cause of God's kingdom. Elders lead clean lives, and are free from all chemical dependence. Elders are honest, humble, clean, and neat in appearance, walk uprightly before God, shun immoral activity and appearance of evil. Elders are constant in prayer, study of scriptures, and in loving service to all people. Elders respond affirmatively in their temporal stewardships and are faithful in duties of their priesthood office and church attendance. Elders are the growing edge of the church's ministry and are constant in study and preparation for greater service.

Supervision: The elder serves under the general guidance of the pastor of the congregation or anyone the pastor may delegate for a specific purpose.

Specific Duties of Office

1.   Is concerned with the quality and integrity of congregational life.
1.1   Presides over a congregation if elected by its members or properly appointed by other jurisdictional officer.
1.2   Presides over pastoral group if appointed by pastor.
1.3   Presides over congregational functions if appointed or elected (evangelism, Christian education, stewardship, youth ministries, or other).
1.4   Organizes and presides over groups to meet emerging or temporary needs of the congregation.
1.5   Organizes congregational life to provide opportunities for all members to give and receive ministry.
1.6   Observes all organized functions of the congregation and recommends needed ministries to pastor.
1.7   When requested, serves as resource person to assist congregational departments and commissions in fulfilling their functions.
1.8   Organizes the congregation around the ministry of witnessing the gospel to the community.
1.9   Serves as advocate for church expansion in all of the congregation's functions.

1.10 Organizes congregational ministries to meet needs of persons in the community.
1.11 Includes nonmembers in appropriate ways in the total life of the congregation.
2.   The elder is concerned with presenting the gospel and the ministry of the congregation to individual persons and families who are not yet members, and to the community at large.
2.1 The elder conducts cottage meetings to share the good news of the gospel with persons and families.
2.2 The elder becomes acquainted with visitors to the congregation and offers needed ministry through home visits, or in other ways.
2.3 The elder offers special ministry of witness to families that are not united in the church.
2.4 The elder presents the ministries of the congregation to its community.
2.5 The elder participates in groups which serve the deepest human needs in the community.
2.6 The elder organizes community programs to meet needs of citizens of the community.
2.7 The elder is aware of existing community programs which provide help to persons and families, and serves as their advocate in community and congregation.
2.8 The elder serves as a "bridge" to ethnic groups to which congregations may offer ministry.
2.9 The elder serves as minister to the dispossessed, lonely, and poor in the community.
2.10 The elder is a minister to the sick and is constantly available for such ministry as they may require.
2.11 The elder may serve as hospital chaplain, chaplain in civic organization service clubs, or public institutions.
3.   The elder participates in and is advocate of the stake, district, or other jurisdictional programs.
3.1 The elder promotes participation of congregational members in appropriate larger jurisdictional programs.
3.2 The elder assists jurisdictional programs in becoming witnessing activities.
3.3 The elder facilitates participation of nonmembers in jurisdictional programs that may lead toward decision for church membership (youth and children's camps, reunions, special weekend activities, or other).
3.4 The elder helps organize special jurisdictional programs to meet needs of dispossessed, lonely, and poor in the congregation and community.
4.   The elder administers the sacraments, preaches the word, and is responsible for the worship life of the congregation.
4.1 The elder takes special care to minister to the deepest spiritual and emotional needs of each person in the congregation.
4.2 The sick, the bereaved, the disappointed and disillusioned all receive special attention and ministry from the elder.
4.3 The elder interprets and administers the sacraments to people's deepest needs emerging from their existential situation and rhythm of life.
4.4 The elders preach the good news of the gospel in conviction, confession, and testimony of its power in their own lives and as promise to others.
4.5 The elder is aware of the deepest needs of the congregation, including those of its number who have not been baptized, and ministers to need rather than promoting a preconceived set of doctrinal or organizational propositions.
4.6 The elders base their ministry on scripture.
4.7 The elder is a student
     a. of scripture;
     b. of interpretative works which provide deeper understanding of the history and meaning of scripture;
     c. of people, their needs, and the disciplines which provide help in meeting those needs;
     d. of the society within which they live as citizen;
     e. of organizational development to gain skills in meeting the missional goals of the church.

Ministries the Elder May Be Requested or Elected to Perform
  1. Presiding officer of a congregation or district
  2. Counselor to presiding officers
  3. Missionary coordinator for a congregation, district, or stake
  4. Bishop's agent, or counselor to stake bishop
  5. Leader of any function of a congregation, district, or stake
  6. Representative of a congregation in community projects or activities
  7. Conductor of evangelistic series or special activities of witnessing
  8. Member or leader of an elder's quorum
  9. Member of a church court

General Duties

The elders are to conduct the meetings of the church as they are led by the Holy Ghost, according to the commandments and revelations of God. Elders are called and ordained to serve as presiding ministers, group enabling ministers, and as ministers of expansion of the church. They are to lead persons and groups into new relationships, new allegiances, expanded participation, and loyalties in life.

The elders invite people to come to Christ and assist all people in developing into witnessing disciples of the Lord Jesus.

CHECKLIST: Check ( ) below the ministries you have offered during the past review period, and those you wish to focus on during the next period.

General Ministries	*Past Period*	*Next Period*
Home Ministry		
Personal Counseling	_____	_____
Cottage Meetings	_____	_____
Public Worship		
Specify _____	_____	_____
Teach classes		
Specify _____	_____	_____
Commission work		
Specify _____	_____	_____
Specific Areas of Calling		
Administer the ordinances.	_____	_____
Preach.	_____	_____
Do missionary work.	_____	_____
Study and teach the scriptures.	_____	_____
Serve as presiding elder or		
assistant.	_____	_____
Preside at meetings of the Saints.	_____	_____
Visit inactive members.	_____	_____
Serve as a traveling minister.	_____	_____
Give hospital ministry.	_____	_____

Visit the sick and administer to
them.   _____   _____

Assist in developing the spiritual
gifts of all.   _____   _____

Assist with priesthood license
renewal process.   _____   _____

Chair the leadership commission.   _____   _____

Other _____   _____   _____

Other _____   _____   _____

Plan for training (list possible courses).

_____

_____

Briefly describe your plan for service for the next three years.

Minister_____   Signature _____

VIII

Timeline for the Introduction of Priesthood Policies

January 1985 — Herald House prints *Guidelines for Priesthood: Ordination, Preparation, Continuing Commitment.*

February 1985 — Members of the Council of Twelve provide for instruction regarding *Guidelines* and their distribution among field administrators.

March 1985 — Calls for women are in process; approvals are obtained.
— Introduce the new position descriptions for priesthood and the new forms for licenses and evaluation.
— Begin the implementation of standards of priesthood and preordination expectations.
— Herald House begins sale and distribution of *Guidelines.*

May 31, 1985 — Instruction process and introduction of *Guidelines* is completed.

November 1985 — First ordinations of women occur.

January 1986 — Policies are made available for field implementation of priesthood organization.
— Begin preparations for the inauguration of priesthood review process, superannuation, and release.

March 1987 — Inaugurate priesthood review procedures and determinations of priesthood status for one-sixth of the priesthood members.

September 1987 — Inaugurate priesthood review procedures and determinations of priesthood status for one-sixth of the priesthood members.

March 1988 — Inaugurate priesthood review procedures and determinations of priesthood status for one-sixth of the priesthood members.

September 1988 — Inaugurate priesthood review procedures and determinations of priesthood status for one-sixth of the priesthood members.

March 1989 — Inaugurate priesthood review procedures and determinations of priesthood status for one-sixth of the priesthood members.

September 1989 — Inaugurate priesthood review procedures and determinations of priesthood status for one-sixth of the priesthood members.

Index to Appendix A

Accountability of Priesthood..64
Calling..61
Categories of Priesthood Activity...66
    Active..66
    Inactive...67
    Release...69
    Silence..68
    Superannuation...66
    Suspension...70
Congregational Needs and Priesthood Calls...............................29, 42
Discerning a Priesthood Call..31
Education, Continuing..58
Education, Preordination Requirements...54
Education, Training for Priesthood...54
Flow Chart for Processing Priesthood Calls.......................................60
Flow Chart for Use of Priesthood Forms..72
Forms:
        Certificate of Ordination: Form A-3...75
        Guidelines for Periodic Priesthood Evaluation with the Presiding Elder: Form D............79
        Letter to Priesthood Member: Form B-2....................................77
        Periodic Priesthood Review Form: Form B-1..............................76
        Periodic Priesthood Review List: Letter, Form A-1.....................73
        Priesthood Self-Evaluation and Feedback Form: Form C...........78
        Plan for Service—Deacon: Form E-1..80
        Plan for Service—Elder: Form E-4..89
        Plan for Service—Priest: Form E-3..86
        Plan for Service—Teacher: Form E-2...83
        Recommendation for Ordination Form..51
        Supplemental Information Regarding
            Periodic Priesthood Review: Form A-2.................................74
Giftedness...61
Guidelines for Calling Officers..24, 53
Historical Perspectives on Priesthood..57
Interview of Priesthood Members............................64–74, 76, 78, 79
Member, Office of..62
Ordination...63
Ordination Ceremony...46
Organization of the Priesthood..21
Pastor's Role Following Ordination...48
Preordination Training..54
Procedures in Priesthood Calls...24, 52
Purpose of Priesthood..25
Qualifications for Priesthood..36
Questions for the Calling Officer..24, 46
Review of Priesthood...See Interview
Setting Apart...63
Structure of Priesthood...21
Temple School and Priesthood Education......................................58–60
Timeline for Policies Implementation...93
Uses of Priesthood..21
Women, Calling to Priesthood..39